DEEP IN THE
Heart

a collection of recipes
Dallas Junior Forum

a collection of recipes from the heart of our
families…friends…and fellow Texans.

Dallas Junior Forum is a non-profit service organization organized in 1977 and designed to serve the needs of the community through its service projects. The objective of Dallas Junior Forum is to create greater interest among young women in civic, educational and philanthropic fields in the Dallas area. Proceeds from the sale of this cookbook support the Cystic Fibrosis Foundation, the Ronald McDonald House, Juliette Fowler Home, schools through "Kids On the Block" puppets, Children's Cancer Fund, Science Place, and The Dallas Children's Advocacy Center.

Additional copies may be obtained by writing:

Dallas Junior Forum
Deep In The Heart
800 E. Campbell, Suite 199
Richardson, TX 75081
(214) 699-9704

First Printing	November 1986	10,000
Second Printing	March 1987	10,000
Third Printing	March 1988	15,000
Fourth Printing	September 1990	10,000
Fifth Printing	September 1991	10,000

Printed in the USA by
WIMMER BROTHERS
A Wimmer Company
Memphis • Dallas

FOREWORD

We're ladies working for common goals.
We're different, yet alike, by performing many roles.
We're wives, mothers, leaders and cooks;
We chauffeur, clean, keep records and books.

The rewards are great when you go and help others;
You see smiles from the young, the old, fathers and mothers.
Serving the community is what we are striving to do;
And by helping them, we help ourselves, too.

When you see the burdens that others must bear,
You open your heart and show that you care.
The women in Forum prove this is true
By the generous, unselfish work that they do.

This cookbook is a collection of recipes from DEEP IN THE HEART of the Dallas Junior Forum members. The recipes have been tested for accuracy and quality and are only a portion of the more than 1200 submitted. They are favorites that we have gathered to share with others and we do not claim that any of them are original. We hope you will enjoy our gift to you as prepared with love from DEEP IN THE HEART of Dallas Junior Forum.

Entertaining is something we like to do,
So favorite recipes we've gathered to share with you.
Most are easy for ladies who lead busy lives
As professionals, mothers, cooks or wives.

In between service and fund-raising, we have many a meeting,
And we always provide some really good eating.
We've decided to share favorite recipes with you
To help with some of the entertaining you do.

Original Cookbook Committee

Debbi Arnold	Ceil Kleinschmidt
Gayle Brown	Beth Layton
Linda Brown	Vicki Layton
Sharon Cravy	Diana Leatherman
Donna Chronister	June Mearns
Barbara Frank	Joanie Moi
Dede Furlong	Patsy Norvell
Pam Hamer	Penny Helms Rivenbark
Lynda Hunter	Anne Sellers
Ann Jones	Karen Smith
Laurie Keeling	Jackie Thornton
Christie Key	Sheryl Turner

Charlene Watson

Past Chairmen

Ann Jones 1985-87

Jackie Thornton & 1987-88
Stephanie Bennett

Vicki Layton & 1988-89
Geraldine Washam

Karen Faulconer & 1989-90
Sally Hamilton

Judy Johns 1990-91

Current Committee

Dede Furlong .... Chairman
Bonita Speer .... Co-Chairman
Sandy Campbell and Judy Johns .... Marketing Promotions

Sharon Gambulos	Laura Martin
Linda Goodall	Judy Nassif
Cindy Gummer	Mary Ann Paul
Judy Humphreyson	Rosalie Rodriguez
Chris LaFaille	Bunny Tibbals
Leah Margerison	Jenny Vestal

Cover and Interior Illustrator

The artist, Heidi Prager Kramer, was born in Austin, Texas. After moving to Florida, she established Heidi's Studio, 326 Lantana Road, Suite 3, Lantana, Florida 33462.

TABLE OF CONTENTS

The Kids
on the Block

A TROUPE OF DISABLED
AND NON-DISABLED PUPPETS

The Kids on the Block programs use puppetry as the medium to address and educate children about disabilities, medical conditions, teen pregnancy prevention and other social issues. The puppets are nearly life-size and, like real children, some have differences such as mental, physical or emotional disabilities, while others have lives touched by abuse, drugs, pregnancy and divorce.

Dallas Junior Forum volunteers have performed a variety of Kids on the Block scripts in area schools for nearly 10 years, delighting and informing thousands of children.

Appetizers and Beverages

Appetizers and beverages can spark up a party
And even please an appetite that really is hearty.
You will find each provides quite a unique flavor
And gives you a taste you surely will savor.

Tortilla Roll-Ups
Tortilla Tempties

3 packages (8 ounces each) cream cheese, softened
1 carton (8 ounces) sour cream
2 Tablespoons picante sauce
½ cup chopped onion
1 jalapeño pepper, chopped
Juice of 1 lime
½ teaspoon garlic salt
48 flour tortillas

Combine all ingredients, except tortillas. Put 1 tablespoon mixture in center of each tortilla and spread evenly. Roll up and chill. When ready to serve, cut each tortilla roll into 3 pieces. Serve with picante sauce. **Yield:** 144 pieces.

Mrs. James Layton (Vicki)

Mexican Dip

1 pound bulk sausage
1 pound ground beef
1 medium onion, chopped
1 teaspoon garlic powder
Tabasco sauce, dash
2 pounds Velveeta cheese
1 can (10½ ounces) cream of mushroom soup
1 can (10 ounces) Rotel tomatoes

Brown and drain sausage, ground beef, and chopped onion. In a large double boiler, melt the cheese and add all other ingredients. Serve in a chafing dish with tostados. **Yield:** 12-15 servings.

Mrs. Ron Souder (Pat)

♥ *Cover a block of cream cheese with jalapeño jelly, Picante sauce, or Picapeppa sauce. Serve with Triscuits, melba toast rounds, or nacho chips.*

Green Chili Won Tons

Won Tons:
½ pound Monterey Jack cheese, grated
1 can (4 ounces) green chilies, chopped
1 package (14 ounces) Won Ton skins
Vegetable oil

Guacamole Dip:
2 large ripe avocados
3 Tablespoons fresh lime juice
½ teaspoon salt
½ teaspoon ground coriander
2 teaspoons minced green onions
3 Tablespoons mayonnaise

Mix cheese and green chilies. Place 1 teaspoon mixture on a Won Ton skin and fold like an envelope. Fry in 2 inches of hot oil until brown, turning so that both sides will be brown. Drain. Serve with guacamole dip.
Guacamole Dip: Mash pulp of avocados and blend in lime juice. Add remaining ingredients and blend until smooth. Cover and refrigerate until ready to use. **Yield:** 6-10 servings.

Note: *Can be frozen ahead.*

                                            Mrs. Jack Hamer (Pam)

Mexican Pick-Up Sticks

2 cans (3 ounces each) French fried onions
1 can (7 ounces) potato sticks
2 cups Spanish peanuts

⅓ cup melted margarine
1 package (1.25 ounces) taco seasoning dry mix

Combine onions, potato sticks, and peanuts. Place in 9x13-inch baking dish. Drizzle with melted butter and stir. Sprinkle with taco seasoning. Mix well. Bake at 250° for 45 minutes, stirring every 15 minutes. **Yield:** 2 quarts.

                                            Mrs. James Layton (Vicki)

Tex-Mex Won Tons

1 pound ground beef	3 teaspoons chili powder
½ cup chopped onion	½ teaspoon ground cumin
4 Tablespoons chopped green pepper	1 package (65 count) Won Ton skins
1 can (15 ounces) refried beans	Salad oil for deep frying
½ cup grated Cheddar cheese	Taco sauce
2 Tablespoons ketchup	

In a skillet cook ground beef, onion, and green pepper until meat is brown and vegetables are tender. Drain off fat. Stir beans, cheese, ketchup, chili powder, and cumin into meat mixture; mix well. Place a Won Ton skin with one point toward you. Put a generous teaspoon of meat mixture onto the center of skin. Fold bottom point of skin over filling; tuck point under filling. Fold side corners over, forming an envelope shape. Roll up toward remaining corner; moisten point and press to seal. Repeat until all skins are filled. Fry, a few at a time, in deep hot oil for about 1 minute per side. Remove with slotted spoon. Serve immediately with taco sauce. **Yield:** 65 Won Tons.

Note: *These may be frozen after fried. Reheat, loosely covered, at 350° for 10-12 minutes.*

Mrs. James Layton (Vicki)

Guacamole Dip
Creamy and Delicious

3 ripe avocados, peeled and seeded	1 Tablespoon lemon juice
1 tomato, chopped	¼ cup picante sauce
½ cup sour cream	½ teaspoon salt, or to taste

Mash avocados and add tomato, sour cream, lemon juice, picante sauce, and salt. Stir well and serve with tortilla chips. **Yield:** 2½ cups.

Note: *Vary amount of picante sauce according to your own taste.*

Mrs. Joe Key (Christie)

Super Nachos
Great Party Dish

1 pound ground beef	1 can (4 ounces) taco sauce
1 large onion, chopped	6 green onions, sliced
1 can (16 ounces) refried beans	1 can (4 ounces) sliced black
1 can (4 ounces) chopped green chilies	olives
1½ cups grated Cheddar cheese	1 cup guacamole
1½ cups grated Monterey Jack cheese	1 cup sour cream

Brown meat and onion in skillet; drain grease. Spread beans in bottom of 9x13-inch oblong casserole. Spread meat and onion on top of beans. Scatter green chilies and Cheddar and Monterey Jack cheeses on top of meat. Dribble taco sauce evenly over all. Bake at 350° for 30 minutes. Top with green onions and black olives. If serving for a main dish, let cool 10 minutes then slice and serve in squares. Pass bowls of guacamole and sour cream. If serving as an appetizer, put a dollop of sour cream on one end and a dollop of guacamole on the other and serve with tortilla chips for dipping. **Yield:** 6-8 main dish servings.

Mrs. Brian Byrne (Veronica)

Tomato Salsa

4 small (2 cups) tomatoes, peeled & chopped	1 teaspoon salt
	Red pepper, dash
½ cup finely chopped onion	½ teaspoon coriander, optional
½ cup finely chopped green pepper	½ teaspoon oregano
	1 Tablespoon lemon or lime juice
1 or 2 jalapeño peppers, seeded & minced	1 Tablespoon vinegar
	1 can (8 ounces) tomato sauce
1 Tablespoon sugar	2 Tablespoons salad oil

Combine all ingredients. Chill for several hours. **Yield:** 3 cups.

Note: *Can be made in blender.*

Mrs. Richard Keeling (Laurie)

11

Gazpacho Dip

1 can (28 ounces) tomatoes, mashed by hand
1 can (8 ounces) tomato sauce
2 Tablespoons vinegar
3 Tablespoons salad oil
1 can (4 ounces) diced green chilies
1 can (4 ounces) chopped ripe olives
1 clove garlic, minced
¼ pound mushrooms, diced
¼ teaspoon salt
¼ teaspoon garlic salt
1 bunch green onions, thinly sliced

Mix together all ingredients in a glass container. Cover and refrigerate overnight. Serve with tortilla chips. **Yield:** 1 quart.

Note: *Prepare 8-10 hours ahead.*

Mrs. Jerry Leatherman (Diana)

Mexican Layer Dip

2 avocados
Lemon juice to taste
Onion salt, dash
Garlic salt, dash
1 can (15 ounces) refried beans, mashed
½ cup picante sauce
1½-2 cups sour cream
1 cup grated Monterey Jack cheese
1 cup grated sharp Longhorn Cheddar cheese
3-4 green onions, including tops, chopped

Make guacamole by blending avocados, lemon juice, onion salt, and garlic salt. Spread in a 7x11-inch dish. Make bean dip by combining refried beans and picante sauce. Spread on top of guacamole. Cover first 2 layers completely with sour cream. Top with grated cheeses. Garnish with chopped green onions. **Yield:** 10-12 servings.

Mrs. Thomas Hunter (Lynda)

Jalapeño Squares

1 pound Monterey Jack cheese, grated	2 eggs
1 pound Cheddar cheese, grated	1 cup flour
½ cup finely chopped jalapeño peppers	1 can (12 ounces) evaporated milk

Arrange cheeses that have been mixed together with chopped peppers in ungreased 9x13-inch ovenproof dish. Mix eggs, flour, and evaporated milk and pour over cheese mixture. Bake in pre-heated oven at 350° for 40 minutes. **Yield:** 48 squares.

Note: *May add 1 can (4 ounces) green chilies to cheeses and ½ teaspoon garlic salt and ½ teaspoon garlic powder to egg mixture as variation.*

Mrs. Jim Conine (Donna)

Empañadas I

2 packages (8 ounces each) Pillsbury crescent rolls	12 stuffed green olives, chopped
1 pound ground beef	1 large tomato, chopped
1 Tablespoon salad oil	Oregano, pinch
1 medium onion, finely chopped	Salt and pepper, dash
1 green pepper, finely chopped	Garlic powder, dash
1 teaspoon capers	Hot sauce

Roll out crescent rolls into one large pastry sheet. Chill while preparing meat mixture. Brown meat in oil and add remaining ingredients except the hot sauce. Cut the pastry sheet into rounds with a cookie cutter. On each round of dough put ½ teaspoon of meat filling. Fold over and flute edges with a damp fork. Fry in hot oil until golden brown. Drain and serve with hot sauce. **Yield:** 55-60 appetizers.

Note: *Should be served hot.*

Mrs. Richard Keeling (Laurie)

Empañadas II

½ medium onion, chopped
1 clove garlic, chopped
1 teaspoon salad oil
1 pound chorizo (Mexican
  sausage)
½ pound ground beef

1 large tomato, peeled and
  chopped
2 jalapeño peppers, chopped
1¼ teaspoons cumin
1 teaspoon chili powder
1 pie crust dough

Sauté onion and garlic in oil. Add meat and brown well. Add tomato, jalapeños, and spices. Simmer until meat is done. Drain excess liquid and cool. Roll out pastry dough and cut into 3-inch rounds. Place as much filling as possible on ½ of round. Fold dough over and pinch edges closed. Bake at 400° on cookie sheet for 20 minutes or until golden brown. **Yield:** About 40.

Note: *Can be frozen and baked later.*

Mrs. William Hollon (Kasey)

Sue's Easy Stuffed Mushrooms

½ pound medium sized
  mushrooms
4 ounces Swiss cheese, shredded
1 hard-boiled egg, finely
  chopped, optional

4 Tablespoons seasoned dry
  breadcrumbs
4 Tablespoons butter, softened

Preheat oven to 350°. Remove stems from mushrooms and clean caps. Mix remaining ingredients and stuff mushroom caps, mounding the filling over caps. Place in lightly buttered casserole, (9-inch round or 2-quart) sides touching and bake for 15-20 minutes. Serve warm. **Yield:** 15.

Note: *May be assembled earlier in the day, or even a day before, and refrigerated. Bake a little longer until cheese is bubbly and browned.*

Mrs. Dennis Furlong (Dede)

Mushrooms Eleganté

48 large mushroom caps
2　cups fresh crabmeat (Snow or
　　King)

1 jar (6 ounces) Chelton House
　hollandaise

Clean mushrooms and remove stems. Poach mushrooms by placing in boiling water and removing from heat. Cover and allow to stand 5 minutes. Remove and pat dry. Mix hollandaise and crabmeat. Spoon into mushroom caps. Broil until brown and bubbly. Serve warm. **Yield:** 48 appetizers.

Mrs. William Hollon (Kasey)

Easy Mushroom Crescent Snacks

3 cups finely chopped fresh
　mushrooms
2 Tablespoons butter or
　margarine, melted
1 teaspoon garlic powder
1 teaspoon finely chopped onion
　or ½ teaspoon instant minced
　onion

1　teaspoon lemon juice
1　teaspoon Worcestershire sauce
1　can (8 ounces) refrigerated
　　quick crescent dinner rolls
1　package (3 ounces) cream
　　cheese, softened
¼ cup grated Parmesan cheese

Brown mushrooms in butter. Add garlic powder, onion, lemon juice, and Worcestershire sauce; stir and cook until liquid evaporates. Set aside. Separate dough into 2 long rectangles. Place in ungreased 9x13-inch pan; press over bottom and ¼ inch up sides to form crust. Spread cream cheese over dough. Top with mushroom mixture and sprinkle with Parmesan cheese. Bake at 350° for 20-25 minutes or until golden brown. Cool 5 minutes, then cut into desired shapes. Serve warm. **Yield:** 24 snacks.

Note: *To make ahead: prepare, cover, and refrigerate up to 2 hours, then bake as directed.*

Mrs. Steve Becker (Frances)

Artichoke Puffs
Excellent Party Appetizers

2 cans (14 ounces each) artichoke
  hearts
Party Rye bread
3 egg whites, at room temperature

¼ cup mayonnaise
¼ cup Parmesan cheese
¼ cup grated Cheddar cheese

Cut artichoke hearts in half or thirds, depending on size. Place each piece face down on a slice of bread. Beat egg whites until stiff. Fold mayonnaise and cheeses into egg whites. It will be lumpy. Place a spoonful on each artichoke. Bake at 375° for 10 minutes until brown. **Yield:** Approximately 36 puffs.

Mrs. Bill Frank (Barbara)

Appetizing Artichoke Squares

1 cup chopped onion
3 Tablespoons butter or olive oil
4 eggs, well-beaten
¼ cup fine dry breadcrumbs
½ teaspoon salt
Pepper, dash
Oregano, dash

Tabasco sauce, 2-3 drops
2 cups shredded Cheddar cheese
2 jars (6 ounces) marinated
  artichoke hearts, drained and
  chopped
Pimiento strips, optional

Sauté onion in butter until transparent. In mixing bowl, combine eggs, breadcrumbs, salt, pepper, oregano, and Tabasco sauce. Stir in onion, cheese, and artichokes. Spread into a greased 7½x11-inch baking pan. Bake at 350° for 18-20 minutes. Cut into 1-inch squares. Serve hot. Garnish with pimiento strips, if desired. **Yield:** 24 squares.

Mrs. Doug Rivenbark (Penny)

♥ *Steam artichokes and serve with your favorite dressing. Allow your guests to feast on artichoke leaves.*

Hot Artichoke Dip

2 cans (14 ounces each) artichoke
  hearts
2 cups grated Parmesan cheese

2 cups mayonnaise
½ cup green onion, tops only
Paprika

Drain artichokes and cut into small pieces. Mix all ingredients together and put into 6½x10-inch casserole dish. Sprinkle with paprika. Bake at 350° for 20-30 minutes. Serve with melba toast, crackers, or vegetable sticks. **Yield:** 6-8 servings.

Mrs. James Layton (Vicki)

Parmesan Artichokes

1 can (14 ounces) artichoke hearts
1 package (3 ounces) cream cheese

Parmesan cheese
Red pepper, dash

Cut artichokes in half. Put ½ teaspoon of cream cheese in center of artichoke pieces. Sprinkle generously with Parmesan cheese. Top with a dash of red pepper. Bake at 350° for 10 minutes. **Yield:** 4 servings.

Mrs. Joe Key (Christie)

Green Chili Egg Squares

½ pound shredded mozzarella
  cheese
½ pound shredded Cheddar
  cheese

8 eggs, beaten
2 cans (4 ounces each) chopped
  green chilies

Grease 7½x11½-inch ovenproof dish. Mix all ingredients together and pour into pan. Bake covered at 350° for 30 minutes. Then lower heat to 250° for 30 minutes longer. Cut in squares and serve warm. **Yield:** 35 squares.

Mrs. William Hollon (Kasey)

Quick Bacon Squares

1 pound bacon, cooked crisp and crumbled
1 bunch green onions, chopped
2 packages (4 ounces each) grated sharp Cheddar cheese

Mayonnaise
1 package (8 ounces) party rye bread

Mix bacon, green onions, and grated cheese with enough mayonnaise to hold mixture together. Spread on bread. Broil 5-7 minutes. **Yield:** 3 dozen.

Note: *May be made ahead and broiled at party time.*

Mrs. Jim Thornton (Jackie)

Spinach Cheese Squares

3 eggs, well beaten
1 cup milk
½ cup butter, melted
1 cup flour
1 teaspoon salt
1 teaspoon baking powder

1 pound sharp Cheddar cheese, grated
1 package (10 ounces) frozen spinach, thawed and drained well
1 teaspoon creole seasoning

Mix together eggs, milk, and butter. Add dry ingredients, then cheese, spinach (squeezed dry) and seasoning. Bake in 3-quart ovenproof dish at 350° for 40 minutes. Cut into 1½-inch squares. **Yield:** 48 squares.

Mrs. Dennis Furlong (Dede)

Rumaki

16 chicken livers
1 cup soy sauce

½ cup sherry
16 slices bacon, halved crosswise

Wash chicken livers and dry with paper towels. Cut each in half, removing any stringy sections. Place in large bowl. Combine soy sauce and sherry. Pour over livers and toss lightly. Wrap each halved liver with one-half slice of bacon. Secure with a wooden toothpick. Arrange on the rack of a broiler pan. Brush both sides with the soy mixture. Broil 3 inches from heat, turning once or twice at 2-3 minute intervals, until bacon is crisp and livers are done. **Yield:** 32 appetizers.

Note: *Water chestnuts may be substituted for chicken livers.*

Mrs. Doug Arnold (Debbi)

Sweet and Sour Chicken Wings

12 chicken wings
Salt and pepper
1 egg
1 teaspoon water
1 teaspoon salad oil
Cornstarch
Salad Oil
1 clove garlic, chopped

Sauce:
¼ cup chicken broth
¼ cup ketchup
1 Tablespoon soy sauce
¾ cup sugar
½ cup cider vinegar
½ cup pineapple chunks, optional
1 can (8 ounces) water chestnuts, optional

Divide wings into two pieces and remove tip. Place tips in saucepan and cover with water. Season with salt and pepper. Simmer for the chicken broth. Beat together egg, water, and oil. Dip wings into egg mixture. Drain on wire rack. Coat with cornstarch. Heat oil and garlic in electric skillet at 350°. Add wings and brown. Drain. Put wings in large baking dish. Combine ingredients for the sauce and pour over chicken. Add pineapple chunks and water chestnuts if desired. Cover and bake at 375° for 40 minutes. **Yield:** 24 wings.

Mrs. Sam Murray (Sandy)

Bourbon Weiners
A Real Crowd Pleaser

½ cup bourbon whiskey
1 cup firmly packed brown sugar
1 cup ketchup

½ cup water
1-2 packages weiners

In a saucepan, mix all ingredients except weiners. Bring to a boil. Cut weiners into bite-size slices and add. Simmer. Transfer to a chafing dish. **Yield:** 2-4 cups.

Note: *Can be frozen.*

Mrs. Bill Frank (Barbara)

Cocktail Meatballs

2 pounds ground chuck
1 envelope (1.25 ounces) onion
  soup mix
1 egg
2 teaspoons monosodium
  glutamate

¼ cup dry breadcrumbs
2 bottles (8 ounces each) cocktail
  sauce
1 jar (10 ounces) grape jelly

In large bowl, mix together first 5 ingredients. Form into bite size meat-balls. Arrange on cookie sheet; cover with plastic wrap and refrigerate (or sauté meatballs until brown in hot butter, cool, and refrigerate). About 30 minutes before serving, combine cocktail sauce and jelly in skillet over medium heat. Add meatballs; simmer covered, about 25 minutes or until heated. Serve in chafing dish with toothpicks. **Yield:** 3 dozen meatballs.

Note: *Cocktail sausages can be substituted for meatballs.*

Mrs. Jerry Brown (Linda)

Teriyaki Steak Roll-Ups

1½ pounds top round steak,
  ¾-inch thick
1 Tablespoon firmly packed
  brown sugar
1 teaspoon ginger
1 can (13¼ ounces) pineapple
  chunks, drained (reserve
  syrup)

½ cup soy sauce
½ cup salad oil
1 clove garlic, minced

Cut steak into strips 3 inches long and ⅛ inch thick. Place in a plastic bag or baking dish. Mix brown sugar and ginger; then stir in reserved pine-apple syrup, soy sauce, salad oil, and garlic. Pour over steak. Close bag or cover dish and refrigerate at least 8 hours. Cut pineapple chunks in half. Roll each steak strip around pineapple chunk. Secure with toothpick. Set oven control to broil. Place roll-ups on rack in broiler pan so tops are 3-4 inches from heat. Broil 2 minutes. Turn and broil 2-3 minutes on other side. Serve immediately. **Yield:** 60 roll-ups.

Note: *Steak strips must be no thicker than ⅛ inch in order to roll them. Steak will be easier to cut if partially frozen.*

Mrs. Steve Moi (Joanie)

Hot Crabmeat Cheese Puffs

½ pound crabmeat
4 green onions, tops and
    bottoms, chopped
½ cup grated Monterey Jack
    cheese
½ cup grated Cheddar cheese
½ cup mayonnaise

1 teaspoon lemon juice
¼ teaspoon curry powder
1 can (5 ounces) water chestnuts,
    drained and chopped
1 package (10 ounces) flaky-style
    refrigerator rolls

Combine all ingredients, except rolls, and mix well. Separate each roll into 3 layers. Place on ungreased cookie sheet and place crabmeat mixture on top. Bake at 400° for about 10 minutes or until golden. **Yield:** 36 puffs.

Note: *This recipe can be doubled and placed in ceramic shells for baking as a main course.*

Cookbook Committee

♥ *A hollowed out pineapple makes a unique container for fruit dip. Spear pieces of fruit with toothpicks and stick them into the outside of the pineapple for easy and pretty servings. This makes a beautiful centerpiece.*

Ham and Cheese Puffs

½ cup butter or margarine,
    softened
1½ cups grated Cheddar cheese
¾ cup ham, cooked and ground

½ teaspoon Worcestershire sauce
⅛ teaspoon red pepper
1 cup sifted flour

In mixing bowl, combine butter, cheese, ham, and seasonings. Mix in flour and shape the dough into small balls (about the size of a large marble). Place on cookie sheet. Bake at 350° for 15-20 minutes. Serve hot. **Yield:** 25-30 puffs.

Note: *Dough may be made ahead of time, wrapped, and either frozen or refrigerated until needed.*

Mrs. Roy Watson (Charlene)

Baked Cheese Puffs

1 loaf Texas toast
½ cup margarine, softened
1 package (3 ounces) cream
   cheese, softened
¼ pound sharp Cheddar cheese,
   grated

¼ teaspoon dry mustard
Salt to taste
Cayenne pepper to taste
2 egg whites, stiffly beaten

Trim crusts from Texas toast, and cut into 1-inch cubes. Combine margarine, cream cheese, grated cheddar, dry mustard, salt, and red pepper in heavy saucepan. Heat on low, stirring until cheese is just melted and ingredients are well combined. Transfer mixture to bowl and fold in stiffly beaten egg whites. Dip bread cubes into cheese mixture to coat and let excess drip off. Place on buttered cookie sheet, chill, loosely covered with foil overnight. Bake at 400° for 8-10 minutes. **Yield:** 60 puffs.

Note: *Can be frozen on cookie sheet and used later.*

Mrs. Paul Carletta (Mary Ann)

Quick Cheese Puffs

¼ cup grated Parmesan cheese
¼ cup grated Cheddar cheese
1 can (10-12 count) refrigerated
   biscuits, separated and
   quartered

4 Tablespoons butter, melted

Preheat oven to 425°. Mix cheeses together. Roll each quarter biscuit in melted butter, then in grated cheeses. Place on cookie sheet ½ inch apart. Bake at 425° for 15 minutes. Serve warm. **Yield:** 40-48 pieces.

Mrs. Dennis Furlong (Dede)

Fried Cheese

1 package (10 ounces) sharp
　Cheddar cheese, cubed
2 eggs, beaten
1 cup Italian seasoned fine
　breadcrumbs

2 Tablespoons sesame seeds
Shortening

Dip cheese cubes in beaten eggs, then in breadcrumbs. Repeat. Dip in sesame seeds. Heat sufficient shortening to fill a frying pan to a depth of 2-3 inches. Fry breaded cheese cubes in the shortening until golden brown. **Yield:** Approximately 35 appetizers.

Mrs. Marvin Chronister (Donna)

Cheese Olive Balls

2 cups shredded sharp Cheddar
　cheese
1 cup flour

½ cup butter
1　jar (5 ounces) green olives

Mix cheese and flour. Melt butter and mix with cheese and flour. Cover olives with mixture to form balls. Bake at 400° for 15-20 minutes. **Yield:** 45-50 appetizers.

Note: *Can be frozen before cooking.*

Mrs. Steve Moi (Joanie)

Ham Balls

1½ pounds smoked ham, ground
1　cup fine breadcrumbs
1　egg, beaten
½　cup milk
1　cup firmly packed brown
　sugar

½ cup water
½ cup pineapple juice
½ cup vinegar
1　teaspoon dry mustard

Mix ham, crumbs, egg, and milk. Form into small balls. Put in 9x13-inch ovenproof dish. Combine remaining ingredients and pour over balls. Bake at 350° for 1 hour. Cook covered first ½ hour then uncover. Serve warm. **Yield:** 50 balls.

Mrs. Bill Frank (Barbara)

Spinach Balls

2 packages (10 ounces each) frozen
  chopped spinach
2 cups herb seasoned stuffing mix
1 cup grated Parmesan cheese

6 eggs, beaten
¾ cup butter, softened
Salt and pepper to taste

Cook spinach according to package directions and drain well. Mix remaining ingredients with spinach. Roll into balls about the size of a walnut. Place on a cookie sheet and bake at 350° for 10 minutes. **Yield:** 60-70 spinach balls.

Note: *These can be made ahead and frozen.*

Mrs. Robert George (Linda)

Pat McGinnis' Asparagus Roll-Ups

12 slices white bread, crust
   removed
1 container (8 ounces) whipped
   cream cheese
2 Tablespoons chives
8 slices bacon, cooked and
   crumbled

1 can (15 ounces) asparagus
   spears
¼ cup margarine, melted
Parmesan cheese

Use rolling pin to flatten each slice of bread. Combine cream cheese, chives, and bacon; stirring well. Spread mixture over bread covering to the edges. Place 2 (1 if large) asparagus spears on each slice; roll and place seam side down on greased cookie sheet. Brush bread with melted margarine and sprinkle with Parmesan cheese. Bake at 400° for 12 minutes. **Yield:** 12 roll-ups.

Mrs. Jim Thornton (Jackie)

Marinated Mushrooms

⅓ cup water	⅛ teaspoon dry mustard
⅓ cup vinegar	1 clove garlic, crushed
¼ cup salad oil	1 Tablespoon sugar
1 Tablespoon finely chopped onion	¼ teaspoon coarsely ground pepper
2 Tablespoons parsley	Tabasco sauce, dash
1 teaspoon lemon juice	1½ pounds small whole
1½ teaspoons salt	mushrooms, cleaned

Combine all ingredients, except mushrooms. Shake to blend. Add mushrooms. Toss gently. Cover and chill. Marinate overnight, stirring occasionally. **Yield:** 4-5 servings.

Mrs. William Hollon (Kasey)

♥ *To freeze mushrooms, wash and dry them quickly. Freeze in a plastic bag. Do not defrost before using. They taste great!*

♥ *When sautéing fresh mushrooms, sprinkle with a little lemon juice to prevent discoloration.*

Hot Crab Muffins

¼ cup margarine, softened	1 package (6) English Muffins, halved
1 jar (5 ounces) Old English cheese	Garlic powder to taste
1½ teaspoons mayonnaise	
1 package (6 ounces) frozen crabmeat, thawed	

Combine first 4 ingredients and spread over 12 halved muffins. Sprinkle with garlic powder; cut into fourths. Bake at 400° for 10-15 minutes; then broil for about 2 minutes or until bubbly. **Yield:** 48 appetizers.

Note: *Can be frozen.*

Mrs. Jim Conine (Donna)

Cream Cheese Crab Bars

1 package (8 ounces) cream cheese
Salt
1 bottle (12 ounces) cocktail sauce
1 can (6 ounces) light crabmeat,
  drained well

Lemon juice
Tabasco sauce
Green onion, including tops,
  chopped

Cut cream cheese bar in half so that it is half as thick. Place halves side by side to form a square. Salt lightly. Pour ⅔ bottle of cocktail sauce on top and sides. Place crabmeat over sauce. Sprinkle with lemon juice. Pour remaining ⅓ bottle of cocktail sauce over crab. Sprinkle with Tabasco. Top with green onions. Serve with crackers. **Yield:** 8 servings.

Note: *May need to blot excess moisture before serving.*

Mrs. Bill Frank (Barbara)

Caviar Pie

2 packages (8 ounces each)
  cream cheese, softened
1 small onion, grated
1 Tablespoon Worcestershire
  sauce
1 Tablespoon lemon juice
½-¾ cup mayonnaise

1 jar (4 ounces) Romanoff caviar
4 eggs, boiled and grated
Fresh parsley, snipped
Paprika

Blend first 5 ingredients. Pour into 8-inch ovenproof dish. Top first with black caviar and then sprinkle with grated eggs. Garnish with parsley and paprika. **Yield:** 6-8 servings.

Mrs. Jim Thornton (Jackie)

Scallops Ceviche
Excellent Compliment to Mexican Food

1½ pounds raw small bay scallops
⅔ cup fresh lime juice
2 ripe tomatoes, finely chopped
½ cup chopped onion
¼ cup olive oil
1 Tablespoon fresh parsley

2 teaspoons finely chopped
 jalapeño peppers
1 teaspoon salt
¼ teaspoon oregano
⅛ teaspoon pepper

Place scallops in a glass bowl. Cover with lime juice. Cover bowl and refrigerate overnight (or at least 6 hours). Stir occasionally. Up to 3 hours prior to serving, add remaining ingredients. Return to refrigerator until served. Drain before serving, reserving ¼ cup juice. Add the reserved juice to salad before serving. **Yield:** 10 cups.

Note: *Serve in glass bowl surrounded by ice to keep cool.*

Mrs. Sam Murray (Sandy)

Tuna and Watercress Tapenade
Elegant Hors d'oeuvre

1 can (7 ounces) chunk white
 tuna, well drained
½ cup mayonnaise
4 ounces cream cheese, room
 temperature
2 Tablespoons fresh lemon juice

¼ teaspoon pepper
2 cups watercress leaves
4 green onions and tops, trimmed
 and chopped
3 Tablespoons small capers

In a food processor, combine tuna, mayonnaise, cream cheese, lemon juice, and pepper. Blend until smooth. Add remaining ingredients and pulsate with on/off switch until mixture is blended. Transfer to bowl, cover, and refrigerate at least 2 hours. Serve with water biscuits, lavash or other crisp crackers. **Yield:** 1½ cups.

Mrs. Dennis Furlong (Dede)

Hot Beef Spread

1 package (8 ounces) cream cheese
1 Tablespoon milk
1 Tablespoon white wine
2 Tablespoons Worcestershire
  sauce

2 Tablespoons chopped onion
1 jar (2½ ounces) dried beef,
  chopped

Combine all ingredients in a medium bowl and microwave on high for 3 minutes. Serve with your favorite crackers. **Yield:** 2 cups.

Mrs. Wallace Brown (Gayle)

Cream Cheese and Olive Spread

2 packages (3 ounces each) cream
  cheese
½ cup mayonnaise

½ cup chopped pecans
1 cup salad olives
Pepper, dash

Blend cream cheese and mayonnaise well. Add other ingredients and refrigerate. Serve with crackers or bread. **Yield:** Approximately 1-1½ cups.

Mrs. Mike Freeman (Cathy)

Hot Mushroom Spread

¼ cup dry minced onion
3 cans (2 ounces each) mushroom
  pieces and stems, drained
2 Tablespoons butter
1 package (8 ounces) cream
  cheese

2 egg yolks, beaten slightly
Salt and pepper to taste
Garlic powder to taste
Party rye bread

Sauté onion and mushroom in butter until soft. Add cheese, egg yolks, and seasonings. Mix until melted and heated. Spread on party rye and bake at 350° for 15 minutes. **Yield:** Approximately 3 dozen appetizers.

Note: *May be made ahead. Simply refrigerate the mixture until ready to spread on bread.*

Mrs. Mac Cravy (Sharon)

Pimiento Cheese Spread

2 pounds Velveeta cheese, grated
8 medium sweet pickles, chopped
8 hard-boiled eggs, chopped
1 jar (6 ounces) chopped
  pimientos, drained

2 cups mayonnaise
3 Tablespoons mustard
3 Tablespoons sugar
Salt and pepper to taste

Mix all ingredients together and chill. **Yield:** Approximately 12 cups.

Mrs. Wallace Brown (Gayle)

Shrimp Spread

1 package (8 ounces) cream
  cheese
1 can (4¼ ounces) baby shrimp,
  drained
½ cup chopped celery

½ cup minced onion
Lemon juice, few drops
3 Tablespoons mayonnaise
Worcestershire sauce, dash

Soften cream cheese. Mash shrimp into bits. Mix all ingredients, and re-frigerate 3-4 hours before serving. **Yield:** 1½ cups spread.

Note: *Serve on crackers or party rye bread.*

Mrs. Mallard Tysseland (Jill)

Ham and Cheese Log

4 ounces sharp Cheddar cheese,
  grated
1 package (8 ounces) cream
  cheese, softened
1 can (4½ ounces) deviled ham
1 can (4½ ounces) ripe olives,
  chopped

1 teaspoon Worcestershire sauce
1 Tablespoon minced onion
½ teaspoon garlic salt
½ cup finely chopped pecans or
  walnuts

Mix all ingredients except nuts. Chill. Shape into log and roll log in nuts. Serve with crackers. Freezes well. **Yield:** 6-8 servings.

Mrs. Bill Frank (Barbara)

Little Pizza Appetizers

1 pound regular bulk pork
  sausage
1 can (8 ounces) tomato sauce
1 can (6 ounces) tomato paste
1 package (6 count) Pepperidge
  Farm club rolls

1 jar (5 ounces) Old English Sharp
  cheese
1 green pepper, finely chopped
Parmesan cheese, grated

Brown sausage, drain fat. Add tomato sauce and tomato paste and simmer a few minutes. Slice rolls ¼ inch thick. Spread with Old English cheese and a heaping teaspoon of meat sauce. Sprinkle with green pepper and Parmesan cheese. Freeze on cookie sheets and package in desired amounts. Bake (frozen) at 450° for 10 minutes. **Yield:** 24 pizzas.

Mrs. Steve Moi (Joanie)

♥ *Place an assortment of cheeses on a tray and garnish with fruit.*

Sausage Swirls

1 package (8 ounces) crescent
  dinner rolls

1 pound sage flavored sausage,
  uncooked

Open package of rolls and smooth out dough with a rolling pin. Cover completely with a thin layer of sausage. Roll carefully into a log. Wrap in wax paper and freeze overnight. Slice into ¼ inch swirls. Place on cookie sheet. Bake at 350° for 20 minutes, or until lightly browned. **Yield:** 60 appetizers.

Note: *This freezes well, and is a great dish for a large meeting or family gathering.*

Mrs. Richard Keeling (Laurie)

Tomato Toasties

½ teaspoon salt
½ cup grated mild Cheddar
   cheese
½ cup mayonnaise
¼ cup chopped green onion,
   stems included

½ pound bacon, cooked and
   crumbled
French style enriched rolls
1 pint cherry tomatoes, sliced
Mayonnaise, to spread

Combine first 5 ingredients. Slice rolls about ¼ inch thick; then cut in half.
Spread mayonnaise on each bread slice. Place sliced tomato on bread. Put
1 teaspoon of mixture on tomato. Broil until lightly browned. **Yield:** 3½
dozen.

Mrs. Bill Frank (Barbara)

Cheese Crispies

1 cup butter
2 cups flour
1 cup grated Cheddar cheese

1 jar (5 ounces) Old English
   cheese
2 cups Rice Krispies

Cut butter into flour. Mix in cheeses. Stir in cereal and form into tiny balls.
Place on cookie sheet and flatten with fork. Bake at 375° for 8-9 minutes.
Yield: 55-60 appetizers.

Note: *Dough can be refrigerated for up to 4 days. Can also bake ahead, freeze and
reheat.*
Variation: *Touch of red pepper adds variation.*

Mrs. Joe Gunn (Sandy)

Blue Cheese Bites

1 package (8 ounces) refrigerator
   biscuits
¼ cup butter

3 Tablespoons crumbled blue
   cheese

Cut each biscuit into quarters. Melt butter and blue cheese together. Roll
biscuit pieces in cheese mixture. Arrange in two 8-inch round baking dishes.
Pour remaining cheese mixture over biscuit pieces, coating well. Bake at
400° for 12-15 minutes until golden. **Yield:** 40 appetizers.

Mrs. Ron Souder (Pat)

31

Salmon Ball

1 package (8 ounces) cream cheese	3 Tablespoons finely chopped onions
1 can (15½ ounces) red salmon, drained and mashed	1 Tablespoon lemon juice
2½ Tablespoons liquid smoke	1 Tablespoon prepared mustard
	Horseradish, dash

Soften cream cheese, mix all ingredients and form into a ball. Serve with party crackers. **Yield:** 10-20 servings.

Mrs. Bill Frank (Barbara)

Seafood Hors d'oeuvre

1 package (8 ounces) cream cheese, softened	2 cans (4¼ ounces each) shrimp, drained and chopped, or 2 cans
1 jar (12 ounces) seafood cocktail sauce	(6 ounces each) crabmeat, drained
Garlic salt to taste	

Spread cream cheese on platter or 8-inch pie pan. Cover with cocktail sauce, using as much as desired. Sprinkle with garlic salt and top with shrimp or crabmeat. Serve with crackers. **Yield:** 6-8 servings.

Note: *Fresh or frozen shrimp or crabmeat may be used.*

Mrs. Jim Conine (Donna)

Curry Clam Dip

1 can (6½ ounces) clams, minced	1 teaspoon parsley
1 package (8 ounces) cream cheese	1 teaspoon Worcestershire sauce
1 teaspoon minced onion	½ teaspoon curry powder
1 Tablespoon lemon juice	

Mix together and add a little milk if needed to blend. **Yield:** 1½ cups.

Note: *Serve cold on crackers. Yummy!!*

Mrs. Bill Crandall (Julie)

Deviled Shrimp Dip

1 pound raw shrimp	Salt and pepper to taste
3 Tablespoons minced onion	6 Tablespoons flour
½ cup butter or margarine, melted	1 cup milk
½ teaspoon dry mustard	1 Tablespoon sherry
Red pepper, dash	½ cup breadcrumbs

Clean shrimp and chop coarsely. Sauté onions until clear in melted butter. Stir in mustard, seasonings, and shrimp. Add flour while stirring constantly. Add milk and cook until mixture boils, continuing to stir constantly. Remove from heat and add sherry. Pour into a greased 1-quart casserole and top with breadcrumbs. Bake at 350° for 30 minutes. Serve with melba rounds. **Yield:** 6-8 servings.

Mrs. Jerry Brown (Linda)

Shrimp Dip
Gets Rave Reviews

1 pound shrimp, cooked and diced	1 Tablespoon horseradish mustard
1½ cups mayonnaise	Juice of ½ lemon
¼ cup chopped fresh parsley	1 teaspoon onion salt
¼ cup frozen chives	

Mix all ingredients together. Refrigerate to allow dip to age. Serve with club crackers. **Yield:** Approximately 3½ cups.

Mrs. William Hollon (Kasey)

Italian Shrimp Dip

2 packages (3 ounces each) cream cheese	½ cup sour cream
1 package (0.7 ounce) Italian dressing, dry	1 Tablespoon lemon juice
	1 can (4¼ ounce) small shrimp

Mix all ingredients. Use as dip for potato chips or tortilla chips. **Yield:** 1 cup.

Mrs. Bill Frank (Barbara)

Spinach Dip

1 package (10 ounces) frozen
  chopped spinach
1 box (1.2 ounces) Knorr vegetable
  soup
1 carton (8 ounces) sour cream

1 cup mayonnaise
1 medium onion, chopped
1 can (8 ounces) sliced water
  chestnuts

Thaw spinach and drain thoroughly. Squeeze all the water out of spinach. Mix all ingredients and refrigerate. **Yield:** Approximately 3 cups.

Note: *Will keep for several days.*

Mrs. Ted Denbow (Connie)

Lo-Cal Vegetable Dip

1 carton (16 ounces) cottage cheese
1 Tablespoon mayonnaise
1 Tablespoon sour cream
2 Tablespoons fresh chopped
  parsley, or dried flakes
2 Tablespoons chopped green
  onion

2 teaspoons Beau Monde
  seasoning
2 teaspoons dill weed
1 teaspoon lemon juice

Put all ingredients into food processor and blend until cottage cheese appears fairly smooth. Serve with a variety of fresh vegetables cut into bite-size pieces for dipping. **Yield:** 2 cups.

Note: *Keeps well in refrigerator for several days.*

Mrs. Ellwood Jones (Ann)

Dill Dip

1 cup mayonnaise
1 cup sour cream
1 teaspoon dill weed
2 teaspoons parsley flakes

1 teaspoon seasoning salt
1 round loaf (1 pound)
  pumpernickel bread, unsliced

Mix all ingredients except bread. Refrigerate overnight. When ready to serve, hollow out middle of bread, leaving bottom and sides and cubing the center. Place dip in the middle of loaf. Use bread cubes to dip. Vegetables may also be used. **Yield:** 2 cups.

Mrs. James Layton (Vicki)

Hot and Cheesy Black-Eyed Pea Dip
Great for New Years

2　jars (5 ounces each) Old
　　English cheese
½-1 cup butter or margarine
½　medium onion, chopped
2　cans (15 ounces each) black-
　　eyed peas, cooked

3 jalapeño peppers, diced and
　seeded
1 can (4 ounces) green chilies,
　chopped
Garlic salt to taste
Corn chips or crackers

Melt cheese over low heat. In a skillet, melt butter and cook onions until soft. Drain peas and add to melted cheese. Add onions, jalapeños, chilies, and garlic salt. Mix well and serve hot in chafing dish with crackers or corn chips. **Yield:** 6 cups.

Mrs. Gerald Box (Pat)

Roquefort Dip

1 medium onion, grated
1 package (8 ounces) cream
　cheese, softened
2 cups mayonnaise

1 package (3 ounces) Roquefort
　cheese, crumbled
Garlic powder, dash

Blend onion, cream cheese, and mayonnaise. Add Roquefort cheese and garlic powder. Serve with fresh vegetables. **Yield:** Approximately 4 cups.

Note: *Good as a salad dressing.*

Mrs. James Samson (Malissa)

Pizza Dip

1 jar (32 ounces) spaghetti sauce
8 ounces mozzarella cheese,
　grated
¼ cup grated Parmesan cheese

2 teaspoons oregano
1 teaspoon instant minced onion
¼ teaspoon garlic salt

Mix all ingredients together and heat until cheeses are melted. Keep warm in chafing dish or fondue pot. Serve with tortilla chips. **Yield:** 4-5 cups.

Note: *Can also be served on English muffins.*

Mrs. Jim Conine (Donna)

Cheese Dip Served In Hawaiian Bread

1 package (8 ounces) cream
  cheese
½ pound Velveeta cheese
1 carton (8 ounces) sour cream
1 jar (2½ ounces) dried beef,
  chopped

Salt and pepper to taste
Garlic salt to taste
1 round loaf (16 ounces) Hawaiian
  bread

Combine ingredients, except the bread, and heat in a double boiler until well blended. Carve out center of Hawaiian bread to make bowl. Pour warm cheese mixture into bread at serving time. Take remaining bread and cut into bite-sized pieces, brown under broiler, and use for dipping into cheese dip. **Yield:** 3 cups.

Mrs. Jim Conine (Donna)

♥ *Scoop out a head of red or green cabbage or a fresh green pepper to use as an interesting container for vegetable dip.*

Broccoli Mushroom Dip

1 package (10 ounces) frozen
  chopped broccoli
1 medium onion, finely chopped
½ cup butter
1 tube (6 ounces) garlic cheese

1 can (10½ ounces) cream of
  mushroom soup
1 can (3 ounces) sliced
  mushrooms, cut twice

Overcook broccoli according to package directions. Sauté chopped onion in butter. Slowly add garlic cheese, mushroom soup, and sliced mushrooms. Mix well. Add broccoli, mix and serve in dip dish over candle or chafing dish. **Yield:** Approximately 3 cups.

Note: *Good as a patty filling for luncheon, as a dip for crackers, or topping on baked potato.*
Variation: *Add ½ cup chopped celery and dash of Tabasco sauce.*

Mrs. Jerry Brown (Linda)

Carol's Cheese Roll

1 package (8 ounces) cream
  cheese, softened
1 jar (5 ounces) Old English Sharp
  cheese
1 Tablespoon butter, softened

1 Tablespoon Worcestershire sauce
Garlic salt, heavy dash
1 cup crushed nuts
1 cup finely chopped black or
  green olives

Combine first 5 ingredients. Shape into a ball and roll in nuts and olives. Serve with crackers. **Yield:** 16 servings.

Mrs. Richard Keeling (Laurie)

Cheese Roll

½ pound American cheese, grated
1 package (3 ounces) cream
  cheese
1 ounce pimiento

½ cup pecans
1 clove garlic
Chili powder

Place all ingredients except chili powder in food processor and mix thoroughly. Shape into 2 rolls and roll in generous amount of chili powder. Wrap in waxed paper and chill well. Serve with crackers. **Yield:** 16-18 servings.

Note: *Will keep for several weeks in refrigerator or can be frozen.*

Mrs. Don Kleinschmidt (Ceil)

Pineapple Cheese Ball

2 packages (8 ounces each) cream
  cheese
¼ cup crushed pineapple
2 Tablespoons chopped green
  pepper

2 Tablespoons chopped green
  onions
2 teaspoons seasoned salt, or less
Chopped nuts

Combine first 5 ingredients. Roll in chopped nuts. **Yield:** 10-12 servings.
Variation: *Garnish with pineapple slices, cherries and parsley.*

Mrs. Robert George (Linda)

Cheese Ball

2 packages (8 ounces each) cream
  cheese, softened
½ pound medium sharp cheese,
  grated
1 can (8 ounces) crushed
  pineapple, drained
¼ cup chopped green pepper

2 Tablespoons chopped onion
Salt, pinch
Sugar, pinch
Red pepper, dash
Paprika, dash
Garlic powder to taste
Pecans, chopped

Combine all ingredients except pecans. Chill for 3 hours. Form into ball
and roll in chopped pecans. **Yield:** 24 servings.

Mrs. Steve Moi (Joanie)

Three-Cheese Ball

2 wedges (3 ounces each)
  Roquefort or blue cheese
2 jars (5 ounces each) processed
  Cheddar cheese spread
4 packages (3 ounces each) cream
  cheese

2 Tablespoons minced onion
1 teaspoon Worcestershire sauce
1 cup ground pecans
¼ cup parsley

Blend all cheeses, onion, and Worcestershire sauce. Roll in ½ cup pecans.
Line bowl with waxed paper and refrigerate cheese ball at least one hour
before serving. Remove and roll in rest of pecans and parsley. **Yield:** 20-
25 servings.

Note: *May be frozen and thawed completely to serve.*

Mrs. John Mearns (June)

Easy and Quick Cheese Ball

2 packages (8 ounces each) cream
  cheese
1 package (10 ounces) frozen
  chopped spinach, thawed and
  drained

1 can (8 ounces) sliced water
  chestnuts
1 package (1.2 ounces) Knorr
  vegetable soup mix

Mix all ingredients. Form into a ball. Serve with crackers. **Yield:** 12 servings.

Mrs. Pete Bennett (Stephanie)

Christmas Wreaths

1 package (8 ounces) cream cheese   Parsley, snipped
1 jar (8 ounces, approximately)
  mammoth-size pimiento stuffed
  olives

Soften cream cheese. Form ¼ inch layer of cream cheese around entire olive. Roll in parsley and refrigerate. Before serving, slice in half to reveal wreath. **Yield:** Approximately 56 halves.

Note: *Fun to make.*

Mrs. William Hollon (Kasey)

Fruit Dip

2   packages (8 ounces each)
    cream cheese, softened
1   package (8 ounces) sour cream
1½ teaspoons cinnamon
½   cup firmly packed brown
    sugar

½   cup granulated sugar
1½ teaspoons vanilla extract
Nuts finely chopped, to taste

Mix all ingredients and refrigerate. Serve as dip with fresh fruits. **Yield:** 2-3 cups.

Note: *Half recipe for a smaller crowd.*

Mrs. Mike Freeman (Cathy)

♥ *Don't cut or peel fruit or vegetables too far ahead of time. Once their flesh is exposed to the air, they lose nutrients and flavor quickly.*

Orange Fluff

1 can (6 ounces) frozen orange
   juice concentrate
1 orange juice can milk
½ orange juice can water

1 egg
2 Tablespoons sugar
2 teaspoons vanilla extract
15-20 ice cubes

In blender, put slightly defrosted orange juice. Add a juice can (6 ounces) full of milk and the other ingredients, then fill blender with ice cubes and process to a slushy consistency. **Yield:** 3-4 cups.

Note: *May use substitute sweetener in place of sugar.*

Mrs. Jim Conine (Donna)

♥ *A china coffee cup contains 6 ounces. A punch cup contains 4 ounces.*

Breakfast Shake
Very Nutritious

1 carton (8 ounces) plain yogurt
1 can (6 ounces) frozen orange
   juice concentrate

¼ cup cold water
1 cup ice cubes

Combine all ingredients except ice cubes in blender. Blend until frothy. Drop in ice cubes and blend. **Yield:** 2-3 servings.

Mrs. Jack Hamer (Pam)

Fruit Ice

1 can (6 ounces) frozen orange
  juice concentrate
1 can (6 ounces) frozen lemonade
  concentrate
1 package (10 ounces) frozen
  strawberries

1 can (8 ounces) crushed
  pineapple
3-4 bananas, sliced
½ cup sugar
2½ cups water

Combine all ingredients in a large bowl. Freeze. Remove from freezer 30-45 minutes before serving. Serve while slushy. **Yield:** 8-10 servings.

Note: *May be frozen in glasses. Children love this as an after-school treat or summer cooler. Can also be served as dessert.*

Mrs. Winston Borum (Jimmie)

Lemonade Tea

2 family-size tea bags
3 quarts water
½ cup sugar

1 can (12 ounces) frozen lemonade
1 quart ginger ale

Steep tea in water. Mix with sugar and lemonade. Add ginger ale just before serving. May garnish with mint leaves. **Yield:** 24 (6 ounce) servings.

Mrs. Jay Settle (Karen)

Strawberry Gelatin Juice Punch
Kids Love This

2 packages (3 ounces each)
  strawberry flavored gelatin
Water
1 can (46 ounces) pineapple juice

1 can (6 ounces) frozen lemonade
  concentrate
2 cups sugar

Dissolve gelatin in 1 quart water and simmer 3 minutes. Add juice, lemonade, sugar, and enough water to make 2 gallons. Chill in refrigerator. **Yield:** 2 gallons.

Mrs. Doug Rivenbark (Penny)

Spicy Hot Cider

3 quarts unsweetened apple cider
2 cinnamon sticks
¾ cup firmly packed brown sugar

3 Tablespoons butter (real butter)
Cinnamon
Nutmeg

Bring cider and cinnamon sticks to a boil. Stir in sugar and butter. Keep hot, but do not let boil. Serve in mugs with a sprinkle of cinnamon and nutmeg. **Yield:** 16-18 cups.

Variation: *One jigger of rum may also be added to each cup, if desired.*

Mrs. Joe Gunn (Sandy)

Cranberry Punch

1 quart cranberry juice
1 can (46 ounces) pineapple juice
1½ cups sugar

1 teaspoon almond extract
1 quart ginger ale

Combine cranberry juice, pineapple juice, sugar, and almond extract. Chill. Just before serving, add ginger ale. Serve over ice. **Yield:** 32 (4 ounce) servings.

Mrs. James Sowards (Nancy)

Cherry Slush Punch

2 packages (3 ounces each) cherry
 flavored gelatin
2 cups boiling water
2 cups sugar

6 cups cold water
2 cans (46 ounces each) pineapple
 juice
2 quarts ginger ale

Mix gelatin in boiling water. Add sugar, cold water, and pineapple juice. Freeze 3 hours. To serve, remove from freezer and thaw. Add ginger ale. Should have a slushy texture. **Yield:** 18-20 servings.

Mrs. Doug Rivenbark (Penny)

Hot Holiday Punch

6 cinnamon sticks
6 whole cloves
1 teaspoon allspice
¼ cup sugar
2 jars (1 quart each) cranberry
  juice

1 can (12 ounces) frozen apple
  juice concentrate
3-4 cups of water

Combine all ingredients in a large pot. Heat. **Yield:** 8 servings.

Mrs. Roy Watson (Charlene)

Christmas Ice Ring and Punch

Water
2 oranges
Red and green maraschino
  cherries
1 bottle (48 ounces) cranberry
  juice

1 can (46 ounces) pineapple juice
½ cup lemon juice concentrate
3 cups white wine
1 bottle (32 ounces) ginger ale or
  lemon-lime beverage

Ice ring: Fill a 6-cup ring mold ⅔ full with water and freeze. Alternate orange wedges peel side down, with red and green cherries (3 in a group) on top of ice. Add thin layer of water and freeze 30 minutes or until oranges and cherries are firmly in place. Slowly add water to top; freeze. To unmold, run warm water on sides of mold, and put in punch bowl.

Punch: Mix well chilled juices and wine together in punch bowl. Just before serving, stir in bottle of carbonated beverage. Place ice ring in bowl. **Yield:** 38 (4 ounce) servings.

Mrs. Ellwood Jones (Ann)

♥ *Decorative ice molds will be crystal clear instead of cloudy if you set aside the amount of water to be frozen. Stir it very well 4-5 times during a 15 minute period to break up and expel the air bubbles which come with newly drawn tap water.*

Christmas Eggnog

¾ cup sugar
10 egg yolks, beaten
4 cups milk, scalded
½ teaspoon salt
10 egg whites

1 cup whipping cream, whipped
½ cup brandy
¼ cup light rum
Nutmeg, grated

Blend ½ cup sugar and the yolks in a double boiler. Stir milk in slowly. Cook over hot water until mixture coats spoon, stirring constantly. Chill well. Add salt to egg whites and beat until stiff. Gradually beat in remaining sugar. Fold egg whites and whipped cream into chilled mixture, separately. Add brandy and rum. Chill for several hours. Pour into punch bowl, sprinkle with nutmeg. **Yield:** 30 (4 ounce) servings.

Mrs. Mallard Tysseland (Jill)

Nona Ingold's Calypso Punch

2 cups canned pineapple juice
1 cup orange juice
3 Tablespoons lemon juice
3 Tablespoons grenadine

2 Tablespoons sugar
1⅓ cups light rum
2 bottles (10 ounces each) club soda

Mix all ingredients except club soda. Refrigerate. Add club soda just before serving. **Yield:** 8 servings.

Mrs. Robert Lusk (Sharon)

Grasshopper Punch
Beware–Habit Forming

1 quart vanilla ice cream
¾ cup green créme de menthe

½ cup white créme de cacao
Chocolate bar for shavings

Blend ice cream and liquers until smooth. Garnish with chocolate shavings. **Yield:** 6 (5 ounce) servings.

Mrs. William Hollon (Kasey)

Milk Punch

6   ounces bourbon
2   cups whole milk
15 ice cubes

2½ Tablespoons sugar
1   teaspoon vanilla extract
Nutmeg, dash

Mix all ingredients in blender. Frappé until ice is crushed and beverage is frothy. Serve with a dash of nutmeg. **Yield:** 2 servings.

Mrs. William Hollon (Kasey)

Tangy Wine Punch

2 cans (12 ounces each) frozen
   limeade concentrate
4 limeade cans white wine

6 limeade cans ginger ale
Sliced oranges

Combine limeade, white wine, and ginger ale in punch bowl. Use the limeade can for measuring the white wine and ginger ale. Add sliced oranges and an ice ring. Serve immediately. **Yield:** 18 cups.

Mrs. Steve Moi (Joanie)

Rosé Party Punch

2   bottles (750 milliliters each)
    rosé wine, chilled
½ cup grenadine syrup

½ cup lemon juice
1   quart ginge ale, chilled

Combine first 3 ingredients in large punch bowl. Add ginger ale. Serve immediately. **Yield:** 22 (4 ounce) servings.

Mrs. Pete Bennett (Stephanie)

Champagne Surprise

1 can (46 ounces) pineapple juice
1 can (6 ounces) frozen limeade
   concentrate

2 fifths champagne, very cold

Combine juices and chill. Before serving gently stir together juices and champagne over block of ice. **Yield:** Approximately 20 (5 ounce) cups.

Mrs. William Hollon (Kasey)

Siberian Warmer
Perfect After-Dinner Drink

1 quart vanilla ice cream   6 ounces dark créme de cacao
6 ounces vodka

Blend all ingredients in a blender until well mixed. Serve in stemmed cocktail glasses. **Yield:** 4 servings.

Mrs. Jack Hamer (Pam)

♥ *Place a spoon in a glass or cup into which a hot liquid is to be poured. The spoon will absorb the heat and keep the glass or cup from breaking.*

Brandy Alexanders

½ gallon creamy vanilla ice cream   ¼ cup créme de cacao
½ cup brandy

Combine all ingredients in container of electric blender; blend well. Freeze until firm. **Yield:** 1 quart.

Note: *May add fresh grated nutmeg on top for extra spice and color.*

Mrs. Sam Murray (Sandra)

Yummy Irish Cream

1¼ cups Irish whiskey   2 Tablespoons chocolate flavoring
1   can (14 ounces) sweetened   2 teaspoons instant coffee
    condensed milk   1 teaspoon almond extract
1   cup whipping cream   1 teaspoon vanilla extract
4   eggs

Mix all ingredients in blender. Refrigerate. Serve cold. **Yield:** 12 (2 ounce) servings.

Note: *Keeps two weeks in refrigerator.*

Mrs. William Hollon (Kasey)

Kahlúa

1 quart distilled water	3 teaspoons vanilla extract
2½ cups sugar	2 cups vodka
9 teaspoons (2 ounces) instant coffee	½ cup brandy

In a saucepan, simmer water, sugar, and coffee slowly, for 3 hours. Cool and add vanilla extract, vodka, and brandy. **Yield:** 1 quart.

Mrs. Mallard Tysseland (Jill)

Mary's Whiskey Slush

7½ cups water	2 cups strong tea (4 tea bags)
1½ cups sugar	2 cups bourbon whiskey
1 can (12 ounces) frozen lemonade concentrate	Club soda
1 can (12 ounces) frozen orange juice concentrate	

Combine all ingredients except club soda. Freeze in plastic container for 24 hours. Spoon slush in glass until ¾ full. Add club soda to fill glass. **Yield:** 12 servings.

Note: *Great for women's luncheon or bridge clubs!*

Mrs. Joe Key (Christie)

Frozen Daiquiri

2 cans (6 ounces each) pineapple juice	6 ounces white rum
1 can (6 ounces) frozen limeade concentrate	

Mix ingredients and freeze for 24 hours or longer. Stir before serving. Return remainder to freezer until ready to serve. **Yield:** 4 (6 ounce) servings.

Mrs. Steven Sellers (Anne)

Bloody Marys

1 can (46 ounces) cocktail
    vegetable juice
1 can (46 ounces) tomato juice
1 cup lemon juice
2 Tablespoons Worcestershire
    sauce

1 teaspoon salt
½ teaspoon seasoned salt
3 cups vodka
Tabasco sauce to taste
Fresh cracked pepper to taste

Combine first 6 ingredients. Mix well. Cover and chill overnight. Stir in vodka, Tabasco, and pepper just before serving. Serve over crushed ice with lime wedge. **Yield:** Approximately 15 cups.

Note: *Celery salt to taste may be added as extra flavoring.*

Mrs. Joe Gunn (Sandy)

Kier Royale

6 ounces créme de cassis, chilled
6 ounces ginger ale, chilled

1 bottle (750 milliliters) dry
    champagne

Pour all 3 ingredients into a punch bowl. Do not stir. **Yield:** 9 (4 ounce) servings.

Mrs. Doug Arnold (Debbi)

Cappuccino
Tested 4 Times and All Rated It Excellent!

2 cups black coffee
2 cups milk
1 Tablespoon sugar
1 Tablespoon cocoa

1½ ounces brandy
1½ ounces créme de cacao
4 cinnamon sticks
Whipped cream, sweetened

Heat all ingredients to a boil. Pour into 4 demitasse cups. Top with sweetened whipped cream and a cinnamon stick. **Yield:** 4 servings.

Mrs. Gerald Box (Pat)

Mary's Canadian Blueberry Tea
It Really Tastes Like Blueberries!

1 ounce Grand Marnier liqueur
1 ounce Amaretto liqueur

¾ cup freshly brewed, strong,
  very hot tea

Combine ingredients in a large cup and sip slowly. **Yield:** 1 serving.

Mrs. Winston Borum (Jimmie)

Spicy Hot Wine

½ cup sugar
¾ cup water
3 whole cloves
3 cinnamon sticks

2 cups orange juice
2 cups pineapple juice
4 cups Burgandy wine

Combine all ingredients except wine. Bring to a slow boil. Simmer 20 minutes. Remove cloves and add wine. **Yield:** 8-10 servings.

Note: *Sliced oranges may be added for color.*

Mrs. Marvin Chronister (Donna)

Hot Butter Rum Mix
An Excellent Holiday Drink

1 quart of the best vanilla ice
  cream available, softened
1 pound brown sugar
1 pound sugar
1 pound butter, softened

2 Tablespoons cinnamon
1 jigger rum
1 cup hot water
Nutmeg

Combine ice cream, sugars, butter, and cinnamon. Store in freezer. To serve use 1-2 tablespoons of mixture with 1 jigger rum and 1 cup of hot water. Top with nutmeg. **Yield:** 70-80 servings.

Note: *Keeps up to 6 months.*

Mrs. Marvin Chronister (Donna)

Instant Cocoa Mix

1 box (8 quarts) dry milk powder
1 jar (11 ounces) non-dairy
  creamer

1 can (16 ounces) instant chocolate
  flavored drink mix
8 ounces powdered sugar

Combine ingredients. To serve, use ¼ cup cocoa mix per cup of hot water.
Yield: Approximately 56 cups.

Note: *Store in an airtight container.*

Mrs. James Sowards (Nancy)

Dry Mix Spiced Tea
Good Gift Item

2 cups Tang
1 cup instant tea
2 cups sugar
2 packages (2 quarts each)
  sweetened lemonade mix

1 Tablespoon cinnamon
1 teaspoon cloves
1 teaspoon nutmeg

Combine all ingredients. Store in airtight jars. Use 1 tablespoon for each
mug of boiling water. **Yield:** 192 mugs.

Mrs. William Hollon (Kasey)

♥ *Use muffin pans to make extra-large ice cubes for punch.*

♥ *Fresh mint frozen in ice cubes makes a lovely addition to iced tea and other
beverages.*

♥ *Decorative ice molds or rings are a beautiful addition to punch. Fill the mold
about ⅓ full of water or fruit juice and freeze. Add lemon, lime, or orange slices,
cherries, strawberries, grape clusters, and / or fresh mint. Cover with cold water or
juice and freeze. Repeat the process making sure that each layer is completely surrounded by clear ice.*

Juliette Fowler Homes
A HERITAGE OF CARING
Serving youth and the aged for over 80 years.

Juliette Fowler Homes, Inc. continues an 80-year tradition of providing physical, emotional and spiritual support to both the young and the elderly. Situated on a 15-acre site in East Dallas, Juliette Fowler Homes supports three facilities: Aged Care, Apartments for Seniors, and Youth & Family Services.

During the past 10 years, Dallas Junior Forum has conducted monthly socials with crafts and bingo for the residents. Dallas Junior Forum funds provided a complete ice cream parlor featuring frozen yogurt and popcorn machines. Additional monies financed a kiln and an innovative therapeutic garden for resident hobby time.

Soups, Salads and Dressings

Soups and salads have started many good dinners,
And we hope you agree that ours are real winners.
They are varied and can be served hot or cold;
They can be light and delicate or richly bold.

Gazpacho

¼ cup olive oil
4 Tablespoons lemon juice
6 cups cocktail vegetable juice
2 cups beef broth
½ cup minced onion
2 tomatoes, peeled and chopped
2 cups minced celery
1 clove garlic, minced

½ teaspoon ground cloves
¼ teaspoon Tabasco sauce
½ teaspoon freshly ground pepper
2 green peppers, chopped
2 cucumbers, diced
Croutons, optional
Green pepper and cucumbers,
    chopped for garnish

Combine oil and lemon juice. Beat. Add remaining ingredients, excluding last 2. Serve with croutons and additional chopped green pepper and cucumbers. **Yield:** 8-10 servings.

Note: *Will keep in refrigerator for several days.*

Mrs. William Hollon (Kasey)

♥ *Garnish your soup! Use lemon or orange slices, chives, parsley, watercress, mint, sliced olives, grated egg, croutons, sliced mushrooms, or sour cream.*

Artichoke Soup

¼ cup finely chopped onion
¼ cup finely chopped celery
3 Tablespoons butter, melted
3 Tablespoons flour
2 cans (14½ ounces each) chicken
    broth

1 Tablespoon lemon juice
Salt and pepper to taste
1 can (8½ ounces) artichokes,
    mashed, juice reserved

Sauté onion and celery in butter. Add flour and cook 1 minute. Stir in broth and lemon juice. Add seasonings, artichokes, and reserved juice. Cover and simmer 20 minutes. **Yield:** Approximately 4½ cups.

Mrs. Jim Conine (Donna)

Iced Avocado Soup

1 avocado
1 can (10¾ ounces) cream of chicken soup
1⅓ cups milk
8 ounces yogurt, plain
1 can (7½ ounces) clams, minced, undrained

8 ounces whipping cream
1 Tablespoon lemon juice
½ teaspoon salt
¼ teaspoon pepper
⅛ teaspoon nutmeg
Parsley for garnish

Mix all ingredients in a blender. Refrigerate. Serve well chilled. Garnish with parsley. **Yield:** 6-8 servings.

Mrs. William Hollon (Kasey)

Black Bean Soup

1 package (16 ounces) black beans, washed and soaked overnight
Ham bone or piece of salt pork
1 onion, chopped
1 bay leaf
½ cup finely chopped celery
1 can (8 ounces) tomato sauce
Tabasco sauce, few drops to taste

Salt and pepper to taste
Garlic powder, dash
Worcestershire sauce, several dashes
Condiments:
Onion
Oil and vinegar
Eggs, hard-boiled
Rice, cooked

Add enough water to cover beans. Add ham bone or salt pork. Cook about 6 hours on simmer. During last 2 hours of cooking, add remaining ingredients except condiments. Before serving, remove ham bone or salt pork. Serve with condiments. **Yield:** 6 servings.

Mrs. Doug Rivenbark (Penny)

♥ *Stock can be frozen in ice cube trays and then stored in plastic bags to be used as needed.*

French Market Bean Soup

1½ cups bean mixture	1 can (15 ounces) tomatoes
2 quarts water	1 large onion, chopped
1 pound ham trimmings and bone	1 clove garlic, chopped
	Salt and pepper to taste

Bean Mixture: Mix together your favorite beans. Stores well. Pretty enough to be given as gifts. Some beans to include: Large Great Northern navy beans, black-eyed peas, small Michigan white navy beans, green split peas, red kidney beans, black turtle beans, garbanzo beans, field peas, baby lima beans, yellow split peas, barley, crowder peas, pinto beans, large white butter beans, and lentils.

Wash bean mixture. Place in water and add ham, tomatoes, onion, and garlic. Bring to a boil, reduce to a simmer, cook 5-6 hours covered. Add salt and pepper to taste. Simmer 30 minutes more. **Yield:** 8 servings.

Note: *Can also be made in crockpot. Freezes well.*

Mrs. William Hollon (Kasey)

Navy Bean Soup

1 pound small white beans	1 clove garlic, minced
1 ham bone or 2 ham hocks	Salt and pepper to taste
1 large onion, chopped	

Sort beans, wash well, and place in a large pot. Cover with plenty of cold water and add remaining ingredients. Simmer until tender 2½-3 hours. Check seasoning after first hour and add more salt, pepper or water as needed. When done, remove ham from bone and add to beans. **Yield:** 6-8 servings.

Note: *Serve with corn bread and salad. Can be frozen.*

Mrs. Donald Hudson (Vickie)

Dried Beef Stew Soup
Great Cold Weather Dish

1 medium potato, peeled and diced	½ teaspoon salt
1 medium onion, diced	1 jar (2½ ounces) dried beef, tear into pieces
1 stalk celery, diced	3½ cups milk
4 Tablespoons butter	1 cup grated American cheese
5 Tablespoons flour	1 cup green peas, frozen

Boil potatoes until tender. Sauté onion and celery in butter. Add flour, salt, and beef. Mix well. Stir in potatoes. Add milk gradually, stirring constantly. Cook until thickened. Add cheese and peas. Cook until cheese is melted. **Yield:** 4 servings.

Mrs. Marvin Chronister (Donna)

♥ *Rub your soup pot with a garlic clove for a lustier soup.*

Cream of Carrot Soup

2 Tablespoons butter	1 cup whipping cream
½ cup chopped onion	⅛ teaspoon Tabasco sauce
1 pound carrots, peeled and sliced	½ teaspoon Worcestershire sauce
1 pound potatoes, peeled and cubed	1 cup milk
6 cups chicken broth	Salt and pepper to taste
1 teaspoon thyme	

In a large pan, melt butter and add onions. Cook briefly. Add the carrots, potatoes, and chicken broth. Bring to a boil. Add thyme. Simmer 30-40 minutes until carrots and potatoes are tender. Cool. Process in a food processor. Return to pan and add remaining ingredients. Heat thoroughly. **Yield:** 6-8 servings.

Note: *This may also be served chilled.*

Mrs. Dan Boyd (Terry)

Creamy Cheese Soup

¼ cup butter
½ cup diced onions
½ cup diced carrots
⅓ cup diced celery
¼ cup flour
1½ Tablespoons cornstarch

3 cups milk
1 can (10 ¾ ounces) chicken broth
⅛ teaspoon baking soda
1 pound American cheese, grated
Salt and pepper to taste

Melt butter in large pan; add onions, carrots, and celery. Sauté until soft. Add flour and cornstarch. Slowly add milk and chicken broth to make a smooth sauce. Add baking soda, grated cheese, salt and pepper. **Yield:** 8 small bowls.

Note: *Never boil this soup.*

Variation: *Add 1 package (10 ounces) frozen, chopped broccoli to make a delicious broccoli soup.*

Mrs. Wallace Brown (Gayle)

Seafood Gumbo

¾ pound bacon, diced
3 large onions, chopped
3 cups chopped celery
3 cups chopped green pepper
1 cup flour
1 can (35 ounces) tomatoes
6 packages (10 ounces each) frozen okra or 3 quarts fresh okra
2 Tablespoons filé or more to taste

3 bay leaves
6 Tablespoons parsley
¾ teaspoon thyme
¾ teaspoon red pepper
3 garlic cloves, minced
18 cups chicken broth
3 pounds shrimp, peeled
1½ pounds crabmeat
4 cups oysters
Salt and pepper to taste
Tabasco sauce to taste

Sauté bacon in a large pot until brown. Add onions, celery, and green pepper. Cook until soft. Add flour and brown. Add tomatoes, okra, filé, bay leaves, parsley, thyme, red pepper, garlic cloves, and broth. Simmer 1 hour. Add seafood. Season with salt, pepper, and Tabasco sauce. Serve in bowls over cooked rice. **Yield:** Approximately 38 cups.

Mrs. William Hollon (Kasey)

Northeast Style Clam Chowder

½ pound bacon
1 small onion, diced
3 stalks celery, diced
2 cans (15 ounces each) clam
  chowder

1 can (16 ounces) new potatoes,
  diced
2 cans (10 ounces each) baby
  clams, diced
1 quart milk

Fry bacon and onions together. When half done, add celery. Drain grease and add rest of ingredients. Simmer. **Yield:** 8-10 servings.

Cookbook Committee

Corn Chowder

5 slices bacon
1 can (16 ounces) whole kernel
  corn, reserve liquid
1 medium onion, thinly sliced
1 cup raw diced potatoes

½ teaspoon salt
1 can (10¾ ounces) cream of
  chicken soup
1½ cups milk

In large saucepan, cook bacon until crisp, remove and reserve drippings. Drain corn into the bacon drippings. Add onion, potatoes, and salt. Cover and simmer for 15 minutes or until vegetables are tender. Add soup, milk, corn, and heat thoroughly. Season to taste with salt and pepper. Crumble bacon on top. **Yield:** 1½ quarts soup.

Note: *Serve with cheese bread.*

Mrs. Jim Thornton (Jackie)

Fancy French Onion Soup

¼ cup butter
4 large onions, thinly sliced
1 teaspoon salt
8 cups beef broth

⅓ cup Madeira wine
Brie cheese
Parmesan cheese, grated

Melt butter. Add onions and salt; cover. Steam for 25 minutes. Add wine. Place slice of Brie on bottom of bowl. Fill with soup and top with Parmesan cheese. **Yield:** 8-10 servings.

Mrs. William Hollon (Kasey)

Easy French Onion Soup

½ cup butter
4 onions, sliced into strips
Salt, dash
Pepper, dash
4 cans (14½ ounces each) beef
   bouillon

2 Tablespoons sherry
Toasted French bread or croutons
Monterey Jack cheese
Parmesan cheese

Melt butter in large pot. Add onions, cover and cook 20 minutes. Add salt, pepper, and bouillon. Add sherry and bring to boil. Put in ovenproof bowls to serve. Drop in slice of toasted French bread or croutons. Cover bowls with thick slices of Monterey Jack cheese and sprinkle with Parmesan cheese. Brown in oven heated to 350°. **Yield:** 6-8 servings.

Mrs. Jerry Brown (Linda)

♥ *To remove all fat from fresh stock, first skim off as much as possible. Next, float ice cubes to congeal any remaining fat. Then float a chilled lettuce leaf on top to collect the congealed fat.*

Microwave French Onion Soup

2 Tablespoons butter
2 medium onions, sliced and
   separated into rings
3 cups water, hot
3 teaspoons instant beef bouillon
½ teaspoon Worcestershire sauce

Pepper, dash
2 slices thin bread, toasted
4 ounces grated mozzarella cheese
4 teaspoons grated Parmesan
   cheese

Combine butter and onion in a 2-quart casserole, cover. Microwave on high for 8-10 minutes or until onions are translucent and tender, stirring once or twice. Add water, bouillon, Worcestershire and pepper. Cover, microwave on high 6-8 minutes or until boiling. Reduce power to medium, microwave 5 minutes. Divide soup into 4 individual bowls, top each with 2 slices toasted bread and 2 tablespoons mozzarella. Sprinkle with Parmesan cheese. Place bowls in microwave and cook on high for 2-3 minutes or until cheese melts. Rotate bowls at 1½ minutes. **Yield:** 4 servings.

Mrs. Jim Conine (Donna)

Split Pea Soup

1 pound dry split peas	½ cup chopped celery leaves
1-1½ quarts water	1 medium onion, chopped
1 pound meaty ham bone	1 bay leaf
2 teaspoons salt	
10 whole peppercorns or ½ teaspoon pepper	

Soak dry peas for 2 hours. Combine all ingredients in crockpot. Cook on low heat 10 hours or high heat for 5-6 hours. **Yield:** 8-10 servings.

Note: *A slice of ham may be substituted for ham bone.*

Mrs. Donald Hudson (Vickie)

♥ *If soup is too salty, add raw potato pieces. Remove before serving.*

Portuguese Soup

2 cups chopped onion	1 head cabbage, cored and chopped
6 cloves garlic, chopped	
6 Tablespoons salad oil	12 small new potatoes, cleaned and quartered
1 pound smoked sausage, sliced	
10 cups beef broth	¼-½ cup vinegar
1 can (16 ounces) kidney beans, undrained	2 cups ketchup
	Salt and pepper to taste

Sauté onions and garlic in oil. When onions are transparent, add sausage slices and brown lightly. Add remaining ingredients and bring to a boil, stirring to prevent scorching. Reduce heat and simmer 35-45 minutes, stirring occasionally. Correct seasonings to taste. **Yield:** 1 gallon or 10 (1½ cup) servings.

Mrs. Joe Key (Christie)

Strawberry Soup

½ cup white wine
½ cup sugar
2 Tablespoons lemon juice

1 teaspoon grated lemon peel
1 pint strawberries

Pour all ingredients (except 4 strawberries) into blender. Cover and process at medium speed until smooth. Cover and refrigerate until chilled. Slice 4 remaining strawberries and garnish soup. **Yield:** 3 servings.

Note: *Serves 4-6 in demitasse.*

Mrs. Jim Conine (Donna)

Zucchini Cream Soup

1 large onion, chopped
4 scallions, minced
¼ cup butter or margarine
3 medium zucchini
3 cups chicken broth

¼ teaspoon basil
¼ teaspoon oregano
Salt and pepper to taste
1½ cups half and half (or milk)

Sauté onion and scallions in butter until opaque but not brown. Grate unpeeled zucchini, add to onion and cook until wilted. Place in food processor and purée. Combine broth, purée with seasonings and heat. Whisk in the half and half. Continue to heat but do not let mixture come to a boil. This can be used as a warm or a cold soup. **Yield:** 2 quarts.

Note: *If serving this cold, chill until serving time and then fold in half and half. Can prepare up to 2 days ahead and refrigerate.*

Mrs. Ellwood Jones (Ann)

♥ *Leftover soups are great used as a substitute for liquids in a casserole.*

Crunchy Hot Chicken Salad

2 cups diced cooked chicken	⅛ teaspoon pepper
1½ cups diced celery	Tabasco sauce, few shakes
¼ cup slivered almonds	½ cup mayonnaise
1 Tablespoon grated onion	1 can (5 ounces) sliced water
1 Tablespoon lemon juice	chestnuts, drained
½ teaspoon salt	½ cup grated cheese

Toss all ingredients together except cheese. Place into greased 9x13-inch baking dish. Top with cheese. Bake at 375° for 30 minutes or until cheese bubbles. **Yield:** 4-6 servings.

Note: *Can be served in patty shells. Add pimiento for color.*

Mrs. Steve Moi (Joanie)

Hot Chicken Salad
Simple and Yummy

2 cups cubed cooked chicken	½ cup mayonnaise
2 cups chopped celery	2 Tablespoons chopped pimiento
1½ cups chopped almonds, toasted	2 Tablespoons lemon juice
½ teaspoon salt	½ can or 5 ounces cream of chicken soup
2 Tablespoons grated onion	3 cups crushed potato chips
½ cup chopped green pepper	½ cup grated American cheese

Toss lightly all ingredients except chips and cheese. Spoon into 1½-quart casserole; spread chips and cheese on top. Bake at 350° for 25 minutes. **Yield:** 3-4 servings.

Mrs. Mike Freeman (Cathy)

Hawaiian Chicken Salad

3 cups cubed cooked chicken
1 cup cubed celery
1 tart apple, peeled and cubed
1 can (11 ounces) mandarin
　oranges, cubed

½ cup macadamia nuts, crushed
1 cup mayonnaise
2 teaspoons curry powder
1 teaspoon salt

Combine all ingredients and chill for at least 2 hours. Serve on a bed of chilled lettuce. **Yield:** 6 servings.

Mrs. Donald Robson (Karen)

Oriental Chicken Salad

2　cups cooked, chopped chicken
1　can (8 ounces) sliced water
　　chestnuts, drained
1½ cups green seedless grapes
½　cup chopped celery

½ cup toasted slivered almonds
⅔ cup mayonnaise
½ teaspoon curry powder
⅓ teaspoon salt
1 teaspoon soy sauce

Combine chicken, water chestnuts, grapes, celery, and almonds. Mix mayonnaise with curry powder, salt, and soy sauce. Combine with chicken mixture and chill thoroughly. Serve over lettuce or cantaloupe slices. Sprinkle with almonds. **Yield:** 5 (1 cup) servings.

Variation: *Top with chow mein noodles instead of almonds.*

Mrs. Mark Layton (Beth)

Wild Chicken Salad

1　box (6 ounces) instant wild rice
3　pounds chicken pieces, boned,
　　skinned, and cooked
1　can (8 ounces) sliced water
　　chestnuts
⅔ cup mayonnaise

⅓ cup milk
⅓ cup lemon juice
4　green onions, finely chopped,
　　including tops of 2
1　cup cashews
2　cups halved seedless grapes

Prepare wild rice according to instructions. Tear chicken into small pieces and mix with rice and water chestnuts. Combine mayonnaise, milk, lemon juice, and onions. Toss with chicken mixture and refrigerate. Before serving, fold in cashews and grapes. **Yield:** 8 servings.

Mrs. Bill Frank (Barbara)

Mexican Fiesta

Chili:
4 pounds ground beef, cooked
　and drained
3 large onions, chopped
2 cans (16 ounces each) tomatoes
2 cans (16 ounces each) tomato
　purée
1 can (16 ounces) tomato sauce
4 Tablespoons chili powder
2 teaspoons cumin
1 teaspoon garlic powder
1 can (46 ounces) Ranch Style
　beans
Salt to taste

Corn chips, crushed
Rice, cooked
Chili
Onions, sliced or chopped
Lettuce, chopped
Fresh tomatoes, chopped
Black olives, chopped
Cheddar cheese, grated
Pecans
Coconut
Picante sauce

Mix together the first 10 ingredients and cook for 45-60 minutes. Place the chili and the remaining ingredients in separate bowls and in the order listed. Encourage guests to take some of all. **Yield:** 20 servings.

Mrs. Thomas Hunter (Lynda)

♥ *Slice tomatoes into wedges to keep them from losing so much of their juice.*

Mexican Salad

1 can (15 ounces) Ranch Style
　beans, drained and rinsed
1 head lettuce, torn
1 onion, chopped
1 cup grated Cheddar cheese
2 tomatoes, diced
1 package (8 ounces) corn chips

1 bottle (8 ounces) Catalina salad
　dressing

Optional:
Ground beef, browned
Avocado, diced
Green peppers, diced

Combine the first 6 ingredients. Add optional ingredients if desired. Toss with salad dressing. **Yield:** 8 servings.

Note: *If not serving immediately, do not mix corn chips and salad dressing to keep chips from getting soggy.*

Mrs. Thomas Hunter (Lynda)

Antipasto Salad

1 can (6 ounces) tuna, drained
  (Albacore in spring water)
1 can (7½ ounces) pitted black
  olives, cut in half
1 can (3 ounces) sliced mushrooms
1 can (9 ounces) artichoke hearts,
  cut in half
1 jar (8 ounces) gardiniera, (Italian
  pickled vegetables)

1 can (8 ounces) tomato sauce
3 Tablespoons olive oil
¼ cup sweet red wine
1 teaspoon salt
2 teaspoons garlic powder
Crackers or garlic toast

Drain tuna, olives, mushrooms, artichoke hearts, and gardiniera thoroughly. Mix together gently. In separate bowl, mix tomato sauce, oil, wine, salt, and garlic. Combine sauce with salad mixture, taking care not to mash tuna. Place in serving dish, cover and refrigerate overnight. Serve with crackers or small slices garlic toast. **Yield:** 6-8 servings.

Mrs. Brian Byrne (Veronica)

Rice and Artichoke Salad

1 box (8 ounces) chicken Rice-
  a-Roni, other flavors may be
  used
2 jars (6 ounces each)
  marinated artichoke hearts,
  reserve oil
½-¾ cup mayonnaise

4 green onions, chopped
½ cup chopped green pepper
1 can (4¼ ounces) black olives,
  sliced or chopped
Salt and pepper to taste, optional

Cook rice according to package directions. Cool. Mix oil from artichokes with mayonnaise. Stir in remaining ingredients. Chill and serve. **Yield:** 4-5 cups.

Note: *May be stuffed into a tomato or avocado.*
Variation: *Four chicken breasts, cooked, boned, and chopped may be added.*

Mrs. Jeff Farmer (Kaliko)

Pasta Salad

1   pound macaroni, cooked and
    drained
⅔ cup cider vinegar
¼ cup safflower oil
¾ cup chopped celery
¾ cup chopped green pepper
8   green onions, chopped
1   jar (2 ounces) pimientos
Worcestershire sauce, 4 dashes
Tabasco sauce, 4 dashes
2   Tablespoons chopped green
    chilies

1   teaspoon salt
1½ teaspoons pepper
1   can (16 ounces) black-eyed
    peas
1   can (16 ounces) corn
1   can (4 ounces) ripe olives,
    chopped
1½ cups mayonnaise
2   Tablespoons picante sauce

Mix together all ingredients. Refrigerate for at least 24 hours. **Yield:** 20-25 servings.

Mrs. Jeff Farmer (Kaliko)

Macaroni Salad

½ package (12 ounces) salad
    macaroni
½ cup sweet pickle relish
½ cup finely chopped onion
3   eggs, boiled and finely
    chopped

1   teaspoon celery seed
1   cup Miracle Whip salad
    dressing
Salt and pepper

Cook macaroni according to package directions. Drain. Add remaining ingredients and mix well. Season with salt and pepper if desired. Cover and refrigerate a few hours before serving. **Yield:** 1½ quarts.

Mrs. Donald Hudson (Vickie)

♥ *Toasted sesame seeds make a marvelous garnish for salads.*

Wild Rice Salad

1 package (6 ounces) long grain and wild rice
½ cup mayonnaise
¼ cup plain yogurt
1 cup chopped celery

1 cup chopped tomatoes
½ cup chopped green onion
2 Tablespoons chopped parsley
⅛ teaspoon salt
⅛ teaspoon pepper

Prepare rice according to directions on package. Cool. Add all remaining ingredients and chill several hours. **Yield:** 6-8 servings.

Variation: *Add ¼ cup sour cream instead of yogurt and 1 cup diced cucumber instead of onions.*

Mrs. Mark Layton (Beth)

Chinese Pea Salad

½ cup mayonnaise
2 Tablespoons lemon juice
¼ teaspoon curry powder
1 Tablespoon soy sauce
⅛ teaspoon garlic salt
1 box (10½ ounces) frozen peas

1 can (6½ ounces) tuna
1 cup chopped celery
½ cup chopped green onions
Lettuce leaves
¼ cups toasted almonds
1 cup chow mein noodles

Mix mayonnaise, lemon juice, curry powder, soy sauce, and garlic salt. Thaw peas in microwave or let thaw naturally for ½ hour. Mix tuna, peas, celery, and onions with curry mixture. Place on lettuce leaf. Sprinkle with almonds and chow mein noodles. **Yield:** 6 servings.

Note: *May chill ahead of time.*

Mrs. Jeff Farmer (Kaliko)

Hot Seafood Salad

1-2 cups King crabmeat	1 cup cubed processed cheese
1 cup cooked and deveined shrimp, chopped	Worcestershire sauce to taste
¼ cup chopped green pepper	¼ cup Cheddar cheese, optional
½ cup chopped celery	½ teaspoon horseradish, optional
¼ cup mayonnaise, approximate	1 cup seasoned breadcrumbs

Combine all ingredients and top with breadcrumbs. Bake at 350° for 30 minutes. **Yield:** 4 servings.

Note: *Can be made ahead and baked just prior to serving.*

Mrs. Donald Robson (Karen)

Shrimp and Crabmeat Salad

1 pound loaf white sandwich bread	1 can (6 ounces) crabmeat, rinsed and drained well
4 hard-boiled eggs, peeled and chopped	2 cans (4¼ ounces each) small shrimp, rinsed and drained well
1 cup chopped celery	
½ large onion, chopped	2-3 cups mayonnaise

Remove crust from bread and cut bread into 1 inch cubes. Combine bread, eggs, celery, and onions in large bowl. Cover and refrigerate overnight. Stir crab and shrimp into bread mixture. Add mayonnaise to desired taste and moistness. Mix well and serve. **Yield:** 8-10 servings.

Note: *Must prepare first step day ahead.*

Mrs. Bill Frank (Barbara)

Shrimply Delicious
New Orleans Without Leaving Home

⅓ cup Miracle Whip salad
    dressing
¼ cup sour cream
1½ Tablespoons lemon juice
¾ teaspoon grated lemon rind
¼ teaspoon salt

½ teaspoon tarragon
½ teaspoon Dijon mustard
½ pound cooked shrimp
¼ teaspoon dill weed
6 lemon wedges

Combine all ingredients except lemon wedges and chill. Use as a stuffing for avocado halves, tomato cups, artichoke bottoms, or beds of Boston lettuce. Garnish with lemon wedges. **Yield:** 4-6 servings.

Note: *Serve as a salad, appetizer, or luncheon dish.*

Mrs. Richard Keeling (Laurie)

Super Spinach Salad I

Dressing:
1 clove garlic
1 teaspoon salt
¾ teaspoon dry mustard
½ cup olive oil
3 Tablespoons lemon juice
Tabasco sauce, dash
Pepper to taste

Salad:
1 package (10 ounces) fresh
    spinach, washed and stems
    removed
½ pint cherry tomatoes
½ pint mushrooms, sliced
2 hard-boiled eggs, sliced

In a wooden bowl pulverize garlic into salt with a wooden spoon. Add remaining dressing ingredients and mix well. Add spinach, tomatoes, and mushrooms. Toss well. Garnish with egg slices. **Yield:** 6-8 servings.

Mrs. Jerry Brown (Linda)

Super Spinach Salad II

Dressing:
3 Tablespoons wine vinegar
6 Tablespoons salad oil
½ teaspoon salt
½ teaspoon pepper
¼ teaspoon dry mustard
2 Tablespoons chopped parsley
1 Tablespoon chopped anchovies
1 clove garlic, cut in half

Salad:
5-6 cups fresh spinach
1 avocado, peeled and sliced
¼ pound fresh mushrooms, sliced

Combine and mix together all dressing ingredients; let stand for 30 minutes. Remove garlic. Wash spinach, remove stems, and dry well. Combine with avocado and mushrooms in salad bowl. Add dressing and toss lightly. Serve immediately. **Yield:** 6 servings.

Mrs. Donald Hudson (Vickie)

Oriental Spinach Salad

1 package fresh spinach, washed and torn
8 slices bacon, cooked and crumbled
2 eggs, hard-boiled and diced
1 can (14 ounces) bean sprouts, drained
1 can (9 ounces) chow mein noodles
1 can (8 ounces) sliced water chestnuts
Mushrooms, optional

Dressing:
1 cup salad oil
½ cup sugar
⅓ cup ketchup
¼ cup red wine vinegar
2 Tablespoons Worcestershire sauce
1 medium onion, quartered
1 teaspoon salt

Mix salad ingredients. Blend all dressing ingredients in blender. Pour over salad before serving. **Yield:** 6-8 servings.

Note: *May serve dressing in separate bowl along with chinese noodles.*

Mrs. Jim Thornton (Jackie)

great w/ Spinach I dressing

Artichokes, Hearts of Palm and Spinach Salad

1 pound fresh spinach, washed
   and torn into bite-sized pieces
1 can (14 ounces) hearts of palm,
   thinly sliced
1 can (14 ounces) artichoke hearts,
   drained and diced
6 slices bacon, cooked and
   crumbled
4 green onions, chopped
3 tomatoes, cut into wedges
2 hard-boiled eggs, chopped
Capers to taste, optional
Pimientos to taste, optional

Dressing:
1 medium red onion, minced
¾ cup sugar
½ cup vinegar
⅓ cup ketchup
⅓ cup salad oil
2 Tablespoons Worcestershire
   sauce
2 teaspoons lemon juice

Combine all salad ingredients. Chill. Combine dressing ingredients. Sprinkle over salad and toss well. **Yield:** 6-8 servings.

Mrs. Richard Keeling (Laurie)

Avocado Salad Bowl
Very Nice Company Salad

1 head Romaine lettuce, washed
   and chilled
1 small red onion, thinly sliced

3 medium ripe avocados
4 ounces oil and vinegar or Italian
   salad dressing

Break Romaine into bite-sized pieces. Place in a medium salad bowl. Separate onion slices into rings. Toss with romaine. Chill. Just before serving, peel and quarter avocados into salad. Shake dressing well, pour over salad and toss gently. **Yield:** 8-10 servings.

Mrs. Roy Watson (Charlene)

♥ *To absorb excess moisture, wrap rinsed salad greens in paper towels and refrigerate for an hour or more.*

♥ *Always tear lettuce for tossed salads, as cutting or slicing gives it a bitter taste.*

Caesar Salad

Salt and pepper to taste
1 large garlic clove, peeled
½ lemon
2 Tablespoons red wine vinegar
1 teaspoon sugar
½ teaspoon horseradish
½ teaspoon dry mustard
2 heaping teaspoons Parmesan cheese
Worcestershire sauce, 2 dashes

A-1 steak sauce, 3 dashes
Tabasco sauce, 3 dashes
⅛ cup olive oil
1 egg yolk, cooked ½ minute
Anchovies, chopped; or anchovy paste to taste
1 head Romaine lettuce, torn into bite-size pieces
Croutons
Parmesan cheese

Sprinkle inside of bowl with salt and pepper. Rub entire surface of bowl with garlic. Discard any piece that remains. Squeeze juice of lemon into bowl; remove seeds. Add vinegar, sugar, horseradish, mustard, Parmesan, Worcestershire, A-1, Tabasco, oil, and egg yolk. Stir together. Add anchovies and lettuce; toss. Top each serving with croutons and additional Parmesan cheese. **Yield:** 4-6 servings.

Note: *This salad is best prepared in a large wooden salad bowl with rough edges.*

Mrs. Burl Turner (Sheryl)

Mock Caesar Salad

Dressing:
Juice of 1 lemon
3 garlic cloves, crushed
¾ cup salad oil
1 teaspoon sugar
½ teaspoon tarragon
Salt and pepper to taste

Salad:
2 heads Romaine lettuce
¼ pound bacon, fried and crumbled
⅔ cup sliced almonds, toasted
2 cups cherry tomatoes, halved
1 cup grated Swiss cheese
⅓ cup grated Parmesan cheese

Combine dressing ingredients and refrigerate for at least 3 hours. Tear the Romaine lettuce and add all other salad ingredients. Toss with dressing just before serving. **Yield:** 10-12 servings.

Mrs. Jerry Leatherman (Diana)

Italian Olive Salad

1 jar (7 ounces) salad olives with
 pimientos
1 can (6 ounces) black olives,
 pitted
1 stalk celery and leaves, cut into
 chunks

½ teaspoon garlic powder
½ teaspoon basil
½ teaspoon oregano
1 onion, cut into chunks
½ cup salad oil

Add all ingredients to food processor and chop (do not purée). Put mixture into large container and refrigerate. The longer you keep it the better the flavor – keeps indefinitely. When ready to use, add 1 cup to prepared greens (Romaine, head lettuce, tomatoes) in salad bowl. Toss with a little Italian dressing. **Yield:** 2 cups.

Note: *Good Louisiana-style salad, great with seafood and gumbos.*

Mrs. Dennis Furlong (Dede)

Mamie's Bermuda Salad

Dressing:
1 cup salad oil
2 Tablespoons vinegar
3 Tablespoons lemon juice
1 Tablespoon sugar
1 teaspoon salt
1 teaspoon dry mustard
1 teaspoon Worcestershire sauce
Paprika, dash
Tabasco sauce, dash

Salad:
½ head cauliflower florets, thinly
 sliced
½ Bermuda onion, thinly sliced
1 cup sliced stuffed olives
1 cup crumbled Roquefort cheese
1 head lettuce, torn

Blend all dressing ingredients in wide-mouth jar and whisk to blend well. Marinate cauliflower, onion, olives and cheese in bowl with ½ cup dressing for several hours before serving. When ready to serve, add torn lettuce and more dressing, if needed. **Yield:** 4-6 servings.

Mrs. Dennis Furlong (Dede)

Mandarin Salad

½ cup sliced almonds
3 teaspoons sugar
½ head iceberg lettuce
½ head Romaine lettuce
1 cup chopped celery
2 whole green onions, chopped
1 can (11 ounces) mandarin
   oranges, drained

Dressing:
½ teaspoon salt
Pepper, dash
¼ cup salad oil
1 Tablespoon chopped parsley
2 Tablespoons sugar
2 Tablespoons vinegar
Tabasco sauce, dash

In a small pan over medium heat, cook almonds and sugar, stirring constantly until almonds are coated and sugar dissolved. Watch carefully as they will burn easily. Cool and store in airtight container. Tear lettuce into bite-size pieces. Toss with celery and onions. Mix all dressing ingredients and chill. Before serving, add almonds and oranges to lettuce and toss with dressing. **Yield:** 4-6 servings.

Mrs. Jack Hamer (Pam)

♥ *To freshen wilted salad greens, douse them quickly in hot water, then in ice water to which a little vinegar has been added.*

Mary's Salad

1 medium head Boston or bibb
   lettuce, torn into pieces
½ avocado, peeled and thinly
   sliced
1 can (11 ounces) mandarin
   oranges, chilled and drained

½ cup chopped pecans, toasted
2 green onions, thinly sliced
Pepper to taste
⅓ cup Italian dressing

Combine all ingredients except dressing in a salad bowl. Just before serving add dressing and toss gently. **Yield:** 6 servings.

Mrs. John Mearns (June)

Snow Pea Surprise

¼ cup sesame seeds
⅔ cup salad oil
2 Tablespoons lemon juice
2 Tablespoons vinegar
2 Tablespoons sugar
1 clove garlic, crushed

1 teaspoon salt
1 pound fresh snow peas
1 head iceburg lettuce, finely shredded
½ cup chopped fresh parsley
½ pound bacon

Brown sesame seeds in oven. Combine with next 6 ingredients. Refrigerate. Remove stems from snow peas and steam for 30 seconds. Chill. Fry bacon until crisp; crumble. Toss peas, lettuce, parsley, and bacon with dressing. Serve immediately. **Yield:** 8-10 servings.

Mrs. William Hollon (Kasey)

Oriental Salad

1 small head cabbage, shredded
3 green onions, sliced
1 package Ramen noodles, broken
1 can (8 ounces) sliced water chestnuts
3 Tablespoons sesame seeds
1 package (2½ ounces) sliced almonds

Dressing:
½ cup salad oil
2 teaspoons sugar
1 teaspoon salt
½ teaspoon pepper
1 teaspoon monosodium glutamate
Garlic salt, pinch
3 Tablespoons vinegar

Combine cabbage, onions, noodles, and water chestnuts. Place sesame seeds and almonds on a cookie sheet and brown slightly in oven; then add to salad. Prepare dressing and pour on salad. Chill. **Yield:** 4-6 servings.

Mrs. Jack Hamer (Pam)

♥ *Quick and easy! Serve cold asparagus on a bed of lettuce topped with mayonnaise and lemon juice. Garnish with pimiento strips.*

Sweet and Sour Cabbage
Family Favorite

6 bacon slices	¼ cup water
2 Tablespoons chopped onion	⅓ cup vinegar
½ cup firmly packed brown sugar	6 cups shredded red cabbage
1 teaspoon cornstarch	1 teaspoon caraway seeds
1 teaspoon salt	

Cook bacon until crisp; drain and crumble. Reserve 3 tablespoons bacon drippings in the skillet. Add chopped onions, brown sugar, cornstarch, salt, water, and vinegar to drippings. Cook, stirring constantly, until mixture thickens slightly and appears clear. Cool. In a large bowl, combine cabbage and caraway seeds. Fold in bacon bits and cooled dressing. Chill and serve. **Yield:** 6 servings.

Mrs. Pete Bennett (Stephanie)

Tomato Aspic
A Cool, Refreshing Salad

3 cups tomato juice	1 cup creamed cottage cheese, optional
1 bay leaf	
8 whole black peppercorns	½ green pepper, cut into rings, optional
2 whole cloves	
2 slices onion	2 hard-boiled eggs, sliced, optional
2 envelopes unflavored gelatin	
½ cup cold water	Mayonnaise, optional
1 teaspoon salt	Salad green beds
1 teaspoon sugar	

Bring tomato juice, bay leaf, peppercorns, cloves, and onion to a boil. Simmer 10 minutes. In a 1-quart bowl soften gelatin in cold water. Strain hot tomato juice mixture into gelatin. Add salt and sugar and stir until completely dissolved; cool. Refrigerate in a shallow 1-quart casserole, or ring mold until firm. If using casserole, cut into squares. Garnish with a dollop of mayonnaise and serve on bed of salad greens. If ring mold is used, fill center with cottage cheese and decorate top of mold with pepper rings and egg slices. **Yield:** 4 servings.

Note: *This is a great do-ahead salad.*

Mrs. Terry Chambers (Dianne)

Copper Pennies
Salad in the Shape of Pennies

2 pounds carrots, sliced
1 can (10¾ ounces) tomato soup
1 teaspoon Worcestershire sauce
½ cup salad oil
¾ cup sugar

¾ cup vinegar
1 teaspoon dry mustard
1 green pepper, diced
1 onion, sliced and quartered

Cook carrots and cool. Mix remaining ingredients. Add to carrots. Refrigerate and serve cold. **Yield:** 8-10 servings.

Note: *Keeps for several weeks in refrigerator.*

Mrs. Marvin Chronister (Donna)

Easy Vegetable Salad

1 pound broccoli
1 can (16 ounces) ripe olives,
   drained and sliced
1 can (8 ounces) sliced water
   chestnuts, drained
1 medium sized green pepper, cut
   into strips

1 medium onion, chopped
4 stalks celery, chopped
½ pound fresh mushrooms, sliced
1 pint cherry tomatoes
1 bottle (8 ounces) Italian
   dressing

In a large bowl, combine all ingredients except dressing. Add dressing and toss gently. Chill 1-2 hours. **Yield:** 10-12 servings.

Mrs. Jim Conine (Donna)

Cauliflower Salad

½ onion, chopped
1 green pepper, chopped
1 pound bacon
1 large head cauliflower, cut into
   florets

½ pound Colby cheese, grated
1 cup mayonnaise
¼ cup sugar

Chop onion and pepper. Fry and crumble bacon. Mix cauliflower, onion, pepper, and cheese with bacon crumbs together. Mix mayonnaise and sugar together and pour over salad. **Yield:** 10-12 servings.

Mrs. Jim Thornton (Jackie)

24 Hour Vegetable Salad

2 cups cauliflower florets
2 cups broccoli florets
1 cup sliced carrots
¼ cup chopped green onion
3 hard-boiled eggs, chopped

½ cup pimiento-stuffed olives
¼ cup mayonnaise
¼ cup sour cream
1 Tablespoon Dijon mustard
1 Tablespoon lime juice

Lightly steam vegetables until tender crisp. Plunge into cold water to stop cooking and keep broccoli green. Drain. Combine vegetables with onion, eggs, and olives. To make dressing, mix mayonnaise, sour cream, mustard, and lime juice. Toss into vegetables. Marinate 24 hours in refrigerator before serving. **Yield:** 8-10 servings.

Mrs. William Hollon (Kasey)

♥ *For more nutritional salads, add thinly sliced, unpared, raw vegetables such as zucchini, broccoli, cauliflower, and yellow squash.*

Cool Vegetable Salad

1 can (16 ounces) French style
  green beans, seasoned
1 can (16 ounces) shoe peg white
  corn
1 can (16 ounces) young small
  sweet peas
1 jar (2 ounces) pimiento, chopped
1 green pepper, chopped

1 cup chopped celery
1 bunch green onions with tops,
   chopped
¾ cup vinegar
1 Tablespoon water
½ cup salad oil
¾ cup sugar
1 Tablespoon salt

Combine vegetables in a bowl. Put remaining ingredients in a saucepan and bring to a boil. Let cool. Pour over vegetables and refrigerate for 2 hours or more. **Yield:** 8-10 servings.

Note: *Yellow corn can be substituted if shoe peg is not available. Even better the second or third day.*

Mrs. Jeff Farmer (Kaliko)

Green Bean and Avocado Salad

1 can (15-16 ounces) French cut
  green beans, drained
6 scallions, chopped, including
  tops
¾ cup prepared Italian salad
  dressing

1 medium avocado, chopped
1 can (6-8 ounces) artichoke
  hearts, drained and chopped

Place green beans in a serving dish with scallions. Pour dressing over mixture. Refrigerate 4 hours or overnight. Before serving, add avocado and artichoke hearts. **Yield:** 6-8 servings.

Mrs. Winston Borum (Jimmie)

German Cucumber Salad

10 cucumbers, thinly sliced
5 onions, thinly sliced
5 cups mayonnaise
2¼ cups apple cider vinegar

2 Tablespoons diced green pepper
7 Tablespoons salt
2 Tablespoons sugar

Combine all ingredients. Refrigerate overnight. **Yield:** Approximately 20 servings.

Mrs. Marvin Chronister (Donna)

Black-eyed Pea Salad

2 cans (15 ounces each) black-
   eyed peas
1½ cups chopped green onions
1½ cups chopped green pepper
1 teaspoon black pepper
1 pound smoked link sausage,
   cooked, reserve 8 slices and
   chop remainder
1 teaspoon chili powder

1 teaspoon basil
¼ teaspoon Tabasco sauce
2 fresh jalapeños, diced, seeds
   removed
1½ cups coarsely chopped tomato
1½ cups peeled and chopped
   cucumber
1 bottle (8 ounces) herb and
   spice dressing

Combine all ingredients except tomatoes, cucumber, and dressing. Toss with dressing and refrigerate for 24 hours. One hour before serving, add tomatoes and cucumber. Toss again. Garnish with sausage slices. **Yield:** 12 servings.

Mrs. Jeff Farmer (Kaliko)

Spring Salad

½ pound fresh asparagus
1 jar (6 ounces) marinated
  artichoke hearts, liquid
  reserved
½ cup sliced mushrooms
¼ cup sliced green onion

1 Tablespoon vinegar
1 teaspoon sugar
1 teaspoon sesame seeds, toasted
¼ teaspoon salt
Tabasco sauce, dash

Cook asparagus for 10-15 minutes. Drain. Place into 6x10-inch dish. Slice artichokes in half and place over asparagus. Add mushrooms and onion. Combine reserved marinade, vinegar, sugar, sesame seeds, salt, and pepper. Pour over vegetables and refrigerate several hours. **Yield:** 4 servings.

Mrs. John Mearns (June)

Marinated Vegetable Salad

1 can (14 ounces) artichoke
  hearts, drained and sliced in
  half
1 can (16 ounces) whole green
  beans, drained
1 can (3¼ ounces) pitted ripe
  black olives, drained
½ pound fresh mushrooms

1 medium purple onion, sliced
Pepper to taste
1 cup sugar
1 cup vinegar
1 teaspoon salt
3 Tablespoons Italian dressing

In a bowl, combine first 6 ingredients. In a saucepan, combine remaining ingredients. Bring to a boil, stirring to dissolve sugar. Cool slightly and pour over vegetables. Refrigerate for at least 24 hours, stirring occasionally to be sure all ingredients are marinated. **Yield:** 4 servings.

Mrs. Steven Sellers (Anne)

♥ *To make colorful onion rings for salads, soak them in beet juice.*

Doug's English Pea Salad

½ cup chopped onion
1 can (17 ounces) English peas
2 hard-boiled eggs, sliced
1 jar (2 ounces) chopped
  pimientos
¾ cup grated American cheese

1½ cups chopped dill pickles
3 heaping Tablespoons
  mayonnaise
1 Tablespoon mustard
Salt and pepper

In a medium bowl carefully combine all ingredients. **Yield:** 6 servings.

Note: *All ingredients can be proportioned according to taste.*

Mrs. Doug Rivenbark (Penny)

Hot Potato Salad
Tastes Wonderful!

8 medium potatoes, cooked,
  peeled and diced
1 pound American cheese, diced
1 cup Miracle Whip salad dressing

½ cup chopped onion
Salt and pepper to taste
3 slices bacon
Sliced green olives, optional

Combine potatoes, cheese, Miracle Whip, onion, salt, and pepper. Pour into greased 9x13-inch baking dish. Top with slices of uncooked bacon and sliced olives. Bake uncovered at 350° for 1 hour. **Yield:** 8-10 servings.

Note: *Can be prepared a day ahead.*

Mrs. Bill Frank (Barbara)

Festive Corn Bread Salad

1 pan (1½-quart) cooked corn
  bread
2 cups mayonnaise
2 celery stalks, chopped
1 large green pepper, chopped

1 jar (4 ounces) chopped
  pimientos
¾ cup chopped green onions
¾ cup chopped pecans
2 large tomatoes, diced

Crumble corn bread into bowl. Add remaining ingredients and stir. Place in refrigerator to chill (about 2½ hours is best). **Yield:** 8-10 servings.

Note: *Great for leftover cornbread. You can't put it down!*

Mrs. Doug Arnold (Debbi)

Taboli Salad

16 ounces taboli wheat
2 fresh tomatoes, chopped
1 cucumber, chopped
2 bunches green onions, chopped
1 green pepper, chopped
2 bunches fresh parsley, stems
　discarded and remainder
　chopped

2 cups salad oil
2 cups lemon juice
2 teaspoons salt
½ teaspoon pepper

Place wheat in large strainer. Rinse well under cold running water and drain. Squeeze excess water out of wheat. Add remaining ingredients to taboli and refrigerate. Prepare at least 8 hours in advance so that flavors have ample time to mingle. **Yield:** 12-16 servings.

Mrs. Richard Keeling (Laurie)

New England Fruit Salad
A favorite holiday or anytime dish

Sauce:
1 cup sugar
5 Tablespoons flour or cornstarch
Reserved liquid from fruit with
　enough milk added to make 1¾
　cups liquid
2 Tablespoons butter or margarine

Salad:
1 can (29 ounces) fruit cocktail,
　drain, reserve liquid
1 can (11 ounces) mandarin
　oranges, drain, reserve liquid
Fresh fruit of choice (banana,
　apple, grapes etc.), chopped into
　bite-size pieces
1 cup miniature marshmallows

Combine sauce ingredients except butter and cook over medium heat, stirring until thick. Add 2 tablespoons butter or margarine, stir into sauce until melted. Set aside to slightly cool. Place all fruits in large bowl. Add marshmallows and sauce. Mix well. **Yield:** 6 servings.

Note: *Can be prepared day ahead, but reserve banana and marshmallows to add just before serving.*

Mrs. Ellwood Jones (Ann)

Katie's Easy Fruit
Kids Love It!

2 cans (21 ounces each) peach pie
  filling
2 cans (11 ounces each) mandarin
  oranges
1 can (20 ounces) pineapple
  chunks, drained

1 carton (16 ounces) frozen
  strawberries
2 bananas, sliced

Combine all ingredients. Chill. This will have a thick texture. **Yield:** 8-10
servings.

Note: *Good afternoon snack.*

Mrs. Jim Thornton (Jackie)

Sour Cream Fruit Salad

1 cup pineapple chunks, drained
1 cup mandarin oranges, drained
1 cup frozen coconut

1 cup miniature marshmallows
1 cup sour cream

Combine all ingredients and refrigerate overnight. **Yield:** 4-6 servings.

Mrs. Terry Chambers (Dianne)

Bing Cherry Salad

1 can (16 ounces) pitted bing
  cherries, drained
1 can (16 ounces) pineapple
  chunks, drained
½ cup nuts

1 cup miniature marshmallows
1 Tablespoon mayonnaise
1 carton (8 ounces) non-dairy
  whipped topping

Combine fruit. Add nuts and marshmallows. Mix mayonnaise and topping together. Fold into fruit. **Yield:** 6 servings.

Note: *Bananas would make a nice addition to this salad.*

Mrs. Terry Chambers (Dianne)

Cherry Salad

1 can (21 ounces) cherry pie filling
1 can (14 ounces) sweetened
  condensed milk
1 can (8 ounces) crushed
  pineapple, drained

1 container (8 ounces) non-dairy
  whipped topping
¼ teaspoon almond extract
¼ teaspoon lemon juice

Stir all ingredients together until well blended. Chill. **Yield:** 8-10 servings.

Note: *Pretty served in a clear glass bowl.*

Mrs. Roy Watson (Charlene)

Toddy's Christmas Salad

3 egg yolks
2 Tablespoons sugar
Salt, dash
2 Tablespoons vinegar
2 Tablespoons pineapple syrup
1 Tablespoon margarine

1 cup whipping cream
2 cups red grapes, seeded
2 cups pineapple chunks
2 oranges, cut into pieces
2 cups miniature marshmallows

In a double boiler cook egg yolks, sugar, salt, vinegar, pineapple syrup, and margarine until thick (won't take long). Let cool. Whip cream and prepare fruit. Fold whipped cream, fruits, and marshmallows into cooked dressing. Chill 24 hours in large covered bowl. **Yield:** 6-8 servings.

Mrs. Jerry Leatherman (Diana)

Coconut Bananas

4 bananas
4 Tablespoons lemon juice

1 carton (16 ounces) sour cream
1¾ cups shredded coconut

Cut bananas into fourths. Place lemon juice, sour cream, and coconut in separate bowls. Dip bananas into lemon juice, roll in sour cream, and then in coconut. Be sure to cover thoroughly. Put in covered bowl and refrigerate several hours or overnight. **Yield:** 16 banana pieces.

Note: *Nice as a brunch fruit.*

Mrs. Doug Arnold (Debbi)

Hot Fruit Salad

1 can (29 ounces) sliced peaches
1 can (16 ounces) apricots
1 can (16 ounces) pineapple
  chunks
1 can (16 ounces) pitted dark
  cherries, well drained

½ cup butter or margarine
2 Tablespoons flour
1 cup firmly packed brown sugar
1 cup grapes
2 bananas, sliced

Drain canned fruits, reserving 1 cup peach juice, ½ cup apricot juice, and ½ cup pineapple juice. Discard juice from cherries. Melt butter in a large saucepan. Add flour, brown sugar, and reserved fruit juices. Heat until bubbly. Add all fruit. Heat on low and keep warm until ready to serve. **Yield:** 11-12 cups.

Mrs. Bill Frank (Barbara)

♥ *To chill sauces or gelatin mixtures quickly, set your mixing bowl in a larger bowl of ice water and refrigerate.*

Apricot Gelatin Salad

1 can (8¼ ounces) crushed
  pineapple
½ cup sugar
1 package (3 ounces) apricot
  flavored gelatin
1 package (3 ounces) cream
  cheese

½ cup ice water
½ cup chopped pecans
1 can (5 ounces) evaporated milk,
  chilled and whipped

Bring pineapple and sugar to a boil. Stir in gelatin until dissolved. Pour into blender or food processor; add cream cheese, and blend. Stir in ice water and pecans. Refrigerate until mushy. Add milk. Pour into a 2-quart flat casserole dish. Chill until firm. Slice into squares and serve. Garnish with a pecan half on each square. **Yield:** 9 servings.

Note: *This does not require a blender or processor, but it makes the job easier.*

Mrs. Thomas Hunter (Lynda)

Blueberry Gelatin Salad

3 cups boiling water
2 packages (3 ounces each)
  blackberry flavored gelatin
1 can (8 ounces) crushed
  pineapple, drained, reserving
  liquid
1 can (15 ounces) blueberries,
  drained

1 package (8 ounces) cream
  cheese
½ cup sugar
1 carton (8 ounces) sour cream
Pecans, chopped

Mix boiling water with gelatin. Add pineapple juice. Chill until slightly congealed. Fold in pineapple and blueberries. Pour into a 6x10-inch pan. Refrigerate until firm. Beat cream cheese, sugar, and sour cream until smooth. Spread over salad and sprinkle with pecans. **Yield:** 8-10 servings.

Note: *Frozen blueberries may be substituted for canned, and black cherry gelatin may be substituted for blackberry.*

Mrs. Don Argenbright (Gail)

Merry Cherry Gelatin

2 packages (3 ounces each) black
  cherry flavored gelatin
1 cup boiling water
1 can (20 ounces) crushed
  pineapple, drained

3 medium bananas, mashed
1 cup chopped walnuts
2 cans (17 ounces each) pitted dark
  cherries
1 carton (16 ounces) sour cream

Dissolve gelatin in boiling water. Immediately add pineapple, bananas, nuts, and cherries plus liquid. Pour half of mixture into bundt pan or 8x12-inch pan. Refrigerate until almost set. Spread sour cream over gelatin. Gently spoon remaining gelatin mixture over cream. Refrigerate until firm. **Yield:** 8 servings.

Mrs. John Mearns (June)

♥ *To peel oranges and grapefruit without the white membranes adhering to the sections, soak the fruit in hot water for five minutes before peeling.*

Holiday Cranberry Salad

1 cup sugar	2 teaspoons grated orange rind
1 cup fresh cranberries, ground	1 can (9 ounces) crushed
1 package (3 ounces) lemon	pineapple
flavored gelatin	½ cup chopped pecans
½ cup boiling water	1 cup chopped celery
1 cup orange juice	

Mix sugar and cranberries together and let stand for several hours. Add gelatin to boiling water, stirring until dissolved. Stir in cranberries and remaining ingredients. Pour into 1-quart mold. Refrigerate until firm. **Yield:** 6-8 servings.

Mrs. Dan Boyd (Terry)

Jeweled Cranberry Shimmer

3½ cups cranberry juice cocktail	½ cup blueberries
1 package (6 ounces) lemon	½ cup green grapes or pitted
flavored gelatin	sweet cherries, cut in half
1 cup peeled and sliced peaches	½ cup slivered almonds
or nectarines	Salad greens or grape clusters

Heat 1½ cups of cranberry juice to boiling in a small saucepan. Pour over the gelatin and dissolve. Stir in remaining 2 cups of cranberry juice. Chill until thickened but not set. Stir in fruits and almonds. Pour into an oiled 6-cup mold. Chill 3-4 hours until firm. To serve, unmold and garnish with salad greens or grape clusters. **Yield:** 6-8 servings.

Mrs. Richard Keeling (Laurie)

Emerald Glow Salad

1 package (3 ounces) lemon	1 can (20 ounces) crushed
flavored gelatin	pineapple, undrained
1 package (3 ounces) lime flavored	1 can (12 ounces) evaporated milk
gelatin	1 cup chopped pecans
1 cup boiling water	

Dissolve gelatin in boiling water. Add pineapple, milk, and nuts. Stir and place in mold or 9x12-inch cake pan. Refrigerate until jelled. Serve on lettuce leaf. **Yield:** 10-12 servings.

Mrs. Jerry Brown (Linda)

Mango Salad

1 can (15 ounces) sliced mangos
2 packages (3 ounces each) lemon
  flavored gelatin

2 packages (8 ounces each) cream
  cheese

Squeeze juice from mangos. Combine juice and enough water to make 1½ cups liquid. Bring to a boil and add gelatin. Stir until dissolved. Blend mangos and cream cheese in food processor. Mix into hot gelatin mixture. Pour into dish or mold and chill until firm. **Yield:** 6 servings.

Note: *For individual servings pour into muffin tins and chill.*

Mrs. Winston Borum (Jimmie)

Congealed Pineapple Salad

2   packages (3 ounces each)
    lemon flavored gelatin
1½ cups hot water
1½ cups cold water
2   cups crushed pineapple,
    undrained

1 cup grated American cheese
1 cup chopped nuts
2 cups whipping cream, whipped

Dissolve gelatin in hot water. Add cold water. Refrigerate until it begins to gel (about 1 hour). Fold pineapple, cheese, and nuts into gelatin. Fold in whipped cream. Pour into 9x13-inch dish. Return to refrigerator to gel. **Yield:** 9-12 servings.

Mrs. Terry Chambers (Dianne)

Raspberry-Applesauce Salad

1 package (3 ounces) raspberry
  flavored gelatin
1 cup boiling water
1 package (12 ounces) frozen
  raspberries

1   cup applesauce
1½ cups sour cream
1½ cups miniature marshmallows

Dissolve gelatin in boiling water. Add raspberries and stir until thawed. Stir in applesauce. Pour into 8x8-inch dish. Chill until set. Combine sour cream and marshmallows. Spread over gelatin. Cover and chill 2 hours or longer. **Yield:** 6-8 servings.

Mrs. Steven Sellers (Anne)

Lemon Gelatin Salad

1 package (3 ounces) lemon
   flavored gelatin
1 cup hot water
¾ cup cold water
1 can (20 ounces) crushed
   pineapple

3 bananas, sliced
1 cup miniature marshmallows
½ cup sugar
2 Tablespoons flour
1 egg
1 cup whipping cream

Mix gelatin according to package directions, using 1 cup hot water and ¾ cup cold water. Let thicken slightly in refrigerator. Drain pineapple, reserving juice. Add pineapple, bananas, and marshmallows. Pour into 9x13-inch pan. Refrigerate. Measure pineapple juice plus enough water to equal 1 cup. Combine with sugar, flour, and egg. Cook until smooth; cool. Whip cream and add to cooled mixture. Spread over gelatin. Serve very cold. **Yield:** 12 servings.

Mrs. Pete Bennett (Stephanie)

Red, White, and Blue Salad

1 box (6 ounces) raspberry
   flavored gelatin
4 cups hot water
1 envelope unflavored gelatin
½ cup cold water
1 cup coffee cream
1 cup sugar
1 teaspoon vanilla extract

1 package (8 ounces) cream
   cheese
1 box (3 ounces) raspberry
   flavored gelatin
1 cup hot water
1 cup chopped pecans
1¾ cups blueberries, drained

Layer 1: Dissolve large gelatin in 4 cups hot water. Pour into 9x13-inch dish. Chill until set.

Layer 2: Soften unflavored gelatin in ½ cup cold water. Combine cream and sugar in saucepan. Heat to boiling, stirring until sugar is dissolved. Add unflavored gelatin and vanilla. Soften cream cheese and blend into hot unflavored gelatin mix. Stir until blended smooth. Cool slightly and pour over bottom layer. Chill until set.

Layer 3: Dissolve small gelatin in 1 cup hot water. Stir in pecans and blueberries. Pour over set cheese layer. Chill again. **Yield:** 10-12 servings.

Note: *Best to make a day ahead for all layers to set.*

Mrs. John Morgan (Marilyn)

Strawberry Delight

2 packages (3 ounces each)
  strawberry flavored gelatin
1 cup boiling water
1 package (10 ounces) frozen
  strawberries, thawed
3 bananas, mashed

1 can (8 ounces) crushed
  pineapple
1 cup chopped pecans
1 package (8 ounces) sour cream
Non-dairy whipped topping,
  optional

Dissolve gelatin in boiling water. Add strawberries, bananas, pineapple, and nuts. Pour half of mixture into oblong dish and chill until firm. Spread sour cream over chilled mixture. Pour remaining half of mixture over sour cream. Refrigerate until firm and ready to serve. Cut into squares. Serve plain or topped with non-dairy whipped topping. **Yield:** 12 servings.

Note: *Can be made a day ahead.*

Mrs. Ellwood Jones (Ann)

♥ *Fruit salads are beautiful served from pineapple boats. Serve large fruit salads from watermelon halves carved like a basket.*

♥ *Frosted grapes make a lovely garnish. Dip grapes into slightly beaten egg whites or fresh lemon juice and then in granulated sugar.*

Frozen Banana Salad

3 large ripe bananas, mashed
2 Tablespoons lemon juice
¾ cup sugar
1 can (8 ounces) crushed
  pineapple, drained
¼ cup finely chopped maraschino
  cherries

¼ cup chopped pecans
1 cup sour cream
1 container (12 ounces) non-dairy
  whipped topping

Mix all ingredients together. Pour into a sheet cake pan sprayed with vegetable cooking spray and freeze. Keep covered in freezer until ready to serve. Slice and serve in squares. **Yield:** 12-14 servings.

Mrs. Ted Denbow (Connie)

Pink Cranberry Freeze

2 packages (3 ounces each) cream
  cheese, softened
2 Tablespoons mayonnaise
2 Tablespoons sugar
1 can (16 ounces) whole cranberry
  sauce

1 can (8¼ ounces) crushed
  pineapple
½ cup chopped nuts
½ cup whipped cream
½ cup powdered sugar
1 teaspoon vanilla extract

Blend together cream cheese, mayonnaise, sugar, fruits, and nuts. Fold in whipped cream to which powdered sugar and vanilla have been added. Pour into loaf pan and freeze at least 6 hours. **Yield:** 10-12 servings.

Mrs. Greg Smith (Katie)

Frozen Fruit Slices
Excellent on a Summer Day

2 packages (3 ounces each) cream
  cheese, softened
1 cup mayonnaise
1 can (1 pound 14 ounces) fruit
  cocktail, well drained

½ cup maraschino cherries,
  drained and quartered
2½ cups miniature marshmallows
1 cup whipping cream, whipped
Food coloring, red or green

Blend cream cheese and mayonnaise. Stir in fruit cocktail, cherries, marshmallows, and whipped cream. Tint with a few drops of food coloring. Pour into 13x9x2-inch glass dish and freeze 10-12 hours. Thaw until easily sliced, about 15-30 minutes. Serve on lettuce leaf. **Yield:** 24 servings.

Note: *You may also use muffin tins or mini-molds. It slips right out and makes serving a breeze.*

Mrs. Bill Frank (Barbara)

♥ *Marshmallows can be cut easily with scissors that are dipped in hot water.*

Frozen Fruit Salad

1 can (12 ounces) evaporated milk, chilled
1 can (17 ounces) fruit cocktail, drained
5 ounces maraschino cherries, halved
3 Tablespoons lemon juice

1 cup miniature marshmallows or 16 large marshmallows, cut into pieces
½ cup chopped pecans
½ cup Miracle Whip salad dressing
Lettuce

In a well chilled bowl, whip milk until stiff. Add remaining ingredients. Pour into 8-inch square dish and freeze. Cut into squares and serve on lettuce cups. **Yield:** 16 (2-inch) squares.

Mrs. Don Kleinschmidt (Ceil)

Blue Cheese Dressing

½ cup whipping cream
4 Tablespoons blue cheese

1 cup mayonnaise
1 teaspoon lemon juice

Whip the cream. Crumble in blue cheese. Fold cream and cheese into mayonnaise. Add lemon juice. Refrigerate 2 hours. **Yield:** 2 cups.

Note: *Thin with 1-2 tablespoons milk to use the next day.*

Mrs. Jack Hamer (Pam)

Dijon Dressing

2 eggs
2 Tablespoons Parmesan cheese
1 clove garlic, crushed
2 Tablespoons Dijon mustard
½ cup salad oil

¼ cup lemon juice
2 teaspoons sugar
Salt to taste
Pepper, freshly ground, to taste

Mix all ingredients with a whisk in a measuring cup. Chill and serve. **Yield:** 1½ cups.

Note: *Great on fresh spinach.*

Mrs. Joe Key (Christie)

Fruit Salad Dressing

⅔ cup pineapple juice
5⅓ Tablespoons lemon juice
2 eggs, beaten

1 cup sugar
2 cups whipping cream, whipped

Combine juices. Add eggs and sugar. Cook in double boiler or pan until thickened. Cool and add whipped cream. Serve with fruit. **Yield:** Approximately 2 cups.

Note: *Good for luncheon salad, dessert or fruit dip. Halve recipe unless feeding 12 or more.*

Mrs. Burl Turner (Sheryl)

Old Fashioned Fruit Sauce

2 cartons (16 ounces each) sour
   cream
½ teaspoon cinnamon
Nutmeg, pinch

3 cups firmly packed brown
   sugar
⅔ cup rum
⅓ cup white raisins

Combine first four ingredients. Blend rum and raisins and add to sour cream mix. Refrigerate. Serve over fresh strawberries, blueberries, raspberries or bananas. **Yield:** 24 servings.

Note: *You may use less rum. This recipe can be halved but why not make it all to have on hand! It keeps forever!*

Mrs. Sam Norvell (Patsy)

Honey Dressing

½ cup mayonnaise
½ cup honey

2 teaspoons poppy seeds

Mix all ingredients until well blended. Serve over fruit. **Yield:** 1 cup.

Mrs. Joe Key (Christie)

Golden Salad Dressing

1½ Tablespoons minced onion	⅔ cup cider vinegar
2 Tablespoons yellow mustard	⅔ cup warm water
4 teaspoons monosodium glutamate	1 teaspoon Worcestershire sauce
	Tabasco, dash
1½ Tablespoons salt	1¾ cups salad oil

Mix the first 6 ingredients in a blender or food processor. Add remaining ingredients, mix thoroughly. **Yield:** Approximately 3 cups.

Note: *Keeps well for several weeks.*

Mrs. Sam Norvell (Patsy)

Honey Mustard Dressing
Great on Spinach Salad

1 cup salad oil	3 teaspoons honey
⅓ cup wine vinegar	1-2 cloves garlic, crushed
6 Tablespoons Durkees sauce	Salt, dash
2 Tablespoons Worcestershire sauce	Pepper, dash

Mix ingredients together. Serve immediately over salad or refrigerate to chill. **Yield:** 2 cups.

Mrs. Richard Keeling (Laurie)

Poppy Seed Dressing

1½ cups sugar	3 Tablespoons onion juice
2 teaspoons dry mustard	2 cups salad oil
2 teaspoons salt	3 Tablespoons poppy seeds
⅔ cup white vinegar	

Combine sugar, mustard, salt, vinegar, and onion juice. Mix well. Add oil slowly, beating constantly with electric beater, until mixture becomes thick. Add poppy seeds and beat a few minutes longer. **Yield:** 3½ cups.

Note: *This can be made in a blender.*

Mrs. Roy Watson (Charlene)

Croutons

Day old bread   **Olive oil**
Clarified butter   **Salad oil**

Cut crusts from slices of day old bread. Cut the bread into cubes. Sauté bread cubes in a small amount of clarified butter, turning to brown on all sides. Drain on paper towels. Or may toast cubes on a cookie sheet which has been lightly spread with a mixture of olive oil and salad oil. Toast at 250° for 30-40 minutes. **Yield:** Approximately 36 cubes per slice.

Note: *Bread cubes may be seasoned with seasonings such as garlic and Parmesan cheese.*

Mrs. Jack Hamer (Pam)

♥ *To clarify butter, melt butter completely over low heat, then remove from heat and let stand a few minutes. Skim fat from top and strain remaining liquid through cheesecloth.*

♥ *Sprinkle Parmesan cheese over most any salad to add looks and good taste.*

♥ *Walnuts or pecans toasted in garlic salt and butter add a delicious taste to salads.*

♥ *To help rid your hands of the odor of onions, rub them with salt or vinegar, rinse in cold water and wash in warm water.*

♥ *Make a fluffy fruit salad dressing by beating 3 tablespoons of mayonnaise into 1 cup of softened vanilla ice cream.*

♥ *You can tell a ripe honeydew by its creamy, off-white, smooth rind and great aroma. Store in the refrigerator wrapped in foil or plastic wrap to prevent its fragrance from perfuming other foods.*

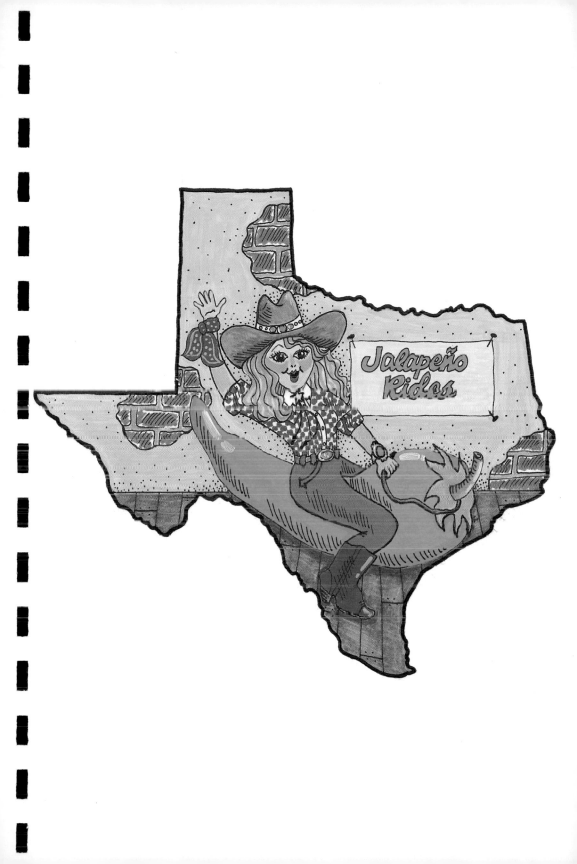

Cystic Fibrosis Foundation

Cystic fibrosis is the most common, fatal genetic disease in the United States. Children with cystic fibrosis inherit the disease from defective genes carried by both parents, occurring in one out of every 2,000 births. The Cystic Fibrosis Foundation supports research, and in August 1989 it was announced that CFF-supported researchers had discovered the cystic fibrosis gene. Funds for CFF are raised through area chapter-supported events such as the Tennis Auction Ball, Bachelor Bid, Reunion Tower Climb and other fund-raising activities.

Dallas Junior Forum has supported the Cystic Fibrosis Foundation during the past eight years, providing volunteers and leadership for events, office assistance and financial support. Dallas Junior Forum funds have paid for brochures, notecards and a cystic fibrosis patient services library.

Breads and Sandwiches

Breads are made with liquid and flour,
And the dough can turn out sweet or sour.
You can make it plain for your favorite spread,
Or add special ingredients for a fancy bread.

Olive Bread

2½ cups flour	1 egg, beaten
⅓ cup sugar	1 cup stuffed green olives, sliced
4 teaspoons baking powder	1 cup chopped pecans
½ teaspoon salt	2 Tablespoons chopped pimiento
1 cup milk	

Thoroughly mix first 4 ingredients. Add milk and egg. Stir in remaining ingredients. Pour into greased 5x9-inch loaf pan. Let stand 20 minutes before baking. Bake at 350° for 1 hour. **Yield:** 1 loaf.

Note: *Good spread with cream cheese for party sandwiches. May be frozen.*

Mrs. Joe Key (Christie)

Beer Bread

3 cups self-rising flour	1 can (12 ounces) beer
3 Tablespoons sugar	¼ cup butter, melted

Combine flour, sugar, and beer. Spread in 9x5-inch bread pan which has been sprayed with vegetable cooking spray. Bake at 350° for 40-45 minutes. Remove from oven. Pour melted butter over hot bread. Bake about 10 minutes more. **Yield:** 1 loaf.

Mrs. Don Argenbright (Gail)

Cheese Bread

2 eggs	2 teaspoons dry mustard
¾ cup water	1½ cups grated Cheddar cheese
2 packages (6 ounces each) biscuit mix	2 Tablespoons butter

Beat eggs in bowl. Stir in water, add biscuit mix, dry mustard, and 1 cup Cheddar cheese. Mix thoroughly and pour into greased 9x5-inch loaf pan. Sprinkle top with remaining cheese and dot with the butter. Bake at 350° for 45 minutes. Let bread cool in pan before removing and slicing. **Yield:** 1 loaf.

Note: *Delicious toasted and with soup or stew.*

Mrs. John Morgan (Marilyn)

Mini-Blinies

24 slices white bread
1 package (8 ounces) cream
   cheese, softened
2 egg yolks

1 cup sugar, divided
½ cup butter, melted
1 teaspoon cinnamon

Trim crust from bread and flatten with a rolling pin. Mix cream cheese, egg yolks, and ½ cup sugar. Spread bread with cream cheese mixture and roll each slice of bread like a jelly roll. Dip in melted butter and roll in mixture of ½ cup sugar and 1 teaspoon cinnamon. Place on a cookie sheet and freeze. When frozen, cut into thirds. Store in freezer. There is no need to thaw before baking. Bake at 350° for 10 minutes. **Yield:** 72 pieces.

Mrs. Steve Moi (Joanie)

Zucchini-Cheddar Bread
A Good Bread with Soup or Salad

¼ cup butter or margarine
1 cup finely chopped onion
2½ cups flour
1 Tablespoon sugar
1 Tablespoon baking powder
1 teaspoon salt

½ teaspoon Italian seasoning
2 eggs
¼ cup milk
1 cup shredded zucchini
1 cup (4 ounces) shredded
   Cheddar cheese

Melt butter in a small skillet and sauté onion until tender (about 5 minutes). Cool slightly. Combine flour, sugar, baking powder, salt, and Italian seasoning in a large bowl. Add onion mixture, eggs, and milk, and stir only until all ingredients are moistened. Press as much moisture as possible out of zucchini, and add to batter. Mix in Cheddar cheese. Batter will be very stiff, so mixing may need to be done with hands. Spread batter evenly in a well buttered 9-inch round cake pan. Bake at 400° for 40-45 minutes, or until a wooden pick inserted in center comes out clean. Serve warm with butter. **Yield:** 6-8 servings.

Note: *Freezes well.*

Mrs. Ellwood Jones (Ann)

Monkey Bread

½ cup sugar
1 teaspoon cinnamon
3 packages (8 ounces each) refrigerator biscuits, cut in quarters

1 teaspoon cinnamon
Sugar
½ cup butter or margarine

Preheat oven to 350°. Combine sugar and cinnamon; roll biscuits in mixture. Layer in a buttered bundt pan. Pour any remaining sugar mixture into an 8 ounce measuring cup. Add 1 teaspoon cinnamon and enough sugar to fill the cup. Melt margarine, stir sugar mixture into it. Spoon over top of biscuits. Bake 30 minutes. **Yield:** 8 servings.

Mrs. Robert Bostwick (Diane)

Pumpkin Bread

3½ cups flour
2 teaspoons baking soda
1½ teaspoons salt
2 teaspoons cinnamon
1 teaspoon nutmeg

3 cups sugar
1 cup salad oil
4 eggs
⅔ cup water
2 cups pumpkin

Sift together flour, baking soda, salt, cinnamon, nutmeg, and sugar. Beat salad oil, eggs, water, and pumpkin. Combine dry and wet ingredients and mix well. Pour into 2 greased 9x5-inch loaf pans. Bake at 350° for 1 hour and 15 minutes. Cool before removing from pan. **Yield:** 2 loaves.

Note: *If using smaller loaf pans (3 loaves), cut baking time to 1 hour.*

Mrs. Jim Conine (Donna)

♥ *Before slicing fresh bread, run a serrated bread knife under hot water, dry it, and slice.*

Zucchini Bread
Stays Fresh in the Refrigerator a Long Time

2 cups uncooked zucchini, sliced	1 teaspoon baking soda
2 cups sugar	½ teaspoon salt
1 cup salad oil	1½ teaspoons cinnamon
3 eggs, beaten	1 cup chopped pecans
3 cups sifted flour	1 teaspoon vanilla extract
¼ teaspoon baking powder	

Chop zucchini in food processor until mixture has no large chunks. Drain. Mix all ingredients. Pour mixture into 2 greased and floured 9x5-inch loaf pans. Bake at 350° for 40-45 minutes. **Yield:** 2 loaves.

Mrs. Marvin Chronister (Donna)

Pennsylvania Applesauce Bread

2 cups flour	¾ cup sugar
1 teaspoon baking powder	½ cup shortening
1 teaspoon baking soda	2 eggs
1 teaspoon salt	1 teaspoon vanilla extract
1 teaspoon cinnamon	1 cup applesauce
½ teaspoon nutmeg	½ cup chopped pecans

Sift together first 6 ingredients. In another bowl, gradually add sugar to shortening; cream well. Blend in unbeaten eggs and vanilla extract. Beat well. Gradually add sifted dry ingredients. Mix well. Stir in applesauce and pecans. Pour into well greased 9x5-inch loaf pan. Bake at 350° for 55-60 minutes. Cool before slicing. **Yield:** 1 loaf bread.

Note: *Bread freezes well. Makes nice muffins also.*

Mrs. Bill Frank (Barbara)

Strawberry Bread

Bread:
3 cups sifted flour
2 cups sugar
1 teaspoon salt
1 teaspoon baking soda
1 Tablespoon cinnamon
4 eggs, beaten
1¼ cups salad oil

1¼ cups chopped pecans
2 cups frozen sliced strawberries
   with juice

Spread:
1 package (8 ounces) cream
   cheese
½ cup strawberries, sliced

Bread: Sift dry ingredients into large mixing bowl. Add remaining ingredients. Mix thoroughly. Pour into 2 greased 9x5-inch loaf pans. Bake at 350° for 1 hour or until it tests done. Let cool 5 minutes before removing from pan.

Spread: Combine cream cheese with sliced strawberries. Keep refrigerated. Spread on sliced strawberry bread. **Yield:** 2 loaves.

Mrs. Jerry Leatherman (Diana)

Holiday Bread

3½ cups sifted flour
3 cups sugar
2 teaspoons baking soda
½ teaspoon salt
1½ teaspoons nutmeg
2 teaspoons cinnamon

4 eggs, beaten
⅔ cup water
1 cup shortening
2 cups cranberry sauce
2 teaspoons vanilla extract
1 cup chopped pecans, optional

Sift together flour, sugar, soda, salt, nutmeg, and cinnamon. Add eggs, water, shortening, cranberry sauce, and vanilla. Mix well and stir in pecans. Fill 5 greased and lightly floured 6¾x3½-inch loaf pans ½ full. Bake at 350° for 1 hour. **Yield:** 5 loaves.

Mrs. Marvin Chronister (Donna)

Poppy Seed Muffins

¼ cup poppy seed
⅔ cup salad oil
1 box (18 ounces) yellow cake mix
1 package (3 ounces) instant coconut cream pudding

⅔ cup water
4 eggs
½ teaspoon almond extract

Mix poppy seed in oil. Blend cake mix, pudding, water, and oil with poppy seed together in mixer at medium speed. Add eggs, one at a time, blending thoroughly after each. Add extract. Pour batter into greased and floured tube pan, or two large muffin tins filled ⅔ full. Bake at 350° 1 hour for cake and 35 minutes for muffins. **Yield:** 18-24 large muffins.

Mrs. Dennis Furlong (Dede)

Fudge Muffins

2 cups unsalted butter, not margarine
8 ounces sweet German chocolate
3½ cups sugar
2 cups flour

Salt, pinch
8 eggs
2 teaspoons vanilla extract
4 cups chopped pecans
36 pecan halves

Preheat oven to 300°. Line muffin tins. Melt butter and chocolate in the top of a double boiler. Combine sugar, flour, and salt in a large bowl. Stir in chocolate mixture. Add eggs and vanilla extract and whisk just enough to moisten all ingredients. Do not over mix! Fold in chopped nuts. Spoon batter into muffin tins until ⅔ full. Top each with a pecan half. Bake 40 minutes. **Yield:** 3 dozen.

Note: *Freezes well.*

Mrs. Sam Murray (Sandra)

♥ *If you grease more muffin cups than you need, fill the empty ones with water to keep the grease from baking on.*

Country Club Muffins

2 eggs	½ cup flour
1 cup firmly packed brown sugar	1 teaspoon vanilla extract
1 cup chopped nuts	2 Tablespoons butter, melted
¼ teaspoon salt	

Preheat oven to 300°. Use a spray shortening and flour mixture on muffin tins and place in oven as it is heating. Beat eggs well. Mix ingredients in order listed. Fill heated muffin tins ¾ full. Bake 22 minutes. **Yield:** 1 dozen large muffins.

Note: *Freezes well.*

Mrs. Joe Key (Christie)

Orange Muffins

2½ cups flour	1⅔ cups sugar
2 teaspoons baking powder	3 eggs, beaten
½ teaspoon salt	1 teaspoon vanilla extract
¾ cup butter or margarine, softened	2 oranges, rind and juice
	Powdered sugar, optional

Sift flour, baking powder, and salt. Set aside. Cream butter and sugar. Add eggs, vanilla, juice of 2 oranges (½ cup), and rind of 2 oranges. Combine liquid and dry ingredients and stir lightly until batter is moist and lumpy. Grease small muffin tins with butter and dust with flour or use small muffin paper liners. Fill each ½ full. Bake at 350° for 15 minutes. **Yield:** 6½ dozen muffins.

Note: *These may be topped with powdered sugar for a sweeter taste.*

Mrs. Jim Conine (Donna)

♥ *A clean toothbrush is a handy gadget for removal of excess rind from your grater.*

Melt In Your Mouth Muffins

¾ cup milk
⅓ cup salad oil
⅓ cup sugar

2 eggs
2 cups Bisquick mix

Combine milk, oil, and sugar. Beat in eggs and add the Bisquick. Stir until well mixed. Mixture may be lumpy. Fill greased cupcake tins ⅔ full. Bake at 425° for 8-10 minutes. **Yield:** 1 dozen muffins.

Note: *You may add 1 cup of drained blueberries to the mixture. Also these may be stored in freezer and reheated in microwave for 30 seconds or less.*

Mrs. Jeff Farmer (Kaliko)

♥ *Place greased pans into the oven for a few minutes before adding batter to make lighter muffins.*

♥ *To keep raisins, currants, and other dried fruit from falling to the bottom of the cake, coat with a small amount of flour before adding them to the batter.*

Harvest Muffins

⅔ cup milk
¾ cup canned pumpkin
1 large egg
½ teaspoon allspice
½ teaspoon cinnamon
½ teaspoon salt
½ cup chopped dates

½ cup chopped pecans or
    walnuts
1½ cups flour
⅔ cup sugar
2 teaspoons baking powder
⅓ cup butter, melted

Beat milk, pumpkin, and egg. Add spices, dates, and nuts. Blend into flour, sugar, and baking powder. Fold in melted butter. Pour into 1 dozen buttered muffin tins. Bake at 400° for 20 minutes. Serve warm with butter. **Yield:** 1 dozen.

Mrs. William Hollon (Kasey)

Bran Muffins
Wonderful and Healthy

1 cup boiling water
2 cups fruit and fiber cereal
1 cup bran cereal
½ cup margarine
1 cup firmly packed brown sugar
½ cup molasses

2 eggs
1 cup chopped prunes or raisins
2 cups buttermilk
2½ cups whole wheat flour
2½ teaspoons baking soda
1 teaspoon salt

Pour boiling water over cereals and butter. Add sugar and molasses. Beat in eggs, then add other ingredients. Pour into greased muffin tins. Bake at 400° about 20 minutes. **Yield:** 24 muffins.

Note: *Can be stored in refrigerator up to 6 weeks before baking.*

Mrs. Winston Borum (Jimmie)

♥ *Lightly oil the cup or spoon used to measure honey or molasses. Nonstick cooking spray works well for this.*

"Six Weeks" Muffins

5 cups flour
2 teaspoons baking soda
2 teaspoons salt
3 cups sugar
1 box (15 ounces) raisin bran
   cereal

4 eggs, beaten
1 cup salad oil
1 quart buttermilk

Sift flour, soda, and salt in large bowl. Add sugar and bran cereal and mix. Next add eggs, oil, and buttermilk. Mix well. Store in covered container in refrigerator. Use as needed. Fill muffin tins ⅔ full. Bake at 400° for 15-20 minutes. **Yield:** Approximately 48 muffins.

Note: *This batter will keep up to 6 weeks.*

Mrs. Bill Crandall (Julie)

No Knead Rolls

1 package dry yeast	1 teaspoon salt
1 cup warm water	½ cup margarine, cold
3 eggs	4 cups flour
3 Tablespoons sugar	

Dissolve yeast in 1 cup warm water and let stand for 5 minutes. Beat eggs until they are light in color, using an electric mixer. Add sugar, salt, and dissolved yeast. Combine these by stirring. Cut cold margarine into small chips and gently stir into egg mixture. Stir in flour until thoroughly combined. Cover bowl with plastic wrap. Let stand (free of draft) for 2 hours. Shape into rolls of any kind. Place on greased cookie sheet and cover with tea towel. Let rise 1 hour. Bake at 350° until lightly brown, about 30 minutes. **Yield:** 8-10 servings.

Note: *Do not make on a humid day.*

Mrs. Jack Hamer (Pam)

♥ *To be sure your yeast is still active, "proof" it. Pour 1 package dry yeast into ½ cup warm water (100-115°) and add 2 teaspoons granulated sugar. Stir and set aside for a few minutes. If mixture swells and bubbles appear on the surface, it is still active.*

Ice Box Rolls

1 cup shortening	1 teaspoon salt, heaping
1 cup hot water	3 Tablespoons sugar
1 package (¼ ounce) yeast	6 cups flour
1 cup cold water	1 cup butter, melted
2 eggs, beaten	

Melt shortening in hot water. Dissolve yeast in cold water. Add to shortening. Combine eggs, salt, and sugar. Stir into shortening. Gradually add flour and mix well. Cover and refrigerate 2-3 hours. Roll dough out. Cut into rolls, and spread 1 cup melted butter over them. Fold each roll in ½ and let rise for 2-3 hours. Bake at 350° for 10-12 minutes until golden brown. Serve warm. **Yield:** 3 dozen.

Mrs. Winston Borum (Jimmie)

Stuffed Dinner Rolls

2-3 green onions, chopped
1 can (4½ ounces) black olives
1½ ounces bacon bits or 2-3 slices
   of fried bacon, crushed
1½ cups grated Cheddar cheese

¼-½ cup mayonnaise
1 dozen Brown N Serve rolls
   or a package of 20 miniature
   rolls

Mix ingredients. Stuff 1-2 tablespoons into roll and brown as instructed.
Yield: 1 dozen rolls.

Note: *You may vary amounts of any or all ingredients to taste. Can be prepared 1-2 days ahead. Just keep refrigerated and do not brown until needed.*

Mrs. Greg Smith (Katie)

♥ *For a delicious way to use leftover hot dog buns, cut horizontally into thin slices, butter, sprinkle with Parmesan cheese or garlic powder, and toast until golden brown.*

Raspberry Jam Puffs

2 cups Bisquick mix
2 Tablespoons sugar
¼ cup margarine, softened
⅔ cup milk

10 teaspoons raspberry jam
1 cup powdered sugar
1 teaspoon vanilla extract
Milk or cream

Preheat oven to 450°. Mix Bisquick, sugar, and margarine. Add milk all at once. Beat no more than 20 strokes to make a soft dough. If over mixed, they will not be light and fluffy. Place one tablespoon of dough into each of 10 paper cupcake liners. Top with 1 teaspoon of jam and another table-spoon of dough. Bake 10-15 minutes or until golden brown. Remove from pan immediately. Blend sugar with vanilla extract and just enough milk or cream to make it easy to spread. Frost puffs. **Yield:** 10 puffs.

Mrs. Jerry Leatherman (Diana)

French Puffs

½ cup sugar
1½ cups flour
1½ teaspoons baking powder
½ teaspoon salt
½ teaspoon nutmeg
1 egg

⅓ cup salad oil
½ cup milk
½ cup butter or margarine, melted
½ cup sugar
1 teaspoon cinnamon

Preheat oven to 350°. Grease small muffin tins. Combine first 5 ingredi-ents. Blend in eggs, oil, and milk. Fill muffin tins and bake 10 minutes. Remove from tins. While still warm, roll in melted butter; then in sugar and cinnamon mixture. **Yield:** 2 dozen small puffs.

Mrs. Robert Bostwick (Diane)

Skip's Tipsy Toast

12 eggs
1 cup milk
1 cup orange juice

1 jigger Grand Marnier liqueur
2-3 loaves French bread
Liquid margarine for frying

Combine first 4 ingredients in large bowl. Slice French bread and soak in mixture for at least 15 minutes. Fry in liquid margarine until crisp and golden. **Yield:** 12 servings.

Note: *Delicious sprinkled with powdered sugar and cinnamon.*

Mrs. Jim Thornton (Jackie)

Puffy French Toast

1 cup flour
1½ teaspoons sugar
1½ teaspoons baking powder
1 teaspoon ground cinnamon
¼ teaspoon nutmeg
½ teaspoon salt

⅛ teaspoon ground cloves
1 cup milk
1 egg, beaten
12 slices white bread
Salad oil for deep frying

Mix all ingredients together. Lightly dip bread slices into batter, coating both sides evenly. Fry in preheated 375° deep oil until golden brown, about 2 minutes on each side. Drain, serve hot. **Yield:** 12 servings.

Note: *Batter can be kept in refrigerator for about a week.*

Mrs. Jim Thornton (Jackie)

♥ *Enhance your favorite waffle recipe by adding crumbled bacon, shredded ham or pecan pieces.*

Alice Skinner's Vegetable Spoon Bread
Great with Ham or Soup

1 package (10 ounces) frozen
  chopped spinach
2 eggs, slightly beaten
1 can (8¾ ounces) cream-style corn

1 cup sour cream
½ cup margarine, melted
1 box (8½ ounces) corn muffin
  mix

Thaw spinach overnight in the refrigerator. Drain well. Combine spinach, eggs, corn, sour cream, and margarine. Mix well. Stir in corn muffin mix. Pour into greased baking pan. Use an 8-inch square pan for thick squares or 7x11-inch pan for thin squares. Bake at 350° for about 35 minutes or until a pick inserted in the center comes out clean. **Yield:** 10-12 servings.

Mrs. Dan Boyd (Terry)

Spoon Cornbread

1 can (16 ounces) creamed corn
1 cup yellow cornmeal
2 eggs, beaten
¾ cup milk
½ cup salad oil

1 teaspoon salt
½ teaspoon baking soda
2 jalapeño peppers, finely chopped
1 cup grated cheese

Mix first 7 ingredients. Put ½ of mixture into greased 9-inch square baking dish. Sprinkle with peppers and ½ cup cheese. Cover with rest of mixture and top with cheese. Bake at 400° for 40 minutes. **Yield:** 6-10 servings.

Mrs. Jay Settle (Karen)

Jalapeño Hush Puppies
Delicious with Fresh Fish or Shrimp

2 cups cornmeal
1 Tablespoon flour
1 teaspoon baking soda
1 teaspoon baking powder
2 teaspoons salt

1 cup buttermilk
1 egg
2 Tablespoons chopped onion
¼ cup chopped jalapeño peppers

Combine all ingredients in bowl and mix until smooth. Drop by table-spoon into hot grease. **Yield:** 2½ dozen.

Mrs. John Morgan (Marilyn)

Best-Ever Cornbread

1 cup yellow cornmeal
½ cup flour
1 teaspoon salt
1 teaspoon baking powder
½ teaspoon baking soda

1 cup buttermilk
½ cup evaporated milk
¼ cup shortening, melted
1 egg

Preheat oven to 450°. Grease 8-inch square pan. Mix cornmeal, flour, and salt. Add remaining ingredients. Stir well and pour into pan. Bake 15 minutes. **Yield:** 4-6 servings.

Mrs. William Hollon (Kasey)

Tex-Mex Cornbread

2 eggs
⅔ cup salad oil
1 cup sour cream
1 cup yellow cornmeal
¾ cup yellow cream-style corn
1 Tablespoon baking powder

1½ teaspoons salt
2 green onion tops, finely chopped
4 small jalapeño peppers, seeded and finely chopped
1 cup grated Cheddar cheese

Combine eggs, oil, sour cream, cornmeal, corn, baking powder, and salt. Add onions, peppers, and ½ of the cheese. Spread in a well greased 8x12-inch baking pan. Cover with remaining cheese. Bake at 425° for 20-25 minutes. **Yield:** 8-10 servings.

Mrs. Doug Rivenbark (Penny)

♥ *For a crusty cornbread, heat bacon drippings or shortening in an iron skillet. Pour in the batter and cook in a hot oven.*

Blue Ribbon Stuffing with Apples

1½ cups chopped onions
½ cup chopped celery
1 cup dry breadcrumbs
2½ cups crumbled cornbread
½ cup butter, melted

Salt and pepper to taste
¼ teaspoon paprika
¾ teaspoon poultry seasoning
1½ cups chopped tart apples
Chicken or turkey broth

Boil onion and celery in 4 cups salted water. Simmer for 10 minutes and drain. Mix with all other ingredients except broth. Add enough broth to mixture to moisten slightly. Bake at 350° in a greased 1½-quart baking dish for 40-50 minutes. **Yield:** 1½ quarts.

Mrs. Doug Arnold (Debbi)

Bacon-Cheese and Olive Melt

12 slices bacon, cooked and
crumbled
1½ cups grated Cheddar or Swiss
cheese
½ cup chopped Spanish olives
1 can (3 ounces) mushrooms,
stems and pieces

2 Tablespoons grated onion
4 eggs, beaten
4 English muffins, toasted and
halved

Preheat oven to 400°. Combine all ingredients, except English muffins.
Spoon mixture on toasted muffin halves. Bake 18 minutes or until melted
and bubbly. **Yield:** 8 muffin halves.

Mrs. Willim Hollon (Kasey)

Fruited Chicken Salad Sandwiches

1 cup cooked chicken, finely
chopped
½ cup finely chopped celery
¾ cup finely chopped apple
⅓ cup crushed pineapple, well
drained
3 Tablespoons mayonnaise

⅛ teaspoon salt
⅛ teaspoon pepper
1 teaspoon lemon juice
¼ teaspoon onion powder
Butter
8 slices bread

Combine chicken, celery, apple, and pineapple in a small bowl. Stir in
mayonnaise, salt, pepper, lemon juice, and onion powder. Mixture may
be refrigerated day before serving. To serve, spread chicken mixture on
buttered bread. Cut as desired. Garnish if desired. **Yield:** 4 whole sandwiches or 32 (2-inch) square appetizer sandwiches.

Note: *May garnish with crushed pineapple or thinly sliced, unpeeled apple.*

Mrs. Doug Arnold (Debbi)

Pizza Open Face
Quick and easy

1 pound bulk sausage
1 package (14 ounces) English
  muffins
1 cup pizza sauce

1 can (4 ounces) mushrooms
6 ounces shredded mozzarella
  cheese

Cook sausage and drain. Split muffins. Layer ingredients on muffins ending with cheese. Broil until cheese melts. **Yield:** 4 servings.

Mrs. Jim Thornton (Jackie)

Foiled Frankfurters
Kids Love This One

8 weiners
½ cup relish, drained
½ cup ketchup
3 Tablespoons margarine
2 Tablespoons mustard

¼ cup chopped onion
Tabasco sauce, dash
¾ cup grated American cheese
8 buns

Cut franks into bite-size pieces. Mix all ingredients together. Spoon into buns and wrap individually in foil. Bake at 375° for 15 minutes. **Yield:** 8 servings.

Note: *Can mix ingredients ahead and put into buns closer to serving time.*

Mrs. Bill Frank (Barbara)

Open-Faced Crab Sandwiches

1 can (7½ ounces) crab or 1 package (6-8 ounces) frozen crab
½ cup grated Cheddar cheese
½ cup mayonnaise
¼ cup chopped ripe olives
¼ cup chopped celery

2 Tablespoons chopped green onions
½ teaspoon grated lemon peel
½ teaspoon garlic salt
2 Tablespoons butter or margarine
3 English muffins, halved

Drain canned crab or defrost and drain frozen crab. Slice crab and combine with cheese, mayonnaise, olives, celery, green onions, lemon peel, and garlic salt. Mix well. Butter English muffin halves and top with crab mixture. Place under broiler until cheese melts and sandwiches are heated through. **Yield:** 6 sandwiches.

Mrs. Bill Frank (Barbara)

Shrimp Tea Sandwiches

2 cans (4½ ounces each) shrimp, finely chopped
1 teaspoon minced green onion flakes
1 rib celery, finely chopped

1 teaspoon lemon juice
¾ cup mayonnaise
2 loaves white bread
Cocktail onions, optional

Combine shrimp, onion flakes, celery, and lemon juice. Mix well and blend in mayonnaise. Spread evenly on 1-inch squares of white bread and top with one cocktail onion if desired. **Yield:** 5 dozen (depending on how thin you cover your bread.)

Note: *Could add green olives or jalapeño peppers for spicier taste.*

Mrs. Pete Cantrell (Wyvonne)

Shrimp Luncheon Sandwiches

1 package (3 ounces) cream
   cheese, softened
2 Tablespoons mayonnaise
1 teaspoon ketchup
1 teaspoon prepared mustard
Garlic powder, dash
1 cup deveined, cooked, and
   chopped shrimp (fresh or
   canned)

¼ cup finely chopped celery
1 teaspoon finely chopped onion
10 slices sandwich bread, lightly
   buttered

Blend cheese and mayonnaise. Add ketchup, mustard, and garlic powder.
Stir in shrimp, celery, and onion. Use as a filling between slices of bread
that have been trimmed and cut into four triangles. **Yield:** 20 sandwiches.

Mrs. Thomas Hunter (Lynda)

Party Sandwich Spread

1 package (8 ounces) cream
   cheese, softened
¾ cup chopped nuts
¼ cup chopped green pepper
¼ cup chopped onion

3 Tablespoons chopped pimiento
1 Tablespoon ketchup
3 eggs, hard-boiled and finely
   chopped

Combine all ingredients and serve on bread. **Yield:** 8 or 9 large sandwiches
or 3 dozen finger sandwiches.

Mrs. Doug Rivenbark (Penny)

Leftover Sandwich Spread
Don't Waste Your Leftovers Anymore!

½-1 pound leftover roast beef or
   ham
¾ cup diced sweet pickles
1 small onion, chopped

2 celery stalks, chopped
2 hard-boiled eggs, chopped
Salt and pepper to taste
Mayonnaise to taste

Grind meat in food processor. Stir into remaining ingredients except mayonnaise. Add enough mayonnaise to thoroughly moisten meat mixture
and refrigerate. **Yield:** 4-6 sandwiches.

Mrs. Marvin Chronister (Donna)

Ronald McDonald House® of Dallas

Since 1981, the Ronald McDonald House of Dallas has served thousands of families of seriously ill children by providing a home away from home while the children are receiviing treatment in area hospitals. Because of the assistance and generosity of concerned individuals, corporations, and community groups, the Ronald McDonald House is able to continue to serve and sustain families when catastrophe strikes the most cherished part of their lives — their children.

Dallas Junior Forum members have provided meals for patient families on a regular basis since 1987, often using recipes from Deep In The Heart. In addition, Dallas Junior Forum provides office staff support and assists in fund-raising events, such as the Wonderland Express, a Christmas train exhibit benefitting the Ronald McDonald House.

Main Dishes

Meal planning really isn't much fun;
And you hope those you serve like what you've done.
You try to fulfill their fondest wishes
By preparing some different and tasty main dishes.

Roger Hicks' Cook-Off Chili

6 pounds coarse ground lean
chili meat
3 onions, chopped
4-6 cloves garlic
3 Tablespoons oil
32 ounces (approximately)
canned tomatoes (½ of
this amount could be
Rotel tomatoes)
24 ounces tomato sauce
3 teaspoons cumin
2 teaspoons paprika
5 Tablespoons chili powder

1-2 Tablespoons ground red chili,
if available
1 square (1 ounce) Baker's
chocolate or 1 Tablespoon
cocoa
1 can (12 ounce) beer
1 Tablespoon sugar
Water, as needed, probably 1
quart as it cooks
Salt and cayenne pepper to taste
2-3 pickled jalapeño peppers, if
you have them

In a very large, heavy cooking pot, brown meat and onions in oil. Add tomatoes and sauce. (Either chop canned tomatoes real fine or break up with spoon and blend lightly with sauce.) Add remainder of ingredients in no particular order. Cook uncovered over low heat, stirring often, and drinking beer, except the one you put in the chili, for at least 4 hours. The longer it cooks and the more beer you drink, the better it will taste! **Yield:** Approximately 20 servings.

Mrs. Jerry Leatherman (Diana)

Special Pepper Steak

Butter
Salt and pepper to taste
8-10 ounces filet steak
1 Tablespoon whole black
pepper, crushed

2-3 Tablespoons mango chutney
1 shot (1½ ounces) brandy

Melt a small quantity of butter in skillet. Salt and pepper filet steak. Sauté in the butter, basting often with accumulated pan juices, until cooked to desired doneness. Sprinkle crushed black pepper on steak and baste for a few more minutes. Add mango chutney and brandy to skillet. Remove steak to serving platter and keep warm. Reduce chutney-brandy mixture to consistency of heavy syrup. Pour over steak to serve. **Yield:** 1 serving.

Mrs. Jack Hamer (Pam)

Wagoner's Grilled Flank Steak

Soy sauce   6-8 slices bacon
1 flank steak, tenderized

Sprinkle soy sauce over both sides of steak and set aside for at least 1 hour. Fry bacon and drain well. Place bacon strips crosswise over steak. Roll steak tightly and secure with skewers. Cut the roll into slices at least ½-inch thick. Grill to desired doneness. **Yield:** 4-6 servings.

Mrs. Ellwood Jones (Ann)

Marinated Flank Steak

1 flank steak   1 clove garlic, minced
⅓ cup soy sauce   ¼ teaspoon dry mustard
⅓ cup cider vinegar   ¼ teaspoon ginger
2 Tablespoons honey   3-4 scallions, chopped
¼ cup corn oil

Cut 3-4 slashes diagonally into flank steak across grain on both sides. Place in shallow dish. Mix remaining ingredients to make marinade. Pour over steak. Marinate in refrigerator overnight or at room temperature for several hours, turning steak several times. Broil steak for 3-8 minutes on each side, basting with marinade once or twice. To serve, slice steak across grain at an angle in ¼-inch thick slices. Remaining marinade may be used as a sauce. **Yield:** 4-6 servings.

Mrs. Dan Boyd (Terry)

♥ *Turning only once while frying, broiling, or charcoal cooking meats, will insure maximum juiciness.*

♥ *Cooking meat at low temperatures retains juice and flavor and reduces shrinkage.*

Burgundy Steak

1 pound lean round steak, sliced thinly into 1-inch strips	2½ teaspoons seasoned salt
3 Tablespoons salad oil	1 Tablespoon Worcestershire sauce
2 cups sliced onion	2 cups diagonally sliced celery
2 cups sliced carrots	2 Tablespoons cornstarch
⅓ cup Burgundy, or any dry red wine	¼ cup water
1¾ cups beef broth	4 cups hot cooked rice
1 can (4 ounces) sliced mushrooms, undrained	

Sauté steak strips in oil until brown. Add onion and cook 2 minutes longer. Stir in carrots, wine, broth, mushrooms with liquid, and seasonings. Bring to a boil. Reduce heat; cover, and simmer 10 minutes. Add celery and cook 10 minutes longer. Dissolve cornstarch in ¼ cup water, then stir into meat mixture. Cook, stirring constantly until thickened. Serve over bed of fluffy, hot rice. **Yield:** 4-6 servings.

Note: *This dish is also great served over cooked egg noodles.*

Mrs. Ellwood Jones (Ann)

Gail's Sukiyaki

1 pound round steak, thinly sliced	½ cup green onions, cut into 1-inch pieces
2 Tablespoons salad oil	1 can (14½ ounces) beef broth
1½ cups sliced celery	3 Tablespoons soy sauce or to taste
1 green pepper, sliced	
1 large onion, thinly sliced	2 Tablespoons cornstarch
1 can (6 ounces) sliced mushrooms	¼ cup water
	4 cups cooked rice

Brown meat in oil. Add vegetables, broth, and soy sauce. Cover and cook over low heat until vegetables are tender, about 5 minutes. Combine cornstarch and water. Add to vegetables and stir until thickened. Serve over rice. **Yield:** 4 servings.

Note: *Use a wok or electric skillet.*

Mrs. Don Argenbright (Gail)

Beef Burgundy

¼ cup salad oil
2 pounds top sirloin or round steak, ½-inch thick
¼ cup flour
1 beef bouillon cube, dissolved in 1 cup water
4 slices bacon, crisp and crumbled
1½ teaspoons salt
¼ teaspoon pepper

¼ teaspoon marjoram leaves
¼ teaspoon thyme leaves
1 garlic clove, pressed and minced
1 cup chopped onion
12 ounces Burgundy wine
8 ounces fresh mushrooms, sliced
Fresh parsley, chopped
Noodles or rice, cooked

Heat oil in a heavy pan. Cut the meat into 1-inch cubes and shake a few pieces at a time in a plastic bag with flour to coat. Brown meat in oil about 10 minutes. Remove to a plate and pour off oil. Do not scrape pan! Return meat to pan and add remaining ingredients except for mushrooms and parsley. Reduce heat, cover, and simmer 1 hour 30 minutes. Add mushrooms and continue simmering for 10 minutes. Garnish with parsley. Serve over noodles or rice. **Yield:** 6 servings.

Note: *To prepare ahead, store in refrigerator without adding mushrooms and parsley. Reheat and proceed as above.*

Mrs. Roger Jones (Janet)

♥ *Flour or breading mix coated on meat or chicken will adhere better during cooking if first allowed to chill for an hour or two.*

Beef Brisket Marinade

8-10 pound brisket, trimmed
Garlic salt to taste
Celery salt to taste

4 Tablespoons Worcestershire sauce
½ bottle liquid smoke

Sprinkle meat liberally with salts. Add Worcestershire sauce and liquid smoke. Marinate overnight. Turn brisket. Cover pan with heavy foil and bake at 225° for 7 hours. **Yield:** 8-10 servings.

Sharon Gardner

Do-Ahead Brisket
Luttrell Family Favorite

5-6 pound brisket, trimmed
Garlic
Pepper

Marinade:
1   bottle (10 ounces)
    Worcestershire sauce
¼   teaspoon per pound
    monosodium glutamate,
    optional
3   Tablespoons liquid smoke

Sauce:
1   cup ketchup
⅓   cup Worcestershire sauce
1   Tablespoon lemon juice
¾   cup firmly packed brown sugar

Begin two days before serving. Season brisket with garlic and pepper. For marinade, mix Worcestershire sauce, monosodium glutamate, and liquid smoke. Pour over brisket and marinate overnight. The next day, cook brisket uncovered at 450° for 30 minutes. Cover; cook for 1 hour per pound at 225°. Reserve broth. Wrap in foil and refrigerate overnight. On serving day slice brisket. Prepare sauce by mixing 2 cups reserved broth, ketchup, Worcestershire, lemon juice, and brown sugar and pour over meat. Cover and heat thoroughly in 350° oven. **Yield:** 6-8 servings.

Mrs. Doug Arnold (Debbi)

Glenna's Brisket

3 pound lean brisket
3 Tablespoons liquid smoke
1 teaspoon garlic salt
1 teaspoon onion salt

2 Tablespoons Worcestershire
  sauce
2 teaspoons celery seed
Barbecue sauce

Place brisket in a baking dish. Combine all ingredients except barbecue sauce and pour over brisket. Cover pan tightly. Bake at 250° for about 5 hours. Top with desired amount of barbecue sauce and bake an additional 15 minutes. **Yield:** 4-6 servings.

Note: *This works great in a crock pot.*

Mrs. Sam Murray (Sandy)

♥ *Place roasts fat side up in the pan. The melting fat will baste the meat as it cooks.*

120

Easy Beef Stroganoff

½ cup sliced white onion
2 Tablespoons butter or
　margarine
1 pound round steak
1 can (10¾ ounces) cream of
　mushroom soup

½ cup sour cream
⅓ cup water
½ teaspoon paprika
Noodles

In skillet, sauté onions in butter until clear. Cut meat into thin strips. Add to onion and cook until brown. Stir in soup, sour cream, water, and paprika. Cover and simmer for 45 minutes. Serve over hot cooked noodles. **Yield:** 4 servings.

Mrs. Jerry Brown (Linda)

♥ *Sprinkle your frying pan with salt to prevent fat from splattering.*

Beef Stroganoff

2 pounds round steak, cut into
　narrow strips
2 Tablespoons salad oil
Water
¼ cup minced onion
1 Tablespoon flour
1 can (10½ ounces) cream of
　mushroom soup

1 can (5 ounces) button
　mushrooms, drained
Salt and pepper to taste
1 cup sour cream
Noodles or rice

Brown steak in oil. Simmer for 15 minutes adding enough water to keep steak from sticking to pan. Add onions. Simmer for another 5 minutes. Add flour, soup, mushrooms, salt, and pepper. Add sour cream just before serving. Serve over cooked noodles or rice. **Yield:** 6 servings.

Note: *A little milk may be added if sauce is too thick.*

Mrs. Jim Conine (Donna)

121

Beef Stew Treat

2 pounds stew meat or sirloin, cubed
1 package (1.25 ounces) onion soup mix
½ cup red wine
1 can (10¾ ounces) cream of mushroom soup

1 can (6 ounces) mushrooms, sliced, whole, or pieces, undrained
Rice or noodles, cooked

Combine all ingredients in roaster and mix. Cover and cook at 300° for 3 hours. Do not open. Serve over rice or noodles. **Yield:** 4-6 servings.

Mrs. Robert George (Linda)

No Peek Stew

2 pounds stew meat
1 can (10½ ounces) cream of mushroom soup
1 package (1.25 ounces) onion soup mix
1 cup thinly sliced carrots
1 cup thinly sliced celery

¾ cup red wine
Marjoram, dash
Thyme, dash
Paprika, dash
Salt and pepper, dash
Minced parsley, dash

Combine all ingredients. Place in 3 to 5-quart baking dish. Cover. Bake at 300° for 3 hours. Don't peek! **Yield:** 6 servings.

Note: *Good served with buttered noodles or rice.*

Mrs. Joe Key (Christie)

♥ *It is easier to remove a garlic clove from stews, spaghetti sauce, and other soupy dishes, if it is speared with a toothpick before placing it in the pot.*

Double Delicious Meatloaf
Great to Have on Hand for a Busy Day!

4 pounds lean ground beef
3 teaspoons salt
½ teaspoon pepper
1 teaspoon oregano
2 teaspoons dried minced onion
3 teaspoons Worcestershire sauce

1 cup chopped mushrooms
1 can (28 ounces) tomatoes,
   undrained
4 eggs, slightly beaten
3 cups breadcrumbs

Combine beef, seasonings, mushrooms, and tomatoes. Add eggs and crumbs. Mix well. Divide into 2 portions. Line 2 loaf pans (9x5-inches each) with foil extending over sides. Place loaves into pans leaving foil open. Bake at 350° for 1 hour. Serve 1 loaf hot from oven. Cool second loaf, seal tightly, and freeze for later use. **Yield:** 4 servings per loaf.

Mrs. Dennis Furlong (Dede)

Meatloaf Supreme

1 pound ground pork
1 pound ground beef
1 cup shredded carrots
1 cup crushed Ritz crackers
1 cup sour cream
¼ cup chopped onion

Mushroom Sauce:
1 beef bouillon cube, crushed
Meatloaf drippings
½ cup sour cream
1 Tablespoon flour
1 can (3 ounces) broiled, sliced
   mushrooms, undrained

Combine first 6 ingredients. Press into a 9x5-inch loaf pan. Bake at 350° for 1 hour-1 hour 30 minutes. Let stand 10 minutes; remove from pan.

Mushroom sauce: Dissolve bouillon cube in meatloaf drippings. Combine with sour cream, flour, and mushrooms. Heat just to boiling. Serve with meatloaf. **Yield:** 4-6 servings.

Note: *Can be prepared ahead and frozen.*

Mrs. Donald Robson (Karen)

Hamburger-Potato Casserole

2 pounds lean ground beef
Salt and pepper to taste
1 medium onion, chopped
1 package (2 pounds) tater tots, frozen

2 cans (10½ ounces each) cream of mushroom soup
1 soup can (10½ ounces) milk
Parmesan cheese

Crumble uncooked ground beef into 9x13-inch pan. Salt and pepper to taste. Add layer of chopped onion, and cover with frozen tater tots. Mix mushroom soup together with 1 soup can milk and pour over tater tots. Sprinkle with Parmesan cheese. Bake at 350° for 1 hour. **Yield:** 8 servings.

Note: *A package of tater tots with onions may be used; but omit the chopped onion. May be made ahead of time and frozen before cooking.*

Mrs. Jim Thornton (Jackie)

♥ *Slip a cookie sheet or sheet of foil under a casserole or fruit pie in the oven to catch spills.*

Seven Layer Casserole
Great Family Dinner

1 cup uncooked rice
1 can (8 ounces) tomato sauce plus ½ can water
Salt and pepper to taste
¼ cup chopped green pepper
1 cup whole kernel corn, drained
¼ cup chopped onion

1½ pounds ground beef, uncooked
1 can (8 ounces) tomato sauce plus ½ can water
Onion rings, green pepper rings, or bacon strips

Layer ingredients as listed in a 2-quart casserole. Garnish top with either onion rings, green pepper rings, or bacon strips. Cover and bake at 350° for 1 hour. Uncover and bake 30 minutes more. **Yield:** 6-8 servings.

Mrs. Winston Borum (Jimmie)

Mexican Meat Pie
Good Family Dish

1½ pounds ground chuck
1 large onion, chopped
1 green pepper, chopped
2 fresh tomatoes, chopped
1 can (10 ounces) Rotel tomatoes
Salt and pepper to taste
1 package (12) corn tortillas

1 can (16 ounces) Ranch Style beans
1 pound Velveeta cheese, thinly sliced
1 can (10½ ounces) cream of chicken soup

Brown meat with onion and pepper. Add tomatoes, salt, and pepper. In a 9x13-inch pan, layer ½ each of the tortillas, meat, beans, and cheese. Repeat. Top with soup. Bake at 350° for 35-40 minutes until bubbly. **Yield:** 6-8 servings.

Mrs.Ellwood Jones (Ann)

Baked Lasagne
Easy and Delicious

1 pound Italian Sausage or ground beef
1 clove garlic, minced
1 Tablespoon parsley flakes
1 Tablespoon basil
1½ teaspoons salt
1 can (28 ounces) tomatoes
2 cans (6 ounces each) tomato paste
10 ounces lasagne or wide noodles

3 cups cream-style cottage cheese
2 eggs, beaten
2 teaspoons salt
½ teaspoon pepper
2 Tablespoons parsley flakes
½ cup grated Parmesan cheese
1 pound mozzarella cheese, thinly sliced

Brown meat slowly, drain grease. Add next 6 ingredients. Simmer uncovered 30 minutes to blend flavors, stirring occasionally. Cook noodles in boiling, salted water until tender. Drain and rinse in cold water. Meanwhile, combine cottage cheese with eggs, seasonings, and Parmesan cheese. Place half the noodles into 9x13-inch baking dish. Spread half the cottage cheese mixture over the noodles. Add half the mozzarella cheese, then half the meat sauce. Repeat layers. Bake at 375° for 30 minutes. Garnish with triangles of mozzarella cheese. Let stand 10-15 minutes. Filling will set slightly. **Yield:** 9-12 servings.

Mrs. Pete Bennett (Stephanie)

Lasagne Bolognese
The Best Authentic Italian Restaurant-Style Lasagne

Meat Sauce:
2 Tablespoons butter
1 cup chopped onion
2 cloves garlic, minced
½ cup chopped celery
2 Tablespoons olive oil
1 pound sweet Italian sausage
1 pound ground round
½ cup dry white wine
2 cups peeled, seeded, and
  chopped fresh tomatoes
4 Tablespoons tomato paste
2 cups beef stock
1 bay leaf
½ teaspoon sugar
½ teaspoon oregano
½ teaspoon basil
⅛ teaspoon allspice
Salt and pepper to taste

Besciamello (Italian Bechamel Sauce):
3 Tablespoons butter
6 Tablespoons flour
2 cups milk
1 cup whipping cream
1 teaspoon salt
⅛ teaspoon nutmeg

Assembly:
1 pound mozzarella cheese, grated
½ pound ricotta cheese
1 pound fresh lasagne noodles, preferably green
½ cup freshly grated Parmesan cheese

Melt butter in skillet and sauté onion, garlic, and celery over low heat until golden. Remove to heavy 3-4 quart saucepan. To same skillet, add olive oil and sauté sausage and beef until lightly browned, stirring to break up lumps. Drain excess grease. Add wine to meat and bring to a boil, stirring constantly, until wine is almost evaporated. Add meat to saucepan containing onion mixture; also add tomatoes, tomato paste, beef stock, bay leaf, sugar, oregano, allspice, and salt and pepper. Simmer, partially covered, for 1 hour, stirring occasionally.

Besciamello: In a heavy 2 to 3-quart saucepan, melt butter over low heat. Stir in flour and cook slowly 2-3 minutes, stirring constantly. Gradually add milk and cream, stirring with a whisk to prevent lumping. Heat to boiling, stirring constantly, until sauce thickens. Remove from heat and add salt and nutmeg. Set aside. Makes approximately 3 cups.

(Continued on next page)

♥ *Before beginning a recipe, gather all the necessary ingredients and utensils, and bring them to your work area. This cuts down on preparation time.*

(Lasagne Bolognese, *continued)*

Assembly: Mix ¾ of the mozzarella cheese with the ricotta cheese and set aside. Butter a 9x13x3-inch baking dish. Cook lasagne noodles until just al dente. When done, drain and cover with cold water; then lift out strips and drain on paper towels. To assemble, spread ¼ inch of meat sauce evenly in dish. Layer with ⅓ of the noodles, then ⅓ of the Besciamella, and ⅓ of the cheese mixture. Repeat twice. Top with the reserved mozzarella and sprinkle with the grated Parmesan. Bake at 350° until bubbly, about 30 minutes. **Yield:** 12 servings.

Note: *Not difficult; just takes time. Freezes beautifully.*

Mrs. Brian Byrne (Veronica)

♥ *To conserve energy, reheat single servings in a microwave or toaster oven.*

Manicotti

1 pound ground beef	20 manicotti shells, uncooked
1 clove garlic, minced	2 cups spaghetti sauce
1 carton (8 ounces) small curd	½ teaspoon oregano
cottage cheese	½ cup Parmesan cheese
8 ounces mozzarella cheese,	
grated	

Cook ground beef with garlic. Drain. Add cottage cheese and mozzarella. Stuff manicotti shells with mixture. Place shells in greased 9x13-inch pan. Pour spaghetti sauce over the shells. Sprinkle with oregano and Parmesan. Cover and refrigerate overnight. Bake uncovered at 350° for 1 hour. **Yield:** 6 servings.

Note: *Must be prepared in advance.*
Variation: *May substitute ricotta cheese for cottage cheese.*

Mrs. James Layton (Vicki)

Our Favorite Lasagne

1 pound Italian sausage in casing
½ pound ground beef
½ cup finely chopped onion
2 cloves garlic, minced
2 Tablespoons sugar
1 teaspoon salt
1 Tablespoon dried basil leaves
½ teaspoon fennel seed
½ teaspoon pepper
¼ cup chopped parsley
1 can (35 ounces) Italian-style tomatoes
2 cans (6 ounces each) tomato paste

½ cup water
½ teaspoon garlic powder
12 lasagne noodles
1 teaspoon salt
1 carton (15 ounces) ricotta cheese
1 egg
Salt
¾ pound mozzarella cheese, thinly sliced
¾ cup grated Parmesan cheese

Remove sausage from casing and chop. In a 5-quart dutch oven, over medium heat, sauté sausage, beef, onion, and garlic. Stir frequently and cook until well browned. Add sugar, salt, basil, fennel, pepper, and half of the parsley and mix well. Stir in tomatoes, tomato paste, and ½ cup water, mashing tomatoes with a wooden spoon. Bring mixture to a boil and then reduce heat to simmer. Cover, simmer for 1 hour, stirring occasionally. Add garlic powder and simmer 30 minutes longer. In an 8-quart kettle bring 3 quarts water and 1 teaspoon salt to boil. Add lasagne noodles 2-3 at a time. Return to boiling and boil uncovered until noodles are just tender. Drain and rinse in a colander under cold water. Dry noodles on paper towels. In a medium bowl combine ricotta, egg, remaining parsley, and salt. Mix well.

Preheat oven to 375°. Into a 9x13-inch baking dish, spoon 1½ cups of sauce. Place 6 noodles lengthwise and overlapping to cover sauce. Spread half of ricotta mixture over noodles and top with ⅓ of mozzarella. Spoon another 1½ cups sauce over cheese and sprinkle with ¼ cup Parmesan. Repeat layering, ending with Parmesan. Spread any remaining cheeses on top. Cover with aluminum foil. Bake for 25 minutes; remove foil and bake uncovered another 25 minutes or until bubbly. Cool for 15 minutes and serve. **Yield:** 8 servings.

Note: *Good Italian sausage really makes this lasagne!*

Mrs. Doug Arnold (Debbi)

Our Family Spaghetti

½ cup chopped onions
2 Tablespoons olive oil
1 pound lean hamburger meat
1 clove garlic, minced
1 can (6 ounces) tomato paste
2 cans (14½ ounces each) whole, peeled tomatoes, one can drained
1 can (15 ounces) tomato sauce
½ teaspoon garlic powder

3 teaspoons Worcestershire sauce
1 teaspoon pepper
1½ teaspoons oregano
½ teaspoon fennel
½ teaspoon sugar
½ teaspoon sweet basil
½ teaspoon garlic powder
Spaghetti, cooked

Sauté onions in olive oil until translucent. Add meat and garlic. Stir until meat is brown. Drain off excess grease. Add all other ingredients, except the last ½ teaspoon of garlic powder. Stir and mash tomatoes until mixed. Bring to a boil and simmer for 1 hour. Add remaining garlic powder. Cover. On low heat, cook for another 20 minutes, stirring occasionally. Serve over spaghetti. **Yield:** 6-8 servings.

Mrs. Doug Arnold (Debbi)

Veal Scallopini with Mushrooms

6 pieces veal scallopini, approximately ¼-inch thick
⅓ cup flour
¼ cup butter or margarine
1 garlic clove

½ pound mushrooms, sliced
½ cup dry vermouth
¼ cup water
1 teaspoon salt
1 Tablespoon chopped parsley

Pound veal ⅛-inch thick. Coat lightly with flour. Melt butter or margarine over low heat. Add garlic and cook until golden. Remove garlic. Increase heat to medium, add veal 2-3 pieces at a time and cook until lightly browned, turning once. Repeat with remaining veal. Transfer to warm platter. To pan drippings, add mushrooms, vermouth, water, and salt. Cook 5 minutes and spoon sauce over meat. Garnish with parsley. **Yield:** 6 servings.

Note: *Chicken breasts can be substituted for veal and are equally as good.*

Mrs. Don Kleinschmidt (Ceil)

♥ *Veal is infant beef and very similar to young chicken. The two are successfully interchanged in recipes.*

129

French Veal Sauté

1½ pounds veal stew meat
2 Tablespoons salad oil
1 can (10½ ounces) cream of mushroom soup
½ cup water
¼ cup white wine
¼ cup chopped onion

½ teaspoon spice parisienne or ¼ teaspoon basil and ¼ teaspoon fresh ground pepper
½ pound mushroom caps
½ cup sour cream
Rice or noodles, cooked

Sauté veal in oil. Add soup, water, wine, onion, and spice. Bring to a boil. Reduce heat. Cover and simmer 1 hour or until veal is fork tender. Stir in mushrooms. Cook 5 minutes. Add sour cream and heat thoroughly. Serve over steamed rice or buttered noodles. **Yield:** 6 servings.

Mrs. William Hollon (Kasey)

Veal Parmesan

8 pieces veal, thinly sliced
¼ cup flour
1-2 eggs, beaten

½ cup Parmesan cheese
4 Tablespoons butter, melted
2 Tablespoons lemon juice

Dip veal slices in flour; shake off excess. Dip in egg and in Parmesan cheese. Sauté in butter until brown, about 5 minutes. Combine butter and lemon juice. Serve with veal. **Yield:** 4 servings.

Mrs. Sam Norvell (Patsy)

Marinated Pork Tenderloin

2 pounds pork tenderloin
½ teaspoon ground ginger
½ medium onion, minced
2 cloves garlic, minced

1 teaspoon crushed basil leaves
1½ teaspoons parsley
3 Tablespoons soy sauce
2 Tablespoons salad oil

Slice tenderloin into ¾-inch medallions. Combine remaining ingredients and process in food processor or blender until well mixed. Pour over meat and marinate for 1 hour or overnight. Grill over hot coals. **Yield:** 4-6 servings.

Mrs. William Hollon (Kasey)

Pork Chops and Orange Sauce

4 pork chops (1 inch thick)	¼ teaspoon cinnamon
Seasoned salt	10 whole cloves
4 Tablespoons water	1-2 teaspoons grated orange rind
5 Tablespoons sugar	½ cup orange juice
1½ teaspoons cornstarch	4 orange slices
Salt, dash	

Brown pork chops. Sprinkle with seasoned salt. Add water, cover, and simmer 1 hour or until tender. Drain any remaining water. Make syrup separately of remaining ingredients, boiling until clear and slightly thickened. Pour over pork chops. **Yield:** 4 servings.

Mrs. Sam Norvell (Patsy)

Sweet and Sour Pork

2 Tablespoons soy sauce	Sauce:
2½ pounds butterfly pork chops, cut into 1½-inch cubes	⅔ cup ketchup
	1⅓ cups water
½ teaspoon salt	2 Tablespoons white vinegar
2 Tablespoons cornstarch	4 Tablespoons firmly packed brown sugar
2 Tablespoons bourbon	
1 teaspoon sugar	
2 cloves garlic, minced	
Salad oil	

Combine first 7 ingredients and marinate for 15 minutes (the meat will absorb most of the liquid). Fry in 2 inches oil in a 12-inch skillet until brown. Mix all sauce ingredients and simmer in a large pot over low heat until sugar is dissolved. Add cooked pork and simmer for 45-60 minutes. Serve over rice. **Yield:** 4-6 servings.

Mrs. Wallace Brown (Gayle)

♥ *Perk up the flavor of pork chops by dipping them in egg beaten with 1 teaspoon prepared mustard before coating with crumbs.*

Polynesian Pork

1 pound pork steak, 2 inches thick	⅓ cup vinegar
1½ teaspoons paprika	1 Tablespoon soy sauce
2 Tablespoons shortening	1 teaspoon Worcestershire sauce
3 Tablespoons firmly packed brown sugar	⅓ cup water
¼ cup instant dry milk powder	1 green pepper, cut into 2x⅛-inch strips
2 Tablespoons cornstarch	1 small onion, thinly sliced
½ teaspoon salt	Rice, cooked
1 can (13½ ounces) pineapple tidbits, drained, reserving syrup	

Cut meat into 2x½-inch strips. Sprinkle with paprika. Brown well in hot shortening in a 10-inch skillet over medium heat. Cover and cook about 3-5 minutes or until tender, stirring occasionally. Drain off drippings. Push meat to one side of skillet. Combine brown sugar, dry milk, cornstarch, and salt in a 1½-quart bowl. If necessary, add water to reserved pineapple syrup to make ⅔ cup. Gradually add syrup, vinegar, soy sauce, Worcestershire sauce, and water to dry ingredients and stir until smooth. Pour into skillet. Cook over low heat until thick and smooth, stirring constantly. Stir in green pepper, onion, and pineapple. Cover and simmer over very low heat 8-10 minutes or until vegetables are tender crisp. Serve over hot rice. **Yield:** 4-6 servings.

Note: *If possible, use Hungarian paprika. Meat is easier to cut if partially frozen.*

Mrs. Doug Arnold (Debbi)

Smothered Pork Chops

6-8 pork chops, center cut	Pepper to taste
1 Tablespoon dehydrated minced onion	1 can (10½ ounces) cream of mushroom soup
Knorr Swiss Aromat Seasoning for Meat to taste	1 cup milk
	2 Tablespoons dry sherry

Place pork chops in 3-quart baking dish and sprinkle with seasonings. In small bowl, mix remaining ingredients and pour over pork chops. Cover and bake at 300° for 2 hours or more. **Yield:** 4-6 servings.

Mrs. Dennis Furlong (Dede)

Pork Chop and Potato Scallop

¼ cup butter	2 medium onions, thinly sliced
¼ cup flour	¾ cup green pepper, coarsely chopped
1 teaspoon salt	Salt and pepper to taste
¼ teaspoon pepper	6 pork chops, center cut, ¾-inch thick
2 cups milk	¼ cup flour
½-1 pound Velveeta cheese	2 Tablespoons salad oil
½ cup sour cream	
4 cups thinly sliced, peeled new potatoes	

Preheat oven to 375°. Melt butter in a small saucepan over moderately low heat. Blend in flour, salt, and pepper. Gradually add milk and cook, stirring constantly, until thick and smooth. Add cheese; stir until melted. Combine slightly cooked cheese sauce and sour cream. In a shallow 2-quart casserole, alternate layers of sliced potatoes, onions, green peppers, and the cheese mixture. Sprinkle each layer of potatoes lightly with salt and pepper. Bake uncovered 30 minutes. Thoroughly coat pork chops with flour. Heat oil in a large skillet over moderately high heat. Place pork chops in skillet and brown evenly on both sides. Remove casserole from oven and stir potatoes. Sprinkle both sides of pork chops with salt and pepper. Place over potatoes. Cover casserole and return to oven for 1 hour and 20 minutes. **Yield:** 6 servings.

Mrs. Carl Smith (Karen)

Creamy Broccoli and Ham Shells

1 package (16 ounces) medium size macaroni shells	½ cup butter or margarine
1 garlic clove, crushed	1 cup whipping cream or half and half
½ pound cooked ham, sliced in slivers or small pieces	1 cup grated Parmesan cheese
1 package (10 ounces) frozen broccoli spears, thawed and cut into ½-inch pieces	

Cook shells according to directions. Sauté garlic, ham, and broccoli in butter until broccoli is tender crisp, approximately 5 minutes. Stir in cream. Cook over medium heat 3 minutes. Stir in cheese. Lower heat and cook until cheese is melted. Toss with shells. **Yield:** 6 servings.

Mrs. Don Kleinschmidt (Ceil)

Denver Brunch
Company Fare

2 cups bite-size Crispy Rice Square cereal
1 cup cooked diced ham
½ cup fresh chopped tomatoes
¼ cup chopped onion
¼ cup chopped green pepper
1 Tablespoon butter
4 eggs, slightly beaten

¼ cup flour
5 drops Tabasco sauce
1 cup milk
¼ teaspoon salt
⅛ teaspoon pepper
2 Tablespoons Parmesan cheese
4 ounces grated mozzarella cheese

Spread cereal evenly in buttered 9-inch pie plate. Sprinkle ham and tomatoes over cereal. Sauté onion and green pepper in butter and spoon over ham and tomatoes. Combine eggs, flour, Tabasco sauce, milk, salt, and pepper. Pour into pie plate. Sprinkle cheeses over top and bake at 325° for 40-50 minutes or until knife inserted comes out clean. **Yield:** 6 servings.

Mrs. Winston Borum (Jimmie)

Egg Portugal

8 slices bread, cubed
¾ pound Cheddar cheese, grated
1½ pounds sausage, browned, drained
2½ cups milk
4 eggs
¾ Tablespoon dry mustard
Salt
¼ cup vermouth

Sauce:
¾ cup butter
¾ cup flour
¾ teaspoon salt
¼ teaspoon pepper
3 cups milk
1 can (4 ounces) mushrooms, drained

Place bread in bottom of 9x13-inch ovenproof dish. Add layer of cheese, then sausage. Mix milk, eggs, mustard, salt, and vermouth. Pour over cheese and sausage. Cover and refrigerate overnight. Bake at 350° for 1 hour. Sauce: In heavy pan, melt butter over low heat. Using a wooden spoon, blend in flour and seasonings. Cook over low heat, stirring until mixture is smooth and bubbly. Add milk and bring to boil, stirring constantly. Boil 1 minute. Add mushrooms and cook until hot. Pour over cooked casserole. **Yield:** 8 servings.

Mrs. Doug Arnold (Debbi)

Sandra Swingle's Breakfast Pizza

1 pound bulk pork sausage
1 package (8 count) refrigerated
  crescent rolls
1 cup frozen hash brown potatoes,
  thawed
1 cup shredded Cheddar cheese

5 eggs
½ cup milk
½ teaspoon salt
⅛ teaspoon pepper
2 Tablespoons fresh grated
   Parmesan cheese

In skillet, cook sausage until brown. Drain. Separate crescent dough into 8 triangles. Place on an ungreased 12-inch pizza pan with points toward the center. Press over bottom and up sides to form crust. Sprinkle with potatoes. Spoon sausage over crust and top with Cheddar cheese. In a bowl, beat together eggs, milk, salt, and pepper. Pour into crust. Top with Parmesan cheese. Bake at 375° for 25-30 minutes. **Yield:** 6-8 servings.

Mrs. Ray Baker (Margaret)

Sausage and Rice Casserole

1 cup rice, uncooked
2 cups chopped carrots
1 large onion, chopped
1 cup chopped celery
½ cup chopped green pepper

1 can (14½ ounces) chicken broth
¼ cup water
1 pound bulk pork sausage
Mushrooms, optional
Parsley, optional

Spread rice evenly in a lightly greased 3-quart casserole. Spoon vegetables over rice. Pour chicken broth and water over the vegetables. Cook sausage until browned; drain well. Spoon sausage over vegetables. Cover and bake at 350° for 30 minutes. Remove from oven, and stir well. Cover and bake an additional 30 minutes. Garnish with mushrooms and parsley if desired. **Yield:** 4-6 servings.

Mrs. Roy Watson (Charlene)

Chicken Pot Pie and I Don't Care

Pastry for double crust pie
1 whole chicken
3 ribs celery, chopped
3 carrots, sliced
1 medium red onion, chopped
1 teaspoon salt
¼ teaspoon pepper
1 package (10 ounces) frozen
 green peas

1 can (10¾ ounces) cream of
 chicken soup
½ cup chicken broth
1 jar (4 ounces) pimientos,
 drained
Nature's Seasonings, dash
Worcestershire sauce, dash

Make pie crust. Roll out half and cover bottom of a 1½ or 2-quart casserole dish. Boil for one hour chicken, celery, carrots, onions, salt, and pepper in enough water to cover. Drain. Skin, bone, and cut chicken into bite-size pieces. Add peas to chicken and vegetables and place in pastry lined casserole dish. Mix cream of chicken soup, broth, pimientos, seasoning mix, and Worcestershire sauce. Pour over chicken and vegetables. Roll out remaining dough and place over chicken and vegetable filling. Pierce dough to allow steam to escape while baking. Bake at 350° for 35-40 minutes or until crust is golden brown. **Yield:** 6 servings.

Mrs. Richard Keeling (Laurie)

Chicken Casserole

2½ pound fryer, cooked, boned,
 and chopped
2 boxes (10 ounces each) frozen
 chopped broccoli
1 can (10½ ounces) cream of
 mushroom soup

1 jar (4 ounces) pimiento
½ cup mayonnaise
1 cup shredded Cheddar cheese
Cheese crackers, crushed

Place chicken in a 9x13-inch dish. Add broccoli. Mix soup, pimiento, and mayonnaise. Pour over chicken and broccoli. Top with Cheddar cheese, then cheese crackers. Bake in 400° oven until brown. **Yield:** 6-8 servings.

Mrs. Greg Smith (Katie)

♥ *Allow approximately 1 pound of chicken, including bones, per serving.*

Luttrell's Crispy Chicken

¼ cup butter
¼ teaspoon garlic powder
¼ cup Romano cheese

4   chicken breasts, skinned and
     boned
2½ cups Italian breadcrumbs

Melt butter in small saucepan and add garlic powder and cheese. Dip chicken in butter mixture and coat with breadcrumbs. Arrange in oven-proof dish. Pour remaining breadcrumbs and butter mixture over chicken. Bake at 350° for 1 hour to 1 hour and 30 minutes. **Yield:** 4 servings.

Note: *Can be stored in refrigerator several hours before baking. Chicken thighs or a whole chicken may be used. (Double the recipe for a whole chicken.)*

Mrs. Doug Arnold (Debbi)

Grilled Chicken Steaks

2 teaspoons Dijon mustard
4 boneless chicken breasts,
   skinned
Pepper

⅓ cup butter or margarine
2   teaspoons lemon juice
½ teaspoon garlic salt
1   teaspoon dried whole tarragon

Spread mustard on both sides of chicken and sprinkle with pepper. Cover and refrigerate 2-4 hours. Melt butter and stir in lemon juice, garlic salt, and tarragon. Cook over low heat 5 minutes; stirring occasionally. Place chicken on grill. Baste with sauce. Grill 50-55 minutes until done; turning and basting every 10 minutes. **Yield:** 4 servings.

Mrs. Jeff Farmer (Kaliko)

Easy Chicken Divan

2 packages (10 ounces each) frozen
   broccoli spears
4 chicken breasts, boned and
   cooked
1 cup mayonnaise

½ teaspoon curry powder
2   cans (10½ ounces each) cream
     of chicken soup
1   Tablespoon lemon juice
½ cup grated Cheddar cheese

Cook broccoli until tender; drain. Arrange in a 9x13-inch dish and place chicken on top. Combine remaining ingredients in saucepan and heat until cheese melts. Pour over chicken. Bake at 350° for 30 minutes or until bubbling. **Yield:** 4 servings.

Mrs. Jim Thornton (Jackie)

Marinated Chicken Breasts

½ cup soy sauce
½ cup pineapple juice
¼ cup salad oil
1 teaspoon dry mustard
1 Tablespoon firmly packed
  brown sugar

1 teaspoon ground ginger
1 teaspoon garlic salt
½ teaspoon pepper
4-6 chicken breasts, boned and
  skinned

Combine all ingredients except chicken. Pour over chicken. Marinate, refrigerated for 24 hours. Grill over coals. **Yield:** 4-6 servings.

Note: *For a real treat, serve with melted butter. Dunk chicken like you would lobster or crab.*

Mrs. William Hollon (Kasey)

♥ *Poultry is easily skinned and boned if slightly frozen. Poultry, veal, and other meats are easily cut if slightly frozen.*

Chicken Kiev
Great for a Dinner Party

12 chicken breasts, skinless and
  boneless
½ cup butter, cut into 12 strips
2 Tablespoons chives
2 Tablespoons tarragon
2 eggs
2 Tablespoons water
½ cup flour

2 cups fresh breadcrumbs
Salad oil for frying
Sauce:
1 can (6 ounces) mushrooms
4 Tablespoons flour
4 Tablespoons butter, softened
1 cup hot chicken broth
1 cup whipping cream

Early in day pound chicken between wax paper until flat and long. Take 1½-inch strips of butter and roll in chives and tarragon. For each kiev, take a 2½x5-inch (approximate) strip of chicken, place a butter strip at one end and roll, tucking the edges. Beat eggs with a little water. Dip chicken into flour, eggs, and water and finally, fresh breadcrumbs. Refrigerate on cookie sheet until ready to fry. Fry like chicken. Keep warm in oven and serve with sauce.

Sauce: In blender mix mushrooms, flour, butter, and chicken broth for 15 seconds. Pour in cream slowly. Heat in saucepan thoroughly. Makes ample amount. **Yield:** 8 servings.

Mrs. William Hollon (Kasey)

Swiss Cheese Chicken Breast

4 chicken breasts, boneless
4 slices Swiss cheese
1 can (10¾ ounces) cream of
  chicken soup

¼ cup white wine
1 cup Pepperidge Farm herb
  dressing mix
⅓ cup butter, melted

Place chicken in casserole dish. Cover with cheese slices. Combine soup and wine and pour over chicken. Sprinkle with crushed dressing mix and drizzle with melted butter. Bake at 350° for 40 minutes. **Yield:** 4 servings.

Mrs. Joe Key (Christie)

Fantastic Chicken

4-5 chicken breasts, boned
1 jar (8 ounces) apricot preserves
1 package (1.25 ounces) dry
  onion soup mix

1 bottle (8 ounces) Russian
  dressing

Place chicken breasts in 9x12-inch ovenproof dish. Combine remaining ingredients. Spoon over chicken. Bake covered at 350° for about 1 hour. Remove cover last 15 minutes to brown. **Yield:** 4 servings.

Note: *If time allows, marinate overnight before baking.*

Mrs. Robert George (Linda)

Chicken Parmesan

4-5 chicken breasts, boneless
½ cup butter, melted

½ cup Parmesan cheese
1½ cups breadcrumbs, 5 slices

Dip chicken in butter, and roll in cheese and breadcrumbs until completely coated. Place in a greased 9x13-inch ovenproof dish; cover with foil. Bake at 375° for 45 minutes. Uncover the last 15 minutes. **Yield:** 4 servings.

Mrs. James Samson (Malissa)

Sherry Mushroom Chicken

4 chicken breasts, split, skinned
   and boned
1 can (4 ounces) sliced mushrooms
1 can (10¾ ounces) cream of
   chicken soup

1 carton (8 ounces) sour cream
¼ cup cooking sherry
Salt and pepper

Place chicken breasts in a 9x13-inch ovenproof dish. Sprinkle mushrooms over chicken breasts. Mix together soup, sour cream, and sherry. Pour over chicken and mushrooms. Season. Bake at 350° for 1 hour. Serve over steamed rice. **Yield:** 8 servings.

Mrs. James Layton (Vicki)

Carolyn Robinson's Quick Chicken and Rice

1 box (8 ounces) chicken Rice-A-
   Roni, cooked according to
   directions
1 chicken or 6 chicken breasts,
   cooked and boned

1 can (10½ ounces) cream of
   mushroom soup
1 cup grated Cheddar cheese

Layer cooked rice, chicken, and soup in casserole. Top with grated cheese. Cover and bake at 350° for 10-15 minutes or until cheese is melted. **Yield:** 6 servings.

Mrs. Robert Lusk (Sharon)

Savory Chicken and Wild Rice

1 package (6 ounces) long grain
   and wild rice
4-6 chicken breasts, boned
¼ cup flour
¼ cup margarine

1 medium onion, quartered
1 cup carrots, quartered
1 bay leaf
1 cup dry white wine
1 cup whipping cream

Prepare rice according to package directions. Flour chicken and slowly brown in margarine. Add onion, carrots, bay leaf, and wine. Cover and simmer 25 minutes. Arrange rice on serving platter. Place chicken on top. Add whipping cream to sauce and heat without boiling. Pour over chicken and rice. **Yield:** 4 servings.

Mrs. King Bourland (Carol)

Chicken and Wild Rice

1 can (10½ ounces) cream of
  chicken soup
1 can (10½ ounces) cream of celery
  soup
1 envelope (1.25 ounces) dry
  onion soup mix

1 soup can dry white wine
1 cup wild rice
3 chicken breasts, boned and cut
  in half

Combine all ingredients except chicken. Let stand for several hours in a 3-quart baking dish. Place chicken under mixture. Cover with foil and bake at 350° for 1 hour. Uncover and bake another hour. **Yield:** 4-6 servings.

Mrs. Wallace Brown (Gayle)

Chicken 'N Apple Cider

3 pounds chicken parts
½ cup apple cider
1 can (10½ ounces) cream of
  chicken soup
1 Tablespoon + 1 teaspoon
  Worcestershire sauce

¾ teaspoon salt
⅓ cup chopped onion
1 can (4-6 ounces) mushrooms,
  sliced and drained
Minced garlic
Paprika

Arrange chicken in 9x13-inch pan. Mix remaining ingredients and pour over chicken. Bake uncovered at 350° for 1 hour to 1 hour 30 minutes. **Yield:** 6-8 servings.

Note: *Makes a good gravy for rice.*

Mrs. Bill Frank (Barbara)

♥ *Cut-up poultry is more perishable than whole birds and turkey more perishable than chicken. It should not be kept more than a day or two before cooking.*

Sandra Swingle's Party Chicken

8 chicken breasts, skinned and
  boned
8 slices of bacon

1 jar (1 ounce) chipped beef
1 can (10¾ ounce) mushroom soup
1 carton (8 ounces) sour cream

Wrap each chicken breast with a slice of bacon. Cover bottom of flat greased 8x12-inch ovenproof dish with chipped beef. Arrange chicken breasts on chipped beef. Mix soup and sour cream and pour over all. Refrigerate. When ready, bake at 275° for 3 hours, uncovered. **Yield:** 8 servings.

Note: *Could be served over rice or noodles.*

Mrs. Ray Baker (Margaret)

♥ *Add several slices of raw potato to reduce an excessively salty taste in stews, soups, or casseroles. Cook for about ten minutes and remove the slices.*

♥ *Cooked chicken should not stand at room temperature. Refrigerate and use in less than three days.*

Nacho Chicken

1 bag (7 ounces) Nacho flavored
  chips
1 large onion, chopped
1 chicken, boiled and boned
1 can (10¾ ounces) cream of
  mushroom soup

1 can (10¾ ounces) cream of
  chicken soup
1 can (10 ounces) Rotel tomatoes
1 cup chicken broth
½ pound Cheddar cheese,
  shredded

Crush chips and put in bottom of 3-quart baking dish. Mix onion, chicken, soups, tomatoes, and broth. Pour over chips. Sprinkle with cheese. Bake at 325° for 30-40 minutes. **Yield:** 6 servings.

Note: *Use ½ can of Rotel tomatoes for milder taste.*

Mrs. Wallace Brown (Gayle)

Chicken Enchiladas

12 corn tortillas
½ cup salad oil
2 cups grated Monterey Jack
  cheese
¾ cup chopped onion
¼ cup butter

3 Tablespoons flour
2 cups chicken broth
1 cup sour cream
2 cups diced boned chicken
1 can (4 ounces) chopped green
  chilies

In a skillet, cook tortillas 5 seconds on each side to soften. Place 2 table-spoons of cheese and 1 tablespoon of onion on each tortilla and roll up. Place seam side down in a 9x13-inch baking dish. Melt butter in large skil-let and blend in flour. Add broth and cook until thick. Stir in sour cream, chicken, and peppers. Cook until heated. (Do not boil.) Pour over tortillas. Sprinkle with remaining cheese. Bake at 350° for 30 minutes. **Yield:** 6 servings.

Mrs. James Layton (Vicki)

♥ *An authentic version of sour cream used in Mexican dishes can be made by combining 2 tablespoons buttermilk with 1 cup whipping cream and allowing it to sit in a covered bowl at warm room temperature for 6 hours or until thickened.*

Chicken Flautas

4 chicken breasts, boned
Salad oil
1 small onion, diced
1 tomato, diced

½   teaspoon garlic salt
3-4 drops Tabasco sauce
1   cup chicken broth
10-12 corn tortillas

Cut chicken into small pieces. Sauté in oil with onion and tomato. Add garlic salt, Tabasco sauce, and chicken broth. Simmer until liquid is gone. Put 2 tablespoons chicken mixture into each tortilla and roll. Secure with toothpicks. Fry until crisp. **Yield:** 6 servings.

Note: *Warming the tortillas briefly in the microwave keeps them from breaking as they are rolled.*

Mrs. Marvin Chronister (Donna)

Chicken Curry

2 Tablespoons chopped onion
2 Tablespoons chopped celery
½ cup butter
½ teaspoon salt
1 Tablespoon curry powder
½ cup flour
3 cups milk (or ½ milk, ½ chicken broth)
1 cup whipping cream
2 Tablespoons sherry
3 cups chicken, cooked and cubed

Approximately ¾ cup of each of the following condiments:
Cooked rice
Chutney
Chopped peanuts
Fried bacon, crumbled
French-fried onions
Hard-boiled egg, chopped
Shrimp, chopped
Black olives, sliced

Sauté onion and celery in butter. Add salt, curry powder, flour, and cook until bubbly. Add milk, cream, and sherry. Stir until thick. Add chicken and heat thoroughly. Serve with the condiments, each in a separate bowl. **Yield:** 6-8 servings.

Mrs. William Hollon (Kasey)

Chicken Chop Suey

4 boneless chicken breasts
3 Tablespoons salad oil
3 small onions, sliced
1 cup diagonally cut celery
½ cup diced red or green pepper
1 can (10½ ounces) chicken broth
3 Tablespoons soy sauce
1 can (14 ounces) bean sprouts, drained

1 can (8½ ounces) bamboo shoots
1 can (8 ounces) water chestnuts, drained
2 Tablespoons cornstarch
2 Tablespoons water
Cooked rice

Cut chicken into strips. Heat oil and sauté chicken for 5 minutes. Push to one side and stir in onions, celery, and pepper. Sauté for 1 minute. Stir in broth and soy sauce. Heat all ingredients to boiling, cover and simmer for 5 minutes. Stir in vegetables. Mix cornstarch with water until smooth; add to mixture. Stir until thick. Serve over hot rice. **Yield:** 4 servings.

Mrs. James Sowards (Nancy)

Spanish Paella
A Delicious Company Dish

3	pounds chicken pieces	⅛	teaspoon pepper
4	Tablespoons salad oil	2	pounds raw shrimp, cleaned and deveined
1	can (10¾ ounces) tomato soup		
1	can (10¾ ounces) onion soup	2	cups uncooked rice
2½	soup cans of water	2	large green peppers, cut into strips
4	medium cloves garlic, minced		
2	teaspoons crushed oregano	1	cup chopped pimiento
2	teaspoons salt	⅔	cup sliced ripe olives

Brown chicken in oil in a very large skillet or in 2 skillets (10 inches each). Pour off fat. Bone the chicken and return to skillet. Stir in soups, water, garlic, and seasonings. Cover. Cook over low heat 15 minutes. Stir in remaining ingredients. Cover and cook over low heat another 30 minutes or until chicken is tender and rice is done. Stir occasionally. **Yield:** 8-10 servings.

Mrs. Bill Frank (Barbara)

Pineapple Chicken with Orange Rice

¼ cup water
¼ cup firmly packed brown sugar
2 Tablespoons cornstarch
1 can (8 ounces) pineapple chunks, drained, reserving juice
¼ cup vinegar
1 Tablespoon soy sauce
½ teaspoon salt
2 cups cooked chicken, cut into bite-size pieces

¾ cup green pepper, cut into pieces
¼ cup sliced green onion

Orange Rice:
1 cup chopped celery
1 can (11 ounces) mandarin oranges, drained
½ cup butter
2 cups cooked rice

Combine first 7 ingredients using pineapple juice (not the chunks). Add cooked chicken and simmer 30 minutes. Add pineapple chunks, green pepper, and onion. Cook an additional 15 minutes.

Orange Rice: Sauté celery and oranges in butter, until tender. Mix with rice. Top with chicken mixture and serve. **Yield:** 4 servings.

Mrs. Don Kleinschmidt (Ceil)

Spicy Chicken Spaghetti

2 cups butter	1 pound mushrooms, sliced
3-4 cloves garlic, minced	2 pounds chicken breasts, cooked and shredded
¼ cup Worcestershire sauce	
1 teaspoon coarse pepper	¾ pound spaghetti
½ teaspoon salt	1 can (2¼ ounces) sliced black olives
4 Tablespoons chili powder	
4 Tablespoons cumin seed	Green onion, chopped
1 medium onion, chopped	Parmesan cheese, grated

In a large skillet, melt butter. Add garlic and spices, and cook for a few minutes. Sauté onion and mushrooms in the mixture. In the meantime, boil chicken until tender and remove from bone. Reserve liquid. Add chicken to mushroom sauce. Cook spaghetti in chicken broth until just done. Rinse and drain. Put spaghetti in a 9x12-inch ovenproof dish. Using two knives, cut spaghetti. Pour in sauce mixture and black olives and toss well. Bake at 350° for 20 minutes. Top each serving with chopped green onion and Parmesan cheese. **Yield:** 8 servings.

Note: *Keeps well and can be made up a day or two in advance. Serve with a green salad and garlic bread.*

Mrs. Brian Byrne (Veronica)

Inez Ashmore's Tetrazzini

2 Tablespoons chopped onion	1 Tablespoon sherry, optional
1 Tablespoon butter or margarine	1 cup diced cooked chicken, ham or turkey
1 can (10½ ounces) cream of mushroom soup	
	2 Tablespoons chopped pimiento
½ cup water	1 Tablespoon chopped parsley
½ cup grated sharp Cheddar cheese	1 package (6 ounces) spaghetti, cooked and drained

In a saucepan cook onion in butter until tender. Blend in soup, water, cheese, and sherry. Cook over low heat until cheese is melted, stirring often. Add meat, pimiento, parsley, and spaghetti. Pour into covered, ovenproof dish. Heat at 300° for 10 minutes. **Yield:** 4-6 servings.

Note: *More shredded cheese may be sprinkled on top for added cheese flavor.*

Mrs. Mike Freeman (Cathy)

Smoked Turkey and Rice Casserole
Great for Leftover Holiday Turkey

12 slices bacon	4 cups diced turkey
½ cup flour	¼ cup pimiento
1 Tablespoon salt	6 cups cooked rice
½ teaspoon pepper	Paprika
1½ quarts milk	
2 packages (6 ounces each) smoked flavored cheese, cubed	

Cut bacon into small pieces and cook until crisp, reserving ½ cup drippings. Combine drippings, flour, salt, and pepper. Blend well. Add milk and stir until thick and smooth. Add ⅔ of the cheese and stir until almost melted. Fold in turkey, pimiento, rice, and bacon. Pour into 2 buttered 1½-quart casseroles. Top with remaining cheese and sprinkle with paprika. Bake at 350° for 20-30 minutes until bubbly. **Yield:** 10-12 servings.

Note: *May substitute smoked turkey and use plain cheddar cheese. Freezes well.*

Mrs. Ellwood Jones (Ann)

♥ *Use dental floss to truss a stuffed chicken or turkey. It won't tear the skin and holds great!*

Turkey Tetrazzini

1¼ cups raw spaghetti, cooked and drained	¼ cup chopped onion
1½-2 cups cooked turkey	1 can (10½ ounces) mushroom soup
1 jar (2 ounces) diced pimiento	½ cup turkey broth
¼ cup chopped green pepper	1¾ cups grated Cheddar cheese

Mix all ingredients together and place in a 9x13-inch casserole. Top with grated cheese. Bake at 350° for 30 minutes. **Yield:** 8 servings.

Mrs. James Sowards (Nancy)

Cheese Soufflé
Great for Overnight Guests

12 slices white bread
2 jars (5 ounces each) Kraft Old
   English cheese spread
Bacon bits, optional

6 eggs
3 cups milk
1 cup butter, melted
Salt and pepper to taste

Spray 7x12-inch glass dish with vegetable cooking spray. Trim crust from bread and cut into four triangles per slice. Using ⅓ of the cheese, place small chunks on bottom of dish. Place ½ of bread triangles on top of cheese. Alternate cheese and bread layers ending with cheese. Bacon may be added to these layers. Beat eggs slightly. Add milk, butter, salt, and pepper and stir. Pour over bread layers. Cover and chill 8 hours. Remove from refrigerator and set at room temperature for 1 hour. Bake at 350° uncoverd for 70 minutes in a pan of water. **Yield:** 6 servings.

Note: *Must be prepared 8 hours earlier.*

Mrs. Bill Frank (Barbara)

Green Chilies and Cheese Soufflé

2 cups grated Monterey Jack
   cheese
2 cups grated Cheddar cheese
1 can (4 ounces) chopped green
   chilies
4 eggs, separated

⅔ cup evaporated milk
1 Tablespoon flour
½ teaspoon salt
⅛ teaspoon pepper
2 tomatoes

Grease soufflé dish. Combine cheeses and green chilies in bottom of dish. Beat egg whites until stiff. Mix egg yolks with milk, flour, and seasonings. Fold into egg whites. Pour into dish over cheeses and chilies. Bake at 350° for 30 minutes. Top with sliced tomatoes and bake an additional 30 minutes. **Yield:** 6-8 servings.

Mrs. James Layton (Vicki)

♥ *Always remove seeds from chilies before using.*

Spinach Supreme Quiche

1 package (10 ounces) frozen
   spinach soufflé, defrosted
1 pound bacon, fried and
   crumbled
2 eggs

3 Tablespoons milk
2 teaspoons chopped onion
1 cup sliced mushrooms, canned
1 cup grated Swiss cheese
1 unbaked 9-inch pie shell

Mix together first 7 ingredients and pour into pie shell. Bake at 425° for 15 minutes. Reduce oven to 325°. Bake 45 minutes longer or until knife inserted in center comes out clean. **Yield:** 6-8 servings.

Mrs. William Hollon (Kasey)

After the Game Quiche

1 unbaked 9-inch pie shell
6 eggs, beaten
½ cup chopped green onions
4 mushrooms, chopped
2 Tablespoons butter
½ cup chopped chicken, ham, or
   turkey

½ cup Parmesan cheese
1 can (10½ ounces) cream of
   celery soup
½ cup half and half
1 teaspoon salt
½ teaspoon pepper
Garlic powder, dash

Brush inside of pie shell with small amount of beaten egg. Prick bottom and sides of shell with fork. Bake at 450° for 5 minutes. Cool. Reduce heat to 375°. In a saucepan, sauté onions and mushrooms in butter. Add chicken and Parmesan. Spread into pie shell. Combine eggs with remaining ingredients. Mix well and pour over chicken mixture. Bake at 375° for 30-35 minutes or until knife inserted in middle comes out clean. Cool 5 minutes before serving. **Yield:** 6 servings.

Mrs. Doug Rivenbark (Penny)

♥ *To prevent a quiche crust from becoming soggy, wait to fill until just before baking.*

Swiss Quiche

25 Ritz crackers, crushed
¼ cup butter, melted
6 slices bacon
½ onion, chopped
2 eggs, beaten

¾ cup sour cream
½ teaspoon salt
Pepper, dash
8 ounces Swiss cheese, grated
½ cup grated Cheddar cheese

Mix crushed crackers and melted butter together in a 9-inch pie pan and press against sides. Cook bacon and dice. Sauté onion in bacon grease. Combine bacon, onion, eggs, sour cream, salt, pepper, and Swiss cheese. Fill pie shell and top with Cheddar cheese. Bake at 375° for 25-30 minutes, until knife comes out clean. Let stand 10 minutes before cutting. **Yield:** 6-8 servings.

Mrs. Dan Boyd (Terry)

Spinach Lasagne

1 large onion, chopped
2 large cloves garlic, minced
2 Tablespoons butter, melted
2 bags (10 ounces each) spinach, stems removed
1 box (8 ounces) lasagne noodles, cooked al dente

1 pound ricotta cheese
1 pound mozzarella cheese, grated
2 eggs, beaten
Salt and pepper to taste
2-3 cups mushroom tomato sauce

Sauté onion and garlic in butter until onion is clear. Add spinach and cook until wilted and all moisture is gone. Set aside to cool. Cook noodles. In separate bowl combine ricotta, ¾ of the mozzarella, eggs, salt, and pepper. Stir in spinach. In 9x13-inch pan, layer noodles and spinach-cheese mixture ending with reserved mozzarella. Cover with foil and bake at 350° for 30 minutes. Uncover and bake an additional 30 minutes until cheese is browned. Cool 10 minutes before cutting into squares and serving. Top with your favorite mushroom tomato sauce. **Yield:** 6-8 servings.

Mrs. Brian Byrne (Veronica)

Spinach Pie Deluxe

1 pound Italian sausage
6 eggs
1 package (16 ounces) shredded
   mozzarella cheese
2 packages (10 ounces each) frozen
   chopped spinach, thawed and
   well drained

⅔ cup ricotta cheese (½ of 16
   ounce container)
¼ teaspoon pepper
¼ teaspoon garlic powder
Pie crust mix for 2-crust pie
1 Tablespoon water

Using a 10-inch skillet over medium heat, remove casing and cook Italian sausage until well browned, stirring often. Spoon off fat. Reserve 1 egg yolk, and in a large bowl combine remaining eggs with sausage, mozzarella cheese, spinach, ricotta cheese, pepper, and garlic powder. Set aside. Prepare pastry according to pie crust directions. Divide pastry into 2 balls with one being slightly larger. On lightly floured surface with lightly floured rolling pin, roll larger ball into a circle. Make it ⅛-inch thick and 2 inches larger all around than a 9-inch pie pan. Line pie pan. Spoon sausage mixture onto pastry.

Roll second ball into a 10-inch circle. Place over filling. With kitchen shears or sharp knife, trim pastry leaving ½-inch overhang. Fold overhang under and press gently all around rim to make standup edge. With sharp knife, cut out a 2-inch circle in center of pastry and cut slits in pastry top. In small bowl, combine reserved egg yolk with water. Brush top of pie with egg mixture. Reroll scraps and cut decorative leaf shaped designs. Place on pie and brush with egg mixture. Bake at 375° for 1 hour and 15 minutes or until golden; chill well. Serve cold or hot. **Yield:** 10 servings.

Note: *Use within 2 days. Freezes well.*

Mrs. Doug Arnold (Debbi)

Sausage Quiche

2½ cups seasoned croutons
2 cups grated sharp Cheddar
  cheese
2 pounds sausage
4 eggs, beaten
¾ teaspoon dry mustard

2½ cups milk
1 can (4 ounces) sliced
  mushrooms, drained
1 can (10½ ounces) mushroom
  soup

Put croutons in 9x13-inch greased casserole dish. Spread with cheese. Cook and drain sausage and spread over cheese. Mix remaining ingredients and pour over sausage. Cover and refrigerate overnight. Bake uncovered at 300° for 1¼ hours. **Yield:** 8-10 servings.

Note: *Must prepare day ahead.*

Mrs. Bill Frank (Barbara)

Good and Cheesy Grits

1 cup grits
1 roll (6 ounces) garlic cheese
½ cup butter or margarine

3 eggs
⅔ cup milk
½ cup grated Cheddar cheese

Cook grits according to directions. Add garlic cheese and butter. Cool; then add eggs and milk. Pour into a greased 2-quart casserole. Bake at 350° for approximately 45 minutes. Top with grated Cheddar cheese the last 10 minutes of cooking time. **Yield:** 6 servings.

Mrs. Jim Thornton (Jackie)

Cheese Grits

6 cups water
1¾ cups grits
½ teaspoon salt
½ cup margarine

¾ pound Velveeta cheese
3 eggs, well beaten
Tabasco sauce, dash

Put 6 cups of water into a deep pan and bring to a boil. Add grits and cook until done. Remove from heat and add salt, margarine, and cheese. Mix and let cool for 30 minutes. Add eggs and Tabasco. Place in deep dish. Bake at 275° for 1 hour. **Yield:** 12 servings.

Mrs. Thomas Hunter (Lynda)

Macaroni and Cheese

½ pound macaroni
1 Tablespoon salt
1 small onion, minced
4 Tablespoons butter
3 Tablespoons flour
½ teaspoon dry mustard
1¼ teaspoons salt

Pepper, speck
3 cups milk
¾ pound Cheddar cheese, shredded
¾ cup breadcrumbs
2 Tablespoons butter, melted

Boil macaroni with salt for 9 minutes. Drain. Put onion in double boiler with 4 tablespoons butter. When butter is melted, stir in flour, mustard, salt, and pepper. Slowly stir in milk; cook until smooth and hot, stirring often. Slowly add about ¾ of the cheese. Stir until cheese is melted. Put macaroni in a 2-quart casserole dish. Pour cheese sauce over macaroni, tossing lightly with a fork. Top with remaining cheese. Toss breadcrumbs with 2 tablespoons butter. Sprinkle over cheese. Bake uncovered at 400° for 20 minutes. **Yield:** 4-6 servings.

Note: *½ to 1½ cups slivered, cooked ham may be added to the cheese sauce. Using fresh breadcrumbs adds to the attractive appearance of this dish.*

Mrs. Carl Smith (Karen)

♥ *One teaspoon dry mustard is equal to 1 tablespoon prepared mustard.*

Melody's Easy Brunch Casserole
Great for Company Breakfast

2 cups croutons, plain or seasoned
1 cup shredded Cheddar cheese
4 eggs, slightly beaten
2 cups milk
½ teaspoon salt

½ teaspoon prepared mustard
⅛ teaspoon onion powder
Pepper, dash
4 slices bacon, cooked and crumbled

Layer croutons in bottom of greased 6x10-inch pan. Sprinkle with cheese. Combine eggs, milk, salt, mustard, onion powder, and pepper. Mix until well blended. Pour into baking dish. Sprinkle with bacon crumbs. Bake at 325° for 55-60 minutes or until eggs are set. **Yield:** 4 servings.

Mrs. Thomas Hunter (Lynda)

Cheese and Bacon Strata
Delicious-Colorful Dish

½ pound bacon, cooked and
   crumbled
½ cup finely chopped celery
¼ cup finely chopped green
   pepper
¼ cup finely chopped onion
8 slices day-old bread, trimmed
4 slices Old English cheese
4 eggs, beaten

2 cups milk
1 teaspoon mustard
1 teaspoon salt
½ teaspoon Worcestershire sauce
¼ teaspoon monosodium
   glutamate
White pepper, dash
Tabasco sauce, dash

Preheat oven to 325°. Combine bacon, celery, pepper, and onion. Mix until
blended. Arrange 4 slices of bread in the bottom of a greased 8-inch square
glass baking dish. Sprinkle with bacon mixture. Place cheese slices over
bacon. Top with remaining bread. Combine remaining ingredients. Blend
well. Pour over sandwiches. Refrigerate for at least 1 hour or overnight.
Bake for 1 hour. Strata will puff up, then fall when cut. Cut into 4 sandwich
size squares. **Yield:** 4 servings.

Mrs. Dan Boyd (Terry)

Make Ahead Breakfast Eggs

18 eggs
½ cup milk
½ teaspoon salt
½ teaspoon pepper
4 Tablespoons butter (2 per
   skillet)

1 carton (8 ounces) sour cream
1 pound bacon, cooked and
   crumbled
1½ cups shredded sharp Cheddar
   cheese

In medium bowl, beat eggs. Stir in milk, salt, and pepper. Set aside. Using
2 (10-inch) skillets (or 1 skillet and repeat process with ½ of egg mixture),
cook egg mixture in 2 tablespoons butter until eggs are beginning to set,
but still moist. Remove from heat to cool. Stir in sour cream and spread
evenly into buttered 9x13-inch pan. Top with bacon and cheese. Cover
with foil and refrigerate overnight. Preheat oven to 300°. Uncover and
bake for 15-20 minutes, or until cheese melts. **Yield:** 8-10 servings.

Note: *May add 1 tablespoon onion flakes and dash of garlic powder for extra flavor.*

Mrs. Dennis Furlong (Dede)

Huevos Rancheros

½ cup chopped onion
1 Tablespoon salad oil
1 can (16 ounces) tomatoes, chopped
1 can (4 ounces) chopped green chilies

¼ teaspoon salt
¼ teaspoon chili powder
⅛ teaspoon garlic powder
4 eggs
Pepper
1 cup shredded Cheddar cheese

Cook onion in oil until soft. Add next 5 ingredients. Cover and simmer 5 minutes. Slide eggs into mixture, taking care not to break yolks. Season with pepper. Cover and poach 3-4 minutes. Place 1 or 2 eggs into serving dish. Spoon on additional sauce. Sprinkle with cheese and put in warm oven until cheese is melted. **Yield:** 2-4 servings.

Mrs. Don Kleinschmidt (Ceil)

Green Chili Bites
Great for Brunch

2 cups chopped green chilies
2 cups grated sharp Cheddar cheese
8 eggs, slightly beaten

Salt, dash
Pepper, dash
8 Tablespoons half and half

Place green chilies in bottom of 11x13-inch pan. Cover with cheese. Mix eggs with salt, pepper, and cream. Pour over chilies and cheese. Bake at 350° for 30 minutes. Let it set for a few minutes before cutting into squares. Serve warm. **Yield:** 10-12 servings.

Mrs. Winston Borum (Jimmie)

♥ *A fresh egg sinks in a bowl of cold water.*

Manicotti

1 can (24 ounces) tomato sauce
   or spaghetti sauce
Basil to taste
Parsley to taste
Salt and pepper to taste
1-2 cloves garlic, minced
Water, as needed
3 pounds ricotta cheese

1 pound cottage cheese
½ cup grated Parmesan cheese
3 eggs
Salt to taste
¼ cup parsley
2-3 packages (8 ounces each)
   manicotti, uncooked
2 cups warm water

Combine tomato sauce and spices. Add enough water to make the sauce thin. Cover bottom of 9x13-inch pan with ½ of the sauce. Combine cheeses, eggs, salt, and parsley. Fill uncooked manicotti shells with cheese filling and place over sauce in pan. Cover with remaining sauce. Add 2 cups warm water. Cover with foil and bake at 350° for 45 minutes. Remove foil and cook another 10-15 minutes. Let stand 15-20 minutes to set. **Yield:** 8-10 servings.

Mrs. William Hollon (Kasey)

Juna's Fettucini

1 pound fettucini noodles
½ cup butter
1 cup whipping cream
2 teaspoons fresh parsley,
   cleaned and chopped

¼ pound Romano or Parmesan
   cheese
Salt and white pepper to taste

Cook noodles in boiling water with 1 teaspoon salt for about 5 minutes. Melt butter in large skillet. Add cream, parsley, salt, and pepper. Cook very low for only a few minutes. Remove from heat and add drained noodles and cheese. Mix together well and serve immediately. **Yield:** 4-6 servings.

Mrs. John Mearns (June)

Chipper Trout

2 pounds Gulf trout fillets
½ cup Caesar salad dressing
1 cup crushed potato chips

½ cup shredded sharp Cheddar
   cheese

Dip fillets in dressing. Place skin side down in baking dish. Combine chips and cheese. Sprinkle over fish. Bake at 500° for 10-15 minutes. **Yield:** 4-6 servings.

Mrs. William Hollon (Kasey)

Fillets with Crabmeat Stuffing
Truly Company Fare!

2 pounds fresh or frozen sole
   fillets
2 packages (6 ounces each) frozen
   crabmeat
⅓ cup butter, melted
½ cup chopped onion
⅓ cup chopped celery

⅓ cup chopped green pepper
2 cups soft bread cubes
2 eggs, beaten
1 Tablespoon chopped parsley
1½ teaspoons salt
½ teaspoon pepper

Thaw fish and crabmeat; drain. Measure ¼ cup melted butter in fry pan. Cook onion, celery, and green pepper until tender. Combine crabmeat, bread cubes, eggs, parsley, 1 teaspoon salt, and pepper. Mix together with the onion mixture. Pour into greased baking dish. Arrange fillets in the mixture. Brush with remaining butter and salt. Bake at 350° for 20-25 minutes. **Yield:** 6-8 servings.

Mrs. Paul Carletta (Mary Ann)

♥ *Remove pulp from lemon halves and use them as cups to hold tartar or cocktail sauce on seafood dishes.*

♥ *The key to successful freezing is proper packaging. Fish keeps better when frozen in water. Game should be frozen quickly and kept at a temperature of 9°.*

Heavenly Broiled Fish

2 pounds fish fillets
2 Tablespoons lemon juice
½ cup grated Parmesan cheese
¼ cup margarine, softened
3 Tablespoons mayonnaise

3 Tablespoons chopped green
   onion
¼ teaspoon salt
Tabasco sauce, dash

Place fillets in a single layer on a well greased baking platter. Brush with lemon juice. Combine remaining ingredients. Broil fillets about 4 inches from heat for 4-6 minutes or until fish flakes easily. Remove from heat and spread with above mixture. Broil 2-3 minutes more or until lightly browned. **Yield:** 6 servings.

Mrs. King Bourland (Carol)

Seafood Creole

¼ cup margarine
¼ cup flour
1 cup hot water
1 can (8 ounces) tomato sauce
½ cup chopped green onions
½ cup chopped parsley (or 2
   Tablespoons dried)
¼ cup chopped green pepper
4 garlic cloves, pressed or finely
   chopped

2 whole bay leaves
1½ teaspoons salt
½ teaspoon thyme
Cayenne pepper, dash
1 lemon slice
1 pound fish fillets, cut into
   1-inch chunks
1 package (6 ounces) shrimp,
   fresh or frozen
Rice, cooked

Prepare roux by heating margarine in large skillet and blending in flour over medium heat. Stir constantly until brown, being careful not to scorch. Add water gradually and cook until thick and smooth. Add remaining ingredients, except shrimp, and simmer for 15 minutes. Add shrimp and cook for about 5 more minutes (until shrimp is completely thawed and hot). Serve over rice. **Yield:** 4 servings.

Mrs. Roger Jones (Janet)

Shrimp Creole

1	cup sliced onion	1½	Tablespoons Worcestershire sauce
1	cup chopped celery		Tabasco sauce, dash
1	clove garlic, chopped	1	teaspoon sugar
2-3	Tablespoons salad oil	1	cup sliced green pepper
1	can (28 ounces) tomatoes, cut up, undrained	1	pound raw shrimp, peeled
1-1½	teaspoons chili powder		Rice, cooked
2	teaspoons salt		

Sauté onion, celery, and garlic in oil until tender but not brown. Add tomatoes and juice, chili powder, salt, Worcestershire sauce, Tabasco sauce, and sugar. Simmer uncovered for 45 minutes. Add green pepper and shrimp. Cover and cook about 10-15 minutes until shrimp and green pepper are done. Serve over cooked rice. **Yield:** 6-8 servings.

Mrs. Donald Hudson (Vickie)

Shrimp Scampi

3	Tablespoons butter	¾	pound medium raw shrimp, shelled and deveined
2	Tablespoons salad oil	¼	teaspoon grated lemon peel
1½	Tablespoons minced green onion	2	Tablespoons minced parsley
4	cloves garlic, minced		Tabasco sauce, dash
2	Tablespoons lemon juice		Lemon wedges
¼	teaspoon salt		

Heat wok over medium heat until hot. Add butter and oil. When butter has melted, add onion, garlic, lemon juice, and salt. Stir-fry until onion is limp, about 30 seconds. Turn heat to high; add shrimp. Stir-fry until pink, about 2 minutes. Add lemon peel, parsley, and Tabasco sauce. Garnish with lemon wedge to squeeze over each serving. **Yield:** 2 servings.

Note: *Serve with hot buttered noodles, rice, or spaghetti.*

Mrs. Mallard Tysseland (Jill)

Saucy Shrimp
Great Party Dish

2 pounds large shrimp, peeled
  and deveined
2 shallots, minced
½ cup butter, melted
1 pound mushrooms, sliced
2 Tablespoons flour

1 teaspoon salt
Pepper to taste
1 carton (16 ounces) sour cream
¼ cup sherry
Rice, cooked

Sauté shrimp and shallots in butter for 5 minutes. Add mushrooms and cook 5 minutes more. Blend in flour, salt, and pepper. Gradually stir in sour cream. Cook until thick, stirring constantly. Remove from heat. Stir in sherry. Serve over hot rice. **Yield:** 6-8 servings.

Mrs. William Hollon (Kasey)

Shrimp and Artichoke Bake

1 pound large raw shrimp,
  unpeeled
1 quart water, boiling
2 Tablespoons vinegar
1 teaspoon pickling spice
1 bay leaf
½ pound fresh mushrooms, sliced
6 Tablespoons butter
1 can (14 ounces) artichoke hearts

4 Tablespoons flour
1½ cups half and half
¼ cup sherry or white wine
1 Tablespoon Worcestershire
  sauce
¼ teaspoon nutmeg
⅓ cup Parmesan cheese, grated
1 teaspoon paprika

Add shrimp to quart of boiling water with vinegar, pickling spice, and bay leaf. Cook 2 minutes. Drain and peel shrimp. Sauté mushrooms in 2 tablespoons melted butter. Reserve in pan with juices. In buttered 2-quart baking dish, layer artichoke hearts, shrimp, and mushrooms with pan juices. Set aside. In medium saucepan, melt 4 tablespoons butter; blend in flour and stir in half and half. Stir constantly until thickened. Add wine, Worcestershire sauce, and nutmeg. Pour sauce over layered mixture, sprinkle with Parmesan and paprika. Bake at 375° for 30 minutes. **Yield:** 6-8 servings.

Note: *Fresh Parmesan cheese is best.*

Mrs. Richard Keeling (Laurie)

Shrimp in Sour Cream

1 pound (18-22 count) shrimp, peeled and deveined
2 Tablespoons chopped green onion
¼ cup butter
8 ounces mushrooms, washed, drained, and sliced
1 Tablespoon flour
1 teaspoon Worcestershire sauce
½ teaspoon salt
¼ teaspoon cracked black pepper
½ teaspoon seafood seasoning or seasoned salt
2 Tablespoons dry sherry
1 cup sour cream
Rice, cooked

In 10-inch skillet, sauté on medium high heat shrimp and onions in butter until shrimp are pink, about 5 minutes. Add mushrooms and cook 5 minutes longer. Sprinkle with flour and seasonings. Add sherry and sour cream and mix well. Simmer over low heat until hot. Do not boil. Serve over cooked rice. **Yield:** 4 servings.

Mrs. Dennis Furlong (Dede)

Spicy Shrimp
An Excellent Cajun Dish

½ cup butter
1 Tablespoon pepper
2 ounces Worcestershire sauce
¼ teaspoon Tabasco sauce
¼ teaspoon garlic powder
2 teaspoons dried parsley
2 pounds raw shrimp, peeled
1 lemon, thinly sliced

Preheat oven to 400°. Melt butter in small saucepan. Add remaining ingredients except shrimp and lemon slices. Put shrimp into a 1½ or 2-quart baking dish. Pour butter mixture over shrimp and top with lemon slices. Cover and cook 5-8 minutes (or until shrimp turns pink). **Yield:** Approximately 4 servings.

Mrs. Marvin Chronister (Donna)

Shrimp-Crab Express

¾ cup butter
⅔ cup flour
2 teaspoons salt
1 teaspoon paprika
¼ teaspoon pepper
3 cups whipping cream

½ cup Chablis wine
3 pounds shrimp, cooked
2 packages (7½ ounces each) frozen crabmeat
Wild rice, cooked

Melt butter. Remove from heat. Stir in flour, salt, paprika, and pepper until smooth. Return to heat and gradually stir in cream. Bring to a boil, stirring constantly. Reduce heat. Simmer 5 minutes. Add wine, shrimp, and crabmeat. Cook over low heat until hot. Do not boil. Serve over wild rice. **Yield:** 6 servings.

Mrs. William Hollon (Kasey)

Crab Au Gratin
Restaurant Cuisine

1 large white onion, chopped
½ bunch green onions, chopped
3 ribs celery, chopped
1 cup butter
4 Tablespoons flour
1 can (12 ounces) evaporated milk

1 can (5 ounces) evaporated milk
2 egg yolks
2 pounds fresh white crabmeat
Salt and pepper to taste
10 ounces Cheddar cheese, grated

Sauté onion and celery in butter until soft. Add flour and blend. Add milk and blend. Cook over low heat until slightly thickened. Remove from heat. Add egg yolks, crabmeat, salt, and pepper. Add cheese to mixture, reserving a little for topping. Place in individual ramekins. Sprinkle with reserved cheese. Bake at 350° for 20 minutes. **Yield:** 6-8 servings.

Mrs. Jerry Brown (Linda)

Crabmeat Rellenos con Queso

2 cans (4 ounces each) whole green chilies, drained
2 eggs
1½ cups buttermilk
1½ cups flour
1½ teaspoons salt
Salad oil for frying
3 cans (7½ ounces each) crabmeat, drained
Avocado, optional

Cheese Sauce:
1 small yellow onion, diced
2 green onions, diced
4 Tablespoons salad oil
4 Tablespoons flour
2 cans (4 ounces each) chopped green chilies, undrained
2 cups milk
1 pound processed cheese, grated
1 teaspoon salt
½ teaspoon pepper
½ teaspoon chili pepper
½ cup picante sauce

Rinse chilies, split from the top to the bottom, and open to form a flat triangle. Soak chilies in mixture of eggs and buttermilk. Mix flour and salt, then cover both sides of chilies with flour mixture. Heat about one cup of oil and sauté chilies until golden brown on both sides. Drain. Place chilies in baking dish and top with crabmeat and enough cheese sauce to lightly cover. Cook under broiler until sauce begins to bubble. **Cheese Sauce:** Sauté onions in oil until tender (4-5 minutes). Turn heat off, add flour, and stir until thoroughly mixed. Turn heat back on to medium and stir in chilies including juice. Cook for about 1 minute. Slowly add milk, stirring constantly, and cook until the mixture becomes a heavy cream. Add cheese and cook until smooth and melted. Add spices and picante sauce. Pour ½ of the cheese sauce over the crabmeat rellenos and reserve the rest of the sauce for tostado dip. **Yield:** 4-6 servings.

Note: *Good garnished with avocado halves.*

Mrs. Marvin Chronister (Donna)

Mary's Salmon Turnovers

Pastry:
1 cup milk
2 eggs
1 Tablespoon salad oil
1 cup flour
¼ teaspoon salt
⅛-¼ teaspoon dill weed
1 Tablespoon butter

Salmon Filling:
2 Tablespoons salad oil
2 cups fresh or frozen chopped broccoli

1 sweet green or red pepper, diced
1 small onion, sliced
1 cup sliced mushrooms
½ cup white wine
1 Tablespoon cornstarch
2 Tablespoons water
1 can (15½ ounces) chunk salmon, drained, and separated
Swiss cheese, grated

Preheat oven to 400°. In a blender, combine first 6 ingredients until smooth. Using butter, grease inside of twelve 4-ounce pyrex cups or muffin tins. Fill each half full with batter. Bake for 20 minutes; lower heat to 350° and bake 15-20 minutes longer. Sauté in oil the broccoli, pepper, onion, and mushrooms until tender. Combine wine, cornstarch, and water. Heat with vegetables. Remove from heat and fold in the salmon. Cut tops off pastry, spoon on salmon filling, and replace tops. Sprinkle with desired amount of cheese. Place under broiler to melt cheese slightly. Serve hot. **Yield:** 12 servings.

Mrs. Doug Arnold (Debbi)

Creamy Shrimp
Great for Ladies Luncheon

2 Tablespoons butter
3 Tablespoons flour
1½ cups milk
½ teaspoon salt

Pepper, dash
¼ cup dry sherry
1 pound cooked shrimp
Parmesan cheese

Melt butter in saucepan. Stir in flour. Add milk and cook until thickened. Add salt, pepper, sherry, and shrimp. Pour into four baking shells or custard cups. Sprinkle each with Parmesan cheese and broil 3-4 minutes or until cheese is brown. **Yield:** 4 servings.

Mrs. Wallace Brown (Gayle)

Tuna Divan

1 package (10 ounces) frozen
   broccoli spears
1 can (6½ ounces) tuna, drained
   and flaked

1 can (10¾ ounces) cream of
   chicken soup
⅓ cup mayonnaise
1 cup grated Cheddar cheese

Cook broccoli spears according to package directions. Drain and arrange in a 1-quart casserole. Top with tuna. Mix soup and mayonnaise together. Pour over tuna. Sprinkle with cheese and bake at 350° for 20 minutes. **Yield:** 4-6 servings.

Note: *Can be prepared in individual au gratin dishes.*

Mrs. Don Kleinschmidt (Ceil)

Chopstick Tuna

1 can (10¾ ounces) cream of
   mushroom soup
¼ cup water
2 cups chow mein noodles
1 can (7 ounces) tuna, drained

1 cup chopped celery
¼ cup chopped onion
½ cup chopped, salted, roasted
   cashews

Combine soup with water. Add 1 cup of noodles and remaining ingredients. Place in ungreased baking dish and top with remaining noodles. Bake at 375° for 15 minutes. **Yield:** 4-6 servings.

Mrs. Jim Thornton (Jackie)

♥ *To convert regular recipes to microwave, cook ¼ of the time. If necessary, add time increments of 30 seconds.*

Super Seafood Supper

1   package (6 ounces) long grain and wild rice, cooked
1   cup chopped green pepper
½   cup chopped celery
½   cup chopped onion
1½ pounds shrimp, cooked
1   cup mayonnaise
1   cup tomato juice
1   can (8 ounces) sliced water chestnuts

2   packages (6 ounces each) frozen crabmeat, thawed
Salt and pepper to taste

Topping:
1   cup sliced toasted almonds
1   cup shredded Cheddar cheese
½   teaspoon paprika

Combine all ingredients except topping. Place in greased 2-quart casserole. Cover with topping. Bake at 350° for 35 minutes. **Yield:** 6-8 servings.

Mrs. William Hollon (Kasey)

♥ *To cook shrimp, drop it into boiling water which has been generously salted. Return water to boil and simmer 2-5 minutes until the shrimp turns pink. Do not overcook.*

Seafood Casserole

4   cups shrimp, cooked
2   cans (6 ounces each) crabmeat
¾   cup minced onion
2   cups chopped celery
1   cup mayonnaise
2   teaspoons Worcestershire sauce

1   teaspoon salt
½   teaspoon pepper
1½ cups breadcrumbs
4   Tablespoons butter, melted

Cut shrimp in half if they are large. Drain and flake crabmeat. Combine the two. Add onion, celery, mayonnaise, Worcestershire sauce, salt, and pepper. Spread in 9x12-inch casserole dish. Mix breadcrumbs with melted butter. Sprinkle over casserole. Bake at 350° for 30 minutes. **Yield:** 8-10 servings.

Mrs. Steven Sellers (Anne)

Windsor Canadian Goose

6-8 pound goose	Sauce:
1 quart buttermilk	½ cup butter
1 package (8 ounces) dried	¼ cup flour
prunes	¾ cup chicken broth
2 apples, sliced	Salt to taste
5 slices bacon	1 cup sour cream
Butter	4 Tablespoons currant jelly

Soak goose in buttermilk for at least 4 hours. Wash and drain. Stuff with prunes and apples. Truss and wrap with bacon. Cover tightly in heavy duty foil. Bake at 325° for about 3-4 hours. Baste with butter to brown.

Sauce: Melt butter in saucepan. Whisk in flour. Add broth and salt and heat, stirring constantly. Just before serving, add sour cream and jelly. Remove fruit from goose and arrange on platter around it. Serve with sauce. **Yield:** 4-6 servings.

Note: *Very nice for Christmas dinner.*

Mrs. Richard Keeling (Laurie)

Baked Wild Goose LaBove

1 wild goose	Gravy:
Salt and pepper to taste	1 Tablespoon flour
Red pepper to taste	½ cup red wine, optional
½ medium onion, sliced	1 can (4 ounces) mushrooms,
1 large green pepper, sliced	optional
1 slice bacon	

Wash goose and pat dry. Make a slit under the breasts and sprinkle inside with salt and peppers. Fill the pocket with onion and several pieces of green pepper. Place a strip of bacon in skillet and brown goose. Then put in roasting pan, breast side down. Place covered roaster in 325-350° oven and cook until tender. Baking time will depend upon size of goose, about 15 minutes per pound.

Gravy: Add a tablespoon of flour to drippings and stir until brown. Add wine and mushrooms if desired, stirring until smooth. Pour gravy over goose. **Yield:** 4-6 servings.

Mrs. Doug Rivenbark (Penny)

Saucy Quail

8 quail breasts	½ cup shortening
Salt and pepper to taste	2 cups sour cream
2 eggs, beaten	4 Tablespoons wine
¼ cup milk	Paprika
1½ cups seasoned breadcrumbs	1 clove garlic, minced

Salt and pepper quail breasts. Combine eggs and milk. Dip quail in egg mixture, then in breadcrumbs. Repeat. Sauté in shortening until golden brown. Place breasts in a 9x13-inch pan. Combine sour cream and wine. Pour over game. Sprinkle with paprika and garlic. Bake at 350° for about 45 minutes. **Yield:** 4 servings.

Mrs. Marvin Chronister (Donna)

♥ *Trim the fat from game because it retains the wild taste.*

♥ *Aging game birds in the refrigerator for 24-48 hours before cooking or freezing removes much of the wild flavor.*

Baked Doves

12-15 dove breasts	1 carton (8 ounces) sour cream
3 Tablespoons butter	1 cup beef bouillon

In a large skillet, brown breasts in butter on all sides. After browning arrange meaty side up in a single layer in skillet. Spread approximately 1 tablespoon sour cream on each breast. Add beef bouillon to the skillet, and cover. Simmer at very low heat or bake at 325° for 1 hour 30 minutes. **Yield:** 6 servings.

Note: *Delicious served over wild rice.*

Mrs. Mac Cravy (Sharon)

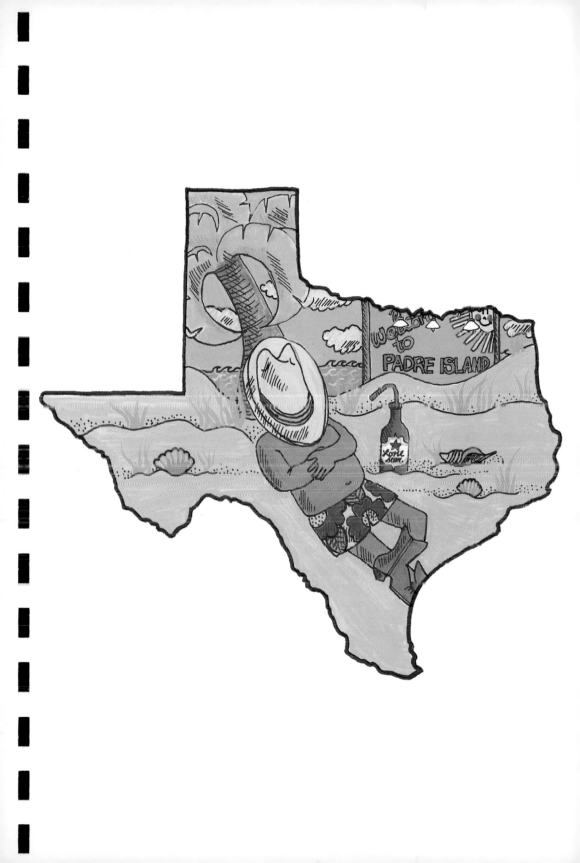

THE SCIENCE PLACE

Southwest Museum of Science and Technology

The Science Place is an innovative museum and learning center devoted to increasing understanding of our scientific and technological society. It offers many hands-on discovery experiences for children and adults, and is one of the fastest growing cultural institutions in Dallas, now more than five times larger than it was only four years ago. In the past two years, attendance has averaged more than 600,000 people annually. The rapidly expanding "ESP" (Exploring the Science Place) cooperative programs are expected to bring more than 10,000 children from surrounding North Texas areas to participate in the overnight and all-day educational programs.

Dallas Junior Forum volunteers conduct school tours through the museum exhibits and provide financial support for specific traveling exhibits.

Vegetables

Vegetables add color to every plate,
And for health, we know they really rate.
You can serve them soft or with a crunch
To enhance your dinner or favorite lunch.

Baked Artichoke Hearts

1 can (8 ounces) artichoke hearts, drained, reserve liquid
4 Tablespoons salad oil
1 small onion, chopped
2 cloves garlic, finely chopped
4 eggs, beaten
⅓ cup Italian seasoned breadcrumbs

1 teaspoon seasoned salt
¼ teaspoon pepper
½ teaspoon oregano
½ teaspoon Tabasco sauce
2 cups grated Cheddar cheese
3 Tablespoons dry parsley

Cut off tops of artichoke hearts, set aside. Cut up artichoke leaves and set aside. Heat oil and ½ cup of reserved liquid and sauté onion and garlic until liquid is reduced. Mix together eggs, breadcrumbs, salt, pepper, oregano, and Tabasco. Fold in cheese, parsley, artichoke leaves, sautéed onion, and garlic. Pour into a greased 9-inch baking dish and top with artichoke tops. Bake at 325° for 30-35 minutes. Cool 35 minutes before cutting. **Yield:** 4 servings.

Mrs. Marvin Chronister (Donna)

Almond Asparagus

1 pound asparagus
3 Tablespoons butter
½ cup slivered almonds, toasted

1 Tablespoon lemon juice
Salt and pepper to taste

Wash asparagus; cut into 1-inch diagonal slices. Melt butter in skillet. Add asparagus and almonds and sauté 3-4 minutes. Cover and steam about 2 minutes or until tender crisp. Toss in the lemon juice and seasonings. **Yield:** 6-8 servings.

Mrs. Dennis Furlong (Dede)

♥ *Don't throw away asparagus stems! They are delicious slivered thinly and stir fried quickly in hot oil.*

Asparagus Au Gratin

1 can (14 ounces) asparagus
  spears
Half and half or milk
2 Tablespoons flour

2 Tablespoons butter, melted
1 cup grated Cheddar cheese
½ cup cracker crumbs (12-14
  crackers)

Drain asparagus, reserving liquid. Add enough half and half or milk to this liquid to equal 1 cup. Set aside. Combine flour and butter in a saucepan; cook over low heat, stirring constantly for about 3 minutes. Gradually stir in asparagus liquid. Cook, stirring constantly until smooth and thickened. Place the asparagus in a lightly greased shallow 1-quart baking dish. Sprinkle with ½ cup cheese. Cover with the white sauce. Sprinkle with cracker crumbs and the remaining cheese. Bake at 350° for 20-30 minutes. **Yield:** 4 servings.

Mrs. Thomas Hunter (Lynda)

Asparagus Casserole

4 Tablespoons butter
2 Tablespoons flour
2 cups milk
¼ teaspoon fresh ground pepper
Salt to taste

4 cups canned "fancy" asparagus
4 eggs, hard-boiled and sliced
½ cup cracker crumbs or seasoned
  breadcrumbs

Melt 2 tablespoons butter; blend in flour. Add milk and cook, stirring constantly until mixture comes to a boil and thickens. Add salt and pepper to taste. Arrange ½ of the asparagus and the egg slices in the bottom of an 8-inch square baking dish. Cover with ½ of the white sauce. Top with remaining asparagus, then remaining white sauce. Sprinkle with crumbs and dot with remaining butter. Bake at 350° for 30-35 minutes or until hot and bubbly. **Yield:** 6 servings.

Mrs. Jerry Brown (Linda)

Asparagus with Sour Cream

1½ pounds asparagus spears
¾ cup sour cream

½ cup grated Parmesan cheese
3 Tablespoons mayonnaise

Snap off tough ends of asparagus. Remove scales with vegetable peeler. Cook asparagus covered in boiling salted water 8 to 10 minutes; drain. Arrange on serving dish and keep warm. Combine sour cream, cheese, and mayonnaise in a double boiler over boiling water. Heat thoroughly, stirring frequently. Pour sauce over asparagus and serve immediately. **Yield:** 6 servings.

Mrs. Joe Key (Christie)

Bailey Green Bean Casserole

2 cans (16 ounces each) or 2 packages frozen French-style green beans, drained
1 can (10½ ounces) cream of celery soup
1 can (10½ ounces) cream of mushroom soup
1 can (8 ounces) sliced water chestnuts, drained

1 small package (2½ ounces) almonds, toasted
Salt and pepper to taste
Picapeppa sauce, dash
Worcestershire sauce, dash
1 can (2.8 ounces) French-fried onions, crumbled

Mix all ingredients except onions. Place in 2-quart casserole. Cover with crumbled onion rings. Bake uncovered at 350° for 30 minutes. **Yield:** 8-10 servings.

Mrs. Richard Keeling (Laurie)

Green Beans and Almonds

2 cans (16 ounces each) French-style green beans
¼ cup almond slivers

¼ cup margarine
½ teaspoon salt
4 Tablespoons lemon juice

Heat beans, then drain. Cook almonds in margarine, salt, and lemon juice until slightly golden brown. Pour over warm green beans. **Yield:** 8 servings.

Mrs. Terry Chambers (Dianne)

Curried Green Beans

2 packages (10 ounces each) frozen
  French-style green beans
2 cups milk
3 Tablespoons margarine, melted
3 Tablespoons flour

1 Tablespoon curry powder
Salt to taste
Red pepper to taste
½ cup grated Cheddar cheese

Cook beans according to package directions and drain well. Combine milk, margarine, and flour. Season with curry, salt, and pepper. Stir into beans and place in a greased 1½-quart casserole. Top with grated cheese. Bake at 350° for 30 minutes. **Yield:** 6 servings.

Mrs. Dan Boyd (Terry)

Green Beans Au Gratin

3 Tablespoons butter
2 Tablespoons flour
1 cup milk
½ cup shredded Swiss cheese
½ teaspoon salt

Pepper, dash
2 cans (16 ounces each) green
  beans, drained
1 cup fresh breadcrumbs
Paprika, dash

Melt 2 tablespoons butter in a saucepan. Blend in flour. Slowly pour in milk, stirring constantly. Continue stirring and cook until thickened. Stir in cheese, salt, and pepper. Do not boil. Place beans in 2-quart baking dish. Pour cheese sauce over beans. Combine remaining butter, crumbs, and paprika. Sprinkle over casserole. Bake at 375° for 20 minutes or until golden brown. **Yield:** 8 servings.

Mrs. Steve Moi (Joanie)

Monterey Jack Green Beans

3 Tablespoons butter
½ cup chopped onion
1 package (9 ounces) French-style green beans, thawed and drained

½ teaspoon salt
½ teaspoon summer savory
⅛ teaspoon pepper
½ cup shredded Monterey Jack cheese

Melt butter in 2-quart saucepan and stir in onion. Cook uncovered over medium heat, stirring occasionally until tender, about 3-5 minutes. Stir in remaining ingredients except cheese. Cover and cook until beans are tender crisp, about 5-7 minutes. Stir occasionally. Sprinkle with cheese, cover, and let stand about one minute. **Yield:** 4-6 servings.

Mrs. John Mearns (June)

Bar-B-Q Baked Beans
Kids Love These!

1 pound ground beef
1½ onions, chopped
2 cans (16 ounces each) pork and beans
½ pound firmly packed brown sugar

¼ cup liquid smoke
½ cup barbeque sauce
2 Tablespoons mustard

Brown meat and onions; drain well. Add remaining ingredients and mix thoroughly. Put into casserole dish. Bake at 350° for 1 hour. **Yield:** 6-8 servings.

Mrs. Donald Hudson (Vickie)

Fancy Baked Beans

1 pound ground beef, browned
1 envelope (1.25 ounces) onion
  soup
2 cans (16 ounces each) pork and
  beans
1 can (16 ounces) kidney beans,
  drained

1 cup ketchup
½ cup cold water
2 Tablespoons mustard
2 teaspoons cider vinegar

Preheat oven to 400°. Combine ingredients and place in greased 2-quart casserole. Bake 30-45 minutes. **Yield:** 8-10 servings.

Note: *Add salad and this is a meal in itself.*

Mrs. Jim Conine (Donna)

Doug's Cajun Red Beans

2 cans (15 ounces each) kidney
  beans
3 slices bacon
1 large onion, chopped
½ cup chopped celery
1 small green pepper, chopped
2 Tablespoons chopped parsley
⅓ cup green onion tops

2 Tablespoons ketchup
1½ teaspoons Worcestershire
  sauce
1 jar (2 ounces) chopped
  pimiento
1 can (8 ounces) tomato sauce
1-2 teaspoons chili powder
Rice, cooked

Place beans in a large saucepan. Fry bacon and crumble into beans. Sauté vegetables in bacon drippings until wilted but not brown, stirring frequently. Add to beans. Add remaining ingredients. Cover and simmer about 30 minutes. Serve over rice. **Yield:** 4 servings.

Note: *Polish sausage, cut into 1-inch sections and prepared according to package directions, may be added at the end of the heating period.*

Mrs. Doug Rivenbark (Penny)

Mamma's Best Beans!

1 pound dried pinto beans	2 Tablespoons firmly packed
¼ pound bacon	brown sugar
1 teaspoon minced garlic	2 teaspoons mustard
1 large onion, chopped	½-1 teaspoon Tabasco sauce
1 large green pepper, chopped	½ teaspoon Worcestershire sauce
2 teaspoons salt	¼ teaspoon pepper
1 can (16 ounces) tomatoes	

Soak beans overnight. Place in a large heavy dutch oven. Cover generously with water to 1 inch below top of pan rim. Bring to a boil. Reduce
heat to simmer, cover, and cook about 1 hour or until tender. Fry bacon
and crumble. In 2 tablespoons of bacon grease, sauté garlic, onion, and
green pepper until onions are translucent. Add to beans along with bacon
and all remaining ingredients. Cover and simmer another hour, stirring
frequently. Add water as necessary. **Yield:** 8-12 servings.

Mrs. Doug Arnold (Debbi)

♥ *Add 1 teaspoon ground ginger to your pot of beans when you start to cook them
to prevent those gas attacks.*

Piquante Beets

1 teaspoon sugar	2 Tablespoons butter
1 Tablespoon vinegar	Nutmeg, dash
½ teaspoon salt	1 can (16 ounces) sliced beets,
1 teaspoon grated onion	not pickled

Cook sugar, vinegar, salt, onion, butter, and nutmeg for 5 minutes. Pour
over hot, drained beets. **Yield:** 4 servings.

Mrs. Terry Chambers (Dianne)

Broccoli Casserole

1 package (10 ounces) frozen chopped broccoli	¼ pound Velveeta cheese
¼ cup butter, melted	⅛ cup milk
	25 Ritz crackers, crushed

Cook broccoli according to directions; drain. Grease 1-quart casserole dish. Place broccoli, ⅛ cup butter, and cheese in dish. Add milk. Combine crackers with remaining ⅛ cup butter. Sprinkle over broccoli. Bake at 350° for 20 minutes. **Yield:** 4-6 servings.

Note: *Broccoli can be cooked in microwave.*

Mrs. Steve Moi (Joanie)

Broccoli Mushroom Casserole

1 large onion, chopped	4 packages (10 ounces each) frozen broccoli spears
½ cup butter	
1 can (10¾ ounces) cream of mushroom soup	1 pound fresh mushrooms, sliced
1½ rolls garlic cheese	1 cup Pepperidge Farm stuffing, crushed

Sauté onion in butter, add soup and cheese. Heat until cheese melts. Cook broccoli spears. Combine with mushrooms and sauce in a buttered 7x11-inch casserole. Sprinkle with stuffing. Bake at 300° for 30 minutes. **Yield:** 10-12 servings.

Mrs. William Hollon (Kasey)

Broccoli Parmesan

1 package (10 ounces) frozen chopped broccoli	½ cup breadcrumbs
5 Tablespoons olive oil	½ cup Parmesan cheese
2 cloves garlic, minced	Salt and pepper, optional

Cook and drain broccoli. In a skillet, heat garlic in olive oil. When hot, add broccoli, breadcrumbs, and Parmesan cheese. Serve when heated thoroughly. Salt and pepper if desired. **Yield:** 4 servings.

Mrs. Ted Denbow (Connie)

Broccoli Supreme

2 packages (10 ounces each)
  frozen chopped broccoli
¼ cup chopped onion
6 Tablespoons butter or
  margarine

2 Tablespoons flour
½ cup water
1 jar (8 ounces) Cheese Whiz
3 eggs, beaten
½ cup cracker crumbs

Thaw and drain broccoli. Sauté onions in 4 tablespoons melted butter. Stir in flour and water and cook until mixed. Blend in cheese. Combine sauce with broccoli and eggs. Put into 1½-quart casserole dish. Mix crumbs with 2 tablespoons melted butter and sprinkle over broccoli mixture. Bake at 350° for 30 minutes. **Yield:** 8 servings.

Mrs. Jeff Farmer (Kaliko)

Champagne Broccoli

2 pounds broccoli, cut
  into florets
4 Tablespoons butter
4 Tablespoons flour
1 cup champagne

1 cup chicken broth
1½ cups grated Gruyère cheese
½ cup grated Monterey Jack
  cheese
½ cup slivered almonds

Steam broccoli lightly, approximately 4 minutes. The broccoli should be undercooked. Rinse, drain, and set aside. In a saucepan, melt butter and stir in flour. Cook over medium heat, stirring for 2 minutes. Add champagne and chicken broth and cook until thickened. Arrange broccoli in a buttered casserole. Sprinkle with grated cheeses. Pour champagne sauce over casserole. Sprinkle with almonds. Bake at 350° for 20-25 minutes. **Yield:** Approximately 8 servings.

Mrs. Richard Keeling (Laurie)

Easy Fancy Broccoli

2 packages (10 ounces each) frozen
  broccoli
1 can (10¾ ounces) cream of
  chicken soup

½ cup mayonnaise
¼ cup breadcrumbs
Paprika

Arrange frozen broccoli in baking dish. Combine soup and mayonnaise and pour over broccoli. Sprinkle with breadcrumbs and paprika. Bake at 300° for 30 minutes. **Yield:** 8 servings.

Mrs. Paul Carletta (Mary Ann)

Myra's Crumb Broccoli

1½ pounds broccoli or 3 boxes (10 ounces each) frozen
1 can (10¾ ounces) cream of mushroom soup
¼ cup mayonnaise
¼ cup grated American cheese
1 Tablespoon pimiento
1½ teaspoons lemon juice
⅓ cup crushed Ritz crackers

Cook broccoli and drain. Put into 1½-quart baking dish. Mix remaining ingredients, and top with crackers. Bake uncovered at 350° for 35 minutes. **Yield:** 4-6 servings.

Mrs. Wallace Brown (Gayle)

Yummy Broccoli and Rice Dish

1 cup chopped onion
1 cup chopped celery
4 Tablespoons butter or margarine
2 packages (10 ounces each) frozen chopped broccoli
1 cup uncooked rice
1 can (10¾ ounces) cream of chicken soup
1 can (5 ounces) evaporated milk
1 jar (8 ounces) Cheese Whiz

Sauté onion and celery in butter. Cook broccoli slightly and drain. Combine broccoli, celery, onion, and rice. Blend soup, milk, and Cheese Whiz. Add to broccoli mixture. Bake at 350° for 30 minutes. **Yield:** 6-8 servings.

Mrs. Pete Bennett (Stephanie)

Broccoli Cauliflower Casserole

1 package (10 ounces) frozen cauliflower
1 package (10 ounces) frozen broccoli
1 cup mayonnaise
1 can (11 ounces) Cheddar cheese soup
1 can (6½ ounces) sliced water chestnuts
2-3 green onions, chopped, including tops
Tabasco sauce to taste
Paprika

Cook cauliflower and broccoli until thawed. Combine all ingredients and sprinkle with paprika. Place in 9x13-inch baking dish. Bake at 375° for 45 minutes. **Yield:** Approximately 8 servings.

Mrs. Jack Hamer (Pam)

Terrific Cauliflower

1 medium head cauliflower
Salt and pepper to taste
1 cup sour cream

1 cup grated sharp American
cheese
3 teaspoons sesame seeds, toasted

Break cauliflower into florets. Cook, covered, in a small amount of salted water for 10-15 minutes. Drain well. Place half of cauliflower in 1-quart dish. Season with salt and pepper. Spread ½ cup sour cream and sprinkle with ½ cup cheese. Top with 1½ teaspoons sesame seeds. Repeat layer. Bake at 350° until cheese melts and sour cream is hot, about 15 minutes. **Yield:** 6 servings.

Mrs. Joe Key (Christie)

♥ *To keep cauliflower white while cooking, add a little milk to the water.*

♥ *Cook vegetables in chicken stock, beef stock, or consummé for a flavor variation.*

Nutty Carrots

5   cups carrot sticks, cut into
    3-inch pieces
1½ cups water
½   teaspoon salt
½   cup butter, melted
2   teaspoons honey
1   teaspoon salt

¼ teaspoon coarsely ground
   pepper
2 Tablespoons fresh lemon juice
¼ teaspoon freshly grated lemon
   peel
½ cup coarsely broken walnuts

Cook carrots in water with salt until tender. Drain completely. Meanwhile, heat all other ingredients, except walnuts. Pour sauce over hot carrots. Toss with walnuts. **Yield:** 8 servings.

Mrs. Jack Hamer (Pam)

Chuckwagon Carrots

3 cups carrots, sliced ¼-inch thick
3 Tablespoons butter
¼ cup bacon, cooked and crumbled
2 Tablespoons thinly sliced green onions

1 Tablespoon firmly packed brown sugar
¼ teaspoon salt
⅛ teaspoon pepper

Bring 1 cup water to a boil in a 2-quart saucepan and add carrots. Cover and cook over medium heat until carrots are tender crisp, about 10-12 minutes. Drain and set aside. In same saucepan, melt butter. Stir in carrots and remaining ingredients. Cover and cook over medium heat, stirring occasionally, about 5-7 minutes. **Yield:** 4 (½ cup) servings.

Mrs. John Mearns (June)

Marinated Carrots

3½ cups sliced carrots
¼ cup Italian dressing
¼ cup Green Goddess dressing
¼ cup grated onion

¼ teaspoon salt
½ teaspoon pepper
1 teaspoon dill seed
1 teaspoon parsley flakes

Cook carrots until tender. Mix remaining ingredients and pour over carrots. Refrigerate 1 day before serving. **Yield:** 6-8 servings.

Note: *Great cold vegetable dish for a luncheon.*

Mrs. Bill Frank (Barbara)

Carrot Casserole

2 pounds carrots, scraped and sliced
1 small onion, chopped
1 green pepper, chopped
½ cup butter or margarine

1 cup mayonnaise
3-4 cups finely crushed Ritz crackers, reserve enough for topping

Cook carrots in boiling water until tender. Drain. Sauté onion and pepper in butter. Blend in carrots and mayonnaise. Sprinkle bottom of 9x13-inch casserole with cracker crumbs. Pour carrot mixture over crackers and top with remaining crumbs. Bake at 350° for 20-30 minutes. **Yield:** 8-10 servings.

Mrs. Joe Key (Christie)

Quick-Easy Carrots with Wine

2 pounds carrots, sliced
  1-inch long
3 ribs celery, chopped
1 onion, chopped
1 cup dry white wine

⅓ cup sugar
¼ cup butter
½ teaspoon dill weed
Salt and pepper, dash

Combine all ingredients. Simmer covered, until carrots are tender crisp, about 25-45 minutes. **Yield:** 8-10 servings.

Mrs. Richard Keeling (Laurie)

Baked Corn

4 Tablespoons margarine
4 Tablespoons flour
2 cups milk
4 eggs, beaten

2 Tablespoons sugar
1 teaspoon salt
2 cans (16 ounces each) corn,
  drained

Melt margarine, add flour and blend. Pour in milk and bring mixture to boil. Boil until thickened. Add eggs, sugar, salt, and corn. Mix well. Pour into 2-quart baking dish. Bake at 350° for 1 hour or until set. **Yield:** 8-10 servings.

Mrs. Jim Conine (Donna)

Grandma's Corn Pudding
As Good as the Frozen Favorite

1½ cups milk, warmed in
  microwave
2 cans (17 ounces each) cream-
  style corn
3 Tablespoons sugar
6 eggs, brought to room
  temperature

2 heaping Tablespoons cornstarch
1 teaspoon salt
4 Tablespoons butter
¼ teaspoon paprika

Combine all ingredients except paprika and mix well. Pour into greased 9x13-inch pan. Bake at 325° for 1 hour. Sprinkle with paprika after baking. **Yield:** 8-12 servings.

Note: *To bring eggs to room temperature more quickly, microwave on the defrost cycle for 2-3 minutes. This dish may be frozen, but will fall somewhat.*

Mrs. Felix Mitchell (Valerie)

Mexican Corn Casserole
Olé–A Nice Change from Beans and Rice when Serving Mexican Food

1 cup butter
2 packages (8 ounces each)
  cream cheese
¾ cup milk
1 can (4 ounces) chopped green
  chilies

4 cans (16 ounces each) shoepeg
  corn, drained
Tabasco sauce, dash
½ cup grated Cheddar cheese

Melt butter in saucepan and blend in cream cheese. Add milk and mix together. Add green chilies, corn, and Tabasco sauce. Put in 9x13-inch casserole dish and top with cheese. Bake at 350° for 30-40 minutes. **Yield:** 12 servings.

Mrs. Winston Borum (Jimmie)

Layered Cheese Vegetable Bake

1 large onion, chopped
1 large green pepper, cut into
  1-inch pieces
1 Tablespoon salad oil
1 eggplant, peeled, cut into
  1-inch pieces
½ pound mushrooms, sliced

1 large tomato, chopped
1 teaspoon salt
½ teaspoon Italian seasoning
¼ teaspoon or less pepper
Butter
1 cup cornbread stuffing
2 cups grated Swiss cheese

Sauté onion and green pepper in oil for 3 minutes. Add eggplant and mushrooms; cook 4 minutes. Stir in tomato and seasoning. Butter a casserole dish and place stuffing on bottom. Layer vegetables and cheese. Repeat. Bake at 350° for 30 minutes. **Yield:** 8-12 servings.

Mrs. William Hollon (Kasey)

Eggplant Patties

1 medium eggplant, pared and cubed	2 Tablespoons chopped onion
1¼ cups crushed Ritz crackers	1 clove garlic, minced
1¼ cups shredded Cheddar cheese	½ teaspoon salt
2 eggs, slightly beaten	⅛ teaspoon pepper
2 Tablespoons minced parsley	Salad oil

In a covered saucepan, cook eggplant in boiling water, about 5 minutes. Drain very well and mash. Stir in remaining ingredients. Shape into patties and fry about 3 minutes on each side in heated oil. **Yield:** 8-10 patties.

Mrs. Jack Hamer (Pam)

♥ *Vegetables that grow underground should be cooked covered. Those that grow above the ground should be left uncovered.*

Perfect Fried Eggplant

2 eggs, beaten	3 Tablespoons grated Parmesan cheese
½ teaspoon salt	
Pepper, dash	1 medium eggplant
1 cup packaged Italian dry breadcrumbs	Salad oil or shortening for frying
	Salt to taste

In a shallow dish mix eggs, salt, and pepper. On waxed paper, mix breadcrumbs and cheese. Cut an unpeeled eggplant crosswise into ⅛-inch thick slices. Dip in egg, then crumb mixture, coating completely. In a large, heavy skillet, slowly heat salad oil (at least ¼-inch deep). Sauté eggplant until golden brown, about 3 minutes on both sides. Drain on paper towels. Sprinkle with salt to taste. Serve with favorite dip. **Yield:** 4 servings.

Mrs. Doug Arnold (Debbi)

Hominy Casserole
Great with Brisket and Ham

2 cans (29 ounces each) white
hominy
Butter
2 cans (4 ounces each) green
chilies, minced

Salt and cracked pepper to taste
1 carton (8 ounces) sour cream
½ cup half and half
1 cup grated Monterey Jack
cheese

Drain and rinse hominy. Generously butter a 3-quart casserole. Layer ingredients as follows: hominy, green chilies, salt, pepper, dots of sour cream, and butter; repeat layers ending with layer of hominy. Dot top with butter and pour half and half over it. Sprinkle with cheese. Bake at 350° for 25-30 minutes. **Yield:** 8-10 servings.

Mrs. Bill Frank (Barbara)

Louise Cole's Cheesy Hominy
Never Neglect Hominy Again

6 slices bacon
1 can (10 ounces) Rotel tomatoes
and green chilies, drained
(reserve ⅓ of liquid)

1 can (15½ ounces) yellow
hominy, drained
1 can (11 ounces) cheese soup
1 small onion, diced

Cook bacon until crisp, then break into pieces. Cut up tomatoes from drained Rotel. Mix all ingredients including ⅓ of the liquid from the Rotel. Bake at 350° for 30 minutes. **Yield:** 6 servings.

Mrs. Marvin Chronister (Donna)

Mushrooms Bourguignon

½ cup butter
1 cup dry red wine or beef broth
1 Tablespoon finely chopped
   green onions
½ teaspoon garlic salt

½ teaspoon dill weed
¼ teaspoon salt
Pepper, dash
1 pound mushrooms

Melt butter in skillet. Add next 6 ingredients. Clean mushrooms and arrange, caps down, in sauce. Cover and simmer 20 minutes. **Yield:** 5-6 servings.

Note: *May cook in microwave on medium setting for 8-10 minutes.*

                                      Mrs. Jim Conine (Donna)

Mushrooms in Wine
This dish is delicious. Do not be dismayed by the time. It's worth it.

1 cup butter
1 cup boiling water
2 beef bouillon cubes
2 chicken bouillon cubes
2 cups Burgundy wine
2 teaspoons Worcestershire sauce
½ teaspoon dill seed

½ teaspoon pepper
1½ teaspoons monosodium
   glutamate
½ teaspoon garlic powder
1½ pounds fresh small
   mushrooms

Combine all ingredients except mushrooms in a large pot. Bring to slow boil over medium heat. Add mushrooms. Reduce to simmer. Cook 5-6 hours with pot covered. Then remove lid. Mushrooms will get very dark. Cook another 3-4 hours. Serve in a chafing dish with picks or as a side dish. **Yield:** 6-8 servings.

Note: *Can be frozen in 2 cup quantities. Use a crock pot if you have one for more carefree cooking. Excellent over brisket or steak.*

                                      Mrs. Gerald Box (Pat)

Baked Curried Onions

1 pound small white cooking onions	¼ teaspoon paprika
1 cup water	2 bouillon cubes
3 Tablespoons butter	1 cup milk
2 Tablespoons flour	3 ounces shredded Longhorn Cheddar cheese
¼ teaspoon Cayenne	6 slices whole wheat bread, toasted and quartered
¼ teaspoon curry powder	

Place onions in saucepan with water, cover and simmer for 10 minutes. Drain and set aside. In a double boiler, melt butter and stir in flour and seasonings. Add bouillon cubes and stir in milk gradually. Add cheese, reserving a few tablespoons to spread on top. Stir constantly until mixture is very thick. Place toast in buttered 2-quart casserole and cover with onions. Pour sauce over onions and top with reserved cheese. Bake at 350° for 20-30 minutes. **Yield:** 4-6 servings.

Mrs. Richard Keeling (Laurie)

Batter for Onion Rings or Vegetables

1½ cups flour	Salt to taste
1 can beer	

Combine ingredients. Let stand 3-4 hours. Dip vegetables of your choice into batter and deep fry. **Yield:** 1¾ cups.

Mrs. Jim Thornton (Jackie)

Green Peas with Celery and Olives

1 Tablespoon butter	20 large pitted ripe olives, halved
1 Tablespoon salad oil	½ teaspoon salt
2 cups celery, ¼-inch sliced	¼ teaspoon pepper
2 packages (10 ounces each) frozen green peas, slightly thawed	

Melt butter; add oil and celery, cover and cook over low heat for 10 minutes. Add peas and continue to cook until peas are heated through. Add olives, salt and pepper. **Yield:** 4-6 servings.

Mrs. Dan Boyd (Terry)

Snow Peas and Water Chestnuts

2 Tablespoons salad oil
¼ cup chopped green onions
1 can (5 ounces) sliced water
   chestnuts, drained
2 cups (½ pound) fresh snow
   peas, ends trimmed
1 teaspoon sugar

1 teaspoon monosodium
   glutatmate
½ cup chicken broth
2 teaspoons cornstarch
Salt
White pepper

Heat oil in large skillet. Add onions; cook and stir until tender (not brown). Add water chestnuts, snow peas, sugar, MSG, and 6 tablespoons of the chicken broth. Bring to a boil; separate pods with a fork. Cover and cook 2 minutes. Blend remaining 2 tablespoons broth and cornstarch; stir into peas. When clear and thick, season with salt and white pepper. **Yield:** 4-5 servings.

Mrs. Sam Norvell (Patsy)

Baked Potatoes with Mushrooms

4 medium baking potatoes,
   washed and pierced with fork
3 Tablespoons butter
2 cups (6 ounces) fresh
   mushrooms, sliced ¼-inch thick

⅓ cup green onion, sliced ⅛-inch
⅛ teaspoon garlic powder
2 Tablespoons crumbled blue
   cheese

Bake potatoes in 350° oven for 60-75 minutes or until fork tender. Meanwhile, melt butter in 8-inch skillet. Stir in remaining ingredients except blue cheese. Cook over medium heat, uncovered, for about 2-4 minutes until mushrooms are tender crisp, stirring occasionally. Remove from heat and stir in blue cheese. Spoon into hot split baked potatoes. **Yield:** 4 servings.

Mrs. John Mearns (June)

♥ *Reheat baked potatoes by dipping them in hot water and baking again in a moderate oven.*

♥ *Mashed potatoes will be fluffier if a pinch of baking soda is added along with the milk and butter. Using hot milk when mashing potatoes keeps them from becoming soggy or heavy.*

Loaded Baked Potatoes

2 large Idaho potatoes
4 strips bacon, quartered
¼ cup chopped shallots
½ cup sour cream
2 Tablespoons Parmesan cheese
½ teaspoon salt

½ teaspoon pepper
3 Tablespoons Miracle Whip
   salad dressing
¼ cup margarine
Paprika

Preheat oven to 400° for 20 minutes. Scrub potatoes well and bake for 1 hour. Cook bacon until crisp, reserving 3 tablespoons fat. Slowly sauté shallots in fat. When potatoes are done, cut in half lengthwise and scoop out into skillet. Retain shells intact. Add bacon, shallots, sour cream, cheese, salt, pepper, Miracle Whip, and margarine and mix thoroughly. Stuff into potato skins and sprinkle with paprika. Turn oven down to 350° and bake for 15-20 minutes. **Yield:** 4 servings.

Note: *May also sprinkle Parmesan cheese on top prior to baking.*

Mrs. Richard Keeling (Laurie)

Baked Potato Casserole

10 medium potatoes, cooked
Butter
2 Tablespoons bacon bits
2 cups sour cream

2 cups grated Cheddar cheese
1 bunch green onions, tops only,
   chopped

Mash potatoes as you would for mashed potatoes. Add extra butter. Combine bacon bits and potatoes and put into 7x11-inch baking dish. Top with sour cream, cheese, and green onions. Bake at 350° about 30 minutes or until cheese melts and casserole is hot. **Yield:** 12 servings.

Note: *May use more bacon and less onion.*

Mrs. Steve Moi (Joanie)

♥ *Fresh potatoes should be cooked in boiling water. Old potatoes should be placed in cold water and brought to a boil.*

Easy Potato Casserole

1 package (32 ounces) frozen shredded hash brown potatoes, thawed
½ cup chopped onion
½ cup chopped green pepper
1 can (10¾ ounces) cream of potato soup

1 can (10¾ ounces) cream of celery soup
1 carton (8 ounces) sour cream
Salt
Pepper
1 cup shredded Cheddar cheese

Preheat oven to 325°. Combine all ingredients except cheese. Toss thoroughly to coat potatoes. Spoon mixture into greased, shallow 2-quart casserole. Bake 1 hour 15 minutes. Sprinkle with cheese and bake an additional 15 minutes. **Yield:** 8-10 servings.

Mrs. Steve Moi (Joanie)

Parmesan Roasted Potatoes

½-¾ cup butter or margarine
1 teaspoon garlic powder
4-6 baking potatoes

1 cup fine breadcrumbs
½ cup Parmesan cheese
Seasoned salt

About 1 hour before preparing potatoes, melt butter and add garlic powder. Peel potatoes and slice lengthwise into quarters. Mix breadcrumbs and cheese. Roll potatoes in butter and then crumb mixture. Sprinkle with seasoned salt. Roast at 350° until golden brown, about 45-60 minutes. **Yield:** 6-8 servings.

Mrs. Joe Key (Christie)

Scalloped Potatoes
Quick, Easy, and Delicious!

4 potatoes
½ cup diced onion
¼ cup celery leaves
1 Tablespoon parsley
3 Tablespoons flour

1 Tablespoon butter
1½ teaspoons salt
½ teaspoon pepper
1½ cups milk
2 cups grated sharp cheese

Peel potatoes, cook slightly, and slice. Place in buttered 2-quart casserole. Combine remaining ingredients except cheese in blender. Pour mixture over potatoes. Top with cheese. Bake at 350° for 1 hour. **Yield:** 6-8 servings.

Mrs. Joe Key (Christie)

Sour Cream Cheese Potatoes

6 medium potatoes
1 can (10¾ ounces) cream of
   chicken soup
4 Tablespoons butter

1½ cups grated Longhorn
   Cheddar cheese
½ cup chopped green onion
1   carton (8 ounces) sour cream

Boil potatoes in jackets until just tender. *Don't overcook.* Slice the cooked potatoes into a 9x13-inch baking pan. In medium saucepan, heat soup, butter, cheese, and onion. When cheese melts, add sour cream, then mix well and pour over potatoes. Bake uncovered at 350° for 40 minutes. **Yield:** 6-8 servings.

Mrs. Greg Smith (Katie)

Oven Fries

4-6 medium baking potatoes
¼ cup salad oil
¼ teaspoon pepper

½ teaspoon seasoned salt
Paprika

Scrub potatoes and cut each into 6 lengthwise wedges. Place potatoes, skin side down, in shallow baking dish or cookie sheet. Combine oil, pepper, and seasoned salt. Brush potatoes with this mixture. Sprinkle lightly with paprika and bake at 400° for 45-50 minutes or until potatoes are tender and lightly browned. Baste once or twice with remaining oil mixture while baking. **Yield:** 4-6 servings.

Mrs. Jack Hamer (Pam)

Easy New Potatoes

2-3 pounds small new potatoes
Salt & pepper to taste

5-6 Tablespoons butter or
   margarine, melted

In salted water, boil potatoes in their skins for 15 minutes. (This can be done early in the day). Drain and refrigerate. One hour before serving, place potatoes into a 9x13-inch pan. Preheat oven to 350°. Cover potatoes with salt, pepper, and butter; turn to coat. Bake for 1 hour, until skins are crispy. **Yield:** 8 servings.

Mrs. Dennis Furlong (Dede)

Joyce's Sweet Potato Casserole
Great for Thanksgiving

2 eggs
1 cup sugar
6 Tablespoons margarine, softened
1 teaspoon vanilla extract
½ cup milk
3 cups cooked and mashed sweet potatoes

Topping:
1 cup firmly packed brown sugar
2 Tablespoons margarine
⅓ cup flour
1 cup chopped pecans

Beat eggs; add sugar, margarine, vanilla, milk, and sweet potatoes. Pour into 1-quart buttered casserole.

Topping: Mix brown sugar, margarine, and flour until it looks like cornmeal. Spread on top of sweet potato mixture. Cover with pecans and pat down with hand. Bake at 350° for 45 minutes. **Yield:** 6-8 servings.

Mrs. Thomas Hunter (Lynda)

♥ *Any fresh or frozen vegetable can be cooked in the oven. Place the vegetable in a covered dish, add salt and 2 tablespoons of butter. Cook at 350° to desired doneness.*

Southern Comfort Sweet Potatoes

4 pounds sweet potatoes
½ cup butter
¼ cup Southern Comfort
⅓ cup orange juice
¼ cup firmly packed brown sugar
½ teaspoon cinnamon

⅛ teaspoon nutmeg
⅛ teaspoon cloves
1 teaspoon salt
½ cup chopped pecans
1 Tablespoon shredded orange rind

Cook washed potatoes in water for 35 minutes. Drain and peel. Mash with butter. Add Southern Comfort, juice, sugar, and spices. Put into a 1½-quart buttered casserole. Top with nuts and orange rind. Bake at 350° for 20-30 minutes. **Yield:** 6-8 servings.

Mrs. William Hollon (Kasey)

Dressed-Up Rice

1 box (14 ounces) instant rice	½ cup chopped parsley
1 medium green pepper, chopped	2½-3 cartons (16 ounces each) sour
½ cup chopped green onion	cream
½ cup butter	1 cup grated Cheddar cheese

Cook the rice per directions on box. Sauté the green pepper and green onions in butter. Add parsley and sauté another minute or two. Stir in the rice, sour cream, and cheese. Place in an 11-inch glass dish or a 2-2½-quart casserole dish. Brown in oven at 350° for about 30 minutes. **Yield:** 12 servings.

Note: *Best if made day before, and it freezes well. Baking time may vary with size and temperature of dish.*

Mrs. Bill Frank (Barbara)

♥ *To keep cooked rice warm, place in a colander over simmering water and cover with cloth or paper towels.*

♥ *Rice will be drier and fluffier if a slice of dry bread is placed on top of it after cooking and draining.*

Jalapeño Rice Texas Style
Rice with a Texas Flair

1 onion, finely chopped	1 can (10¾ ounces) beef bouillon
1 cup uncooked rice	3 cups grated Cheddar cheese
2 Tablespoons salad oil	Half and half
1-3 jalapeño peppers, finely chopped	

Brown onion and rice in hot oil. Add jalapeños and bouillon. When rice has absorbed all liquid, layer rice and cheese in a 2-quart baking dish. Pour cream to the top of the rice. Cover tightly with foil and bake at 350° for 45 minutes. **Yield:** 6 servings.

Note: *Beef bouillon may be made with a cube.*

Mrs. Doug Rivenbark (Penny)

Fantastic Rice

1 package (5 ounces) brown and wild rice mix
½ cup chopped green onion
2 cups sliced fresh mushrooms

3 Tablespoons butter, melted
½ teaspoon garlic salt
¼ cup dry white wine
½ cup sliced natural almonds

Prepare rice according to package directions. Sauté onion and mushrooms in butter. Add garlic salt and wine. Cook over medium high heat until all the liquid is absorbed. Stir this mixture into the rice, add the almonds, and mix well. **Yield:** 4-6 servings.

Mrs. Thomas Hunter (Lynda)

Green Chili Rice
Great with Ham or Brisket

1 cup chopped onion
¼ cup butter, melted
4 cups cooked rice
1 carton (16 ounces) cottage cheese
1 carton (16 ounces) sour cream

2 cups grated Cheddar cheese
2 cans (4 ounces each) chopped green chilies, drained
⅔ teaspoon salt
⅛ teaspoon pepper
¼ cup chopped parsley

Sauté onion in butter. Combine all ingredients in a large casserole. Mix well. Bake at 375° for 30 minutes. **Yield:** 8-12 servings.

Note: *Can be made ahead, refrigerated, and baked when needed.*

Mrs. James Layton (Vicki)

♥ *Scorched rice can be helped by placing a piece of fresh white bread crust over the rice and covering the pot. Within a few minutes, remove the bread and the scorched taste will have disappeared.*

♥ *Toss rice with two forks or stir with one fork, as the use of a spoon bruises the grains and makes them sticky.*

Golden Rice

½ cup thinly sliced green onions
½ cup shredded carrot
2 Tablespoons butter
1 cup apple or orange juice
1 cup water
1 cup uncooked long grain rice
½ cup golden raisins
1 Tablespoon firmly packed
   brown sugar

1 teaspoon salt
¼ teaspoon pepper
½ teaspoon curry powder
¼ teaspoon cinnamon
¼ teaspoon ginger
½ cup chopped peanuts or
   cashews

In a medium saucepan, cook and stir onions and carrot in butter until tender crisp. Stir in juice, water, and remaining ingredients except peanuts. Heat to boiling. Reduce heat. Cover and simmer until rice is tender and liquid is absorbed; 20-30 minutes. Stir in nuts just before serving. **Yield:** 4-6 servings.

Note: *This is a great accompaniment for chicken curry dishes!*

Mrs. Richard Keeling (Laurie)

♥ *Burned food can be removed from an enamel saucepan by filling the pan with cold water containing 2-3 tablespoons salt, and allowing to stand overnight. The next day cover and bring water to a boil.*

Rice with Mushrooms
Simple and Delicious

1⅓ cups long grain rice, uncooked
2 cans (10½ ounces each) beef
   consummé
1 can (4 ounces) mushrooms,
   drained

1 medium onion, chopped
1 stick margarine

Mix uncooked rice, consummé, mushrooms, and onion in 2-quart casserole dish. Cut stick of margarine into slices (about 10) and place on top. Cover. Bake at 425° for 45 minutes or until consummé is absorbed. **Yield:** 6 servings.

Mrs. Terry Chambers (Dianne)

Spanish Rice

½ cup margarine
1 medium onion, chopped
1 cup chopped celery
2 large ripe tomatoes, chopped

½ teaspoon salt
1 can (4 ounces) mushrooms, drained
2 cups rice, cooked

Melt margarine in skillet. Sauté onion, celery, tomatoes, and salt. Add mushrooms and cook for 1 minute. Pour over rice and toss. Let stand for 15-20 minutes before serving. **Yield:** 6 servings.

Mrs. Terry Chambers (Dianne)

Tuta Roberts' Curried Rice

6 Tablespoons margarine
1½ teaspoons salt
1 teaspoon curry powder
1½ cups Uncle Ben's converted rice

2 cans (14½ ounces each) chicken broth, unsalted

Mix margarine, salt, and curry powder in skillet. Melt, stirring constantly. Add rice and brown lightly. Be careful not to burn margarine. Add one can of broth. Stir. Cover and cook slowly until tender. Do not bring to rapid boil. Add second can of broth as needed, adding small amount at a time. **Yield:** 4 servings.

Mrs. Robert Lusk (Sharon)

Spinach Au Gratin with Artichoke Hearts

1 can (14 ounces) artichoke hearts (8-10 hearts)
1 Tablespoon butter
3 packages (10 ounces each) frozen chopped spinach

1 package (8 ounces) cream cheese, softened by adding
2 Tablespoons milk
Salt and pepper to taste
1 cup grated Swiss cheese or
½ cup Parmesan cheese

Sauté artichoke hearts in melted butter. Place in 3-quart casserole and set aside. Cook spinach as directed on package and drain so that no moisture remains. Mix with softened cream cheese and salt and pepper. Spread over artichokes. Sprinkle with cheese. Cook uncovered at 350° for 15 minutes or until cheese melts and browns. **Yield:** 6-8 servings.

Mrs. John Mearns (June)

Spinach Provencale

1 onion, chopped
½ pound fresh mushrooms,
    thinly sliced
¼ cup butter
2 packages (10 ounces each)
    frozen chopped spinach,
    cooked and drained or 2 bags
    (10 ounces each) fresh spinach,
    cooked and chopped
1 Tablespoon lemon juice

1 teaspoon Dijon mustard
½ teaspoon salt
½ cup sour cream
2 large ripe tomatoes, sliced
    ¼-inch thick
Salt and pepper to taste
1 cup grated sharp Cheddar
    cheese
1 cup grated mozzarella cheese

Preheat oven to 375°. In a large skillet, sauté the onion and mushrooms in butter until soft. Add the next five ingredients and remove from heat. Place spinach mixture in bottom of a shallow baking dish. Layer ½ of the tomatoes, salt, pepper, and ½ of the cheeses. Repeat layer. Bake for 30 minutes or until bubbly. **Yield:** 8 servings.

Mrs. Donald Robson (Karen)

Fresh Spinach Casserole
Great Side Dish

1 package (10 ounces) fresh
    spinach
3 eggs, beaten
6 Tablespoons flour
1 teaspoon salt

¼ teaspoon pepper
Onion powder, dash
2 cups low fat cottage cheese
2 cups grated Cheddar cheese

Wash, remove spine and chop spinach. Beat eggs and flour until smooth. Mix all ingredients together and place into a 2-quart casserole. Bake uncovered at 350° for 1 hour. Let stand a few minutes before serving. **Yield:** 6-8 servings.

Mrs. Dennis Furlong (Dede)

Special Spinach
Easy and Excellent

2 packages (10 ounces each) frozen chopped spinach
6 slices bacon, diced
4 green onions, tops and bottoms, chopped

1 small onion, chopped
¼ cup breadcrumbs
1 cup sliced mushrooms
Salt and pepper to taste

Cook spinach according to directions, drain. Fry bacon, remove from pan and dice. Sauté onions in drippings. Add breadcrumbs, mushrooms, spinach, bacon, and seasonings. Bake in casserole at 350° for 20 minutes. **Yield:** 8-10 servings.

Mrs. William Hollon (Kasey)

Baked Tomatoes

1 quart stewed tomatoes
3 ounces seasoned croutons
6 Tablespoons firmly packed brown sugar

¼ teaspoon salt
¼ teaspoon pepper
Basil, pinch
¼ cup butter or margarine, melted

Combine all ingredients. Mix well. Place in 7-inch glass dish. Cover and bake at 350° for 1 hour. **Yield:** 8 servings.

Note: *May add another ½ can of tomatoes and more seasoned croutons for extra servings.*

Mrs. Bill Frank (Barbara)

Baked Puff Tomatoes

3 tomatoes, cut in half
Morton Nature's Seasons

1 cup mayonnaise
4 Tablespoons Parmesan cheese

Place tomato halves in shallow ovenproof dish. Sprinkle with seasoning. Warm in 300° oven for 5-10 minutes. Cool. Combine mayonnaise and cheese; spread over tomatoes. Before serving, place tomatoes under broiler until puffy and lightly browned. **Yield:** 6 servings.

Mrs. Jerry Leatherman (Diana)

Spinach Stuffed Tomatoes

1 package (10 ounces) frozen
  spinach
¼ cup whipping cream
1 teaspoon lemon juice
⅓ cup buttermilk salad dressing

¼ cup grated Parmesan cheese
¼ teaspoon white pepper
3 medium tomatoes, fully ripe
Salt and pepper to taste
Butter or margarine

Defrost spinach and drain by squeezing until dry. Combine cream, lemon juice, dressing, cheese, and white pepper. Add spinach. Cut tomatoes in half and remove pulp. Salt and pepper the remaining shell. Fill with spinach mixture and dot with butter. Bake at 375° for 20 minutes. **Yield:** 6 servings.

Note: *Nice served with shrimp.*

Mrs. Jerry Brown (Linda)

Stuffed Tomatoes

6 tomatoes
1 onion, chopped
1 green pepper, chopped
¼ cup butter

¼-½ cup herb stuffing
Sour cream
Parmesan cheese, grated

Cut tomatoes in half. Scoop out pulp and place in mixing bowl. Sauté onion and green pepper in butter. Stir into the tomato pulp. Add enough stuffing to thicken and stuff tomatoes. Top with sour cream. Sprinkle with cheese. Broil for 10 minutes. **Yield:** 6 servings.

Mrs. Greg Smith (Katie)

Skillet Squash

¼ cup margarine
4 cups thinly sliced yellow
  squash
1 onion, sliced

1 teaspoon salt
Pepper
2 tomatoes, sliced
½ cup grated American cheese

Melt margarine in large skillet. Add all other ingredients except cheese. Cook covered until tender. Do not overcook. Sprinkle with cheese and heat until melted. **Yield:** 4-6 servings.

Mrs. Wallace Brown (Gayle)

Harvest Acorn Squash
Great for the Holidays

2 medium acorn squash
½ cup water
¼ cup butter, softened
⅓ cup chopped pecans

¼ cup firmly packed brown sugar
¼ teaspoon mace, optional
2 teaspoons vanilla extract

Preheat oven to 400°. Cut squash in half lengthwise and remove seeds. Place squash in ungreased 8x12-inch baking dish, cut side up. Pour water into dish and set aside. Combine remaining ingredients and mix. Divide mixture between squash halves evenly. Cover and bake for 35-45 minutes, or until tender. **Yield:** 4 servings.

Mrs. John Mearns (June)

Country Squash Pie

1 unbaked 10-inch pie shell
2 medium zucchini, thinly sliced
2 medium yellow crookneck
  squash, sliced
1 small onion, sliced
1 medium tomato, chopped
1 small green pepper, chopped
1 stalk celery, chopped

1 clove garlic, minced
1 teaspoon salt
½ teaspoon pepper
½ teaspoon basil
2 Tablespoons butter, melted
3 eggs, beaten
½ cup whipping cream
¼ cup Parmesan cheese

Bake pie shell at 450° for 8 minutes or until lightly browned. Cool. Sauté vegetables, garlic, salt, pepper, basil, and butter in a large skillet until tender. Spoon into pie shell and spread evenly. Combine eggs and cream, mixing well. Pour over vegetables. Sprinkle with cheese. Bake at 350° for 30 minutes. **Yield:** 6-8 servings.

Mrs. Richard Keeling (Laurie)

Scrumptious Baked Squash

3 pounds yellow summer squash, sliced
½ cup chopped onion
¾ cup cracker meal or breadcrumbs
½ teaspoon pepper

2 eggs
1 teaspoon sugar
½ teaspoon salt, optional
½ cup butter, melted
8-10 crackers

Cook sliced squash in water until tender. Drain well and mash with potato masher. Add all ingredients except ½ of the melted butter and the crackers. Pour mixture into non-greased loaf baking dish, then pour the rest of the butter and cracker crumbs on top. Bake at 375° for 50 minutes or until brown. **Yield:** 4-6 servings.

Mrs. Doug Arnold (Debbi)

Squash Au Gratin

1-2 pounds squash
½ cup chopped onion
½ cup chopped green pepper
½ cup chopped water chestnuts
¼ cup butter
½ cup grated Cheddar cheese

½ cup mayonnaise
1 teaspoon sugar
1 egg, beaten
Salt and pepper to taste
Club crackers, crushed
Paprika

Wash, remove skin, and slice squash. Steam or cook in boiling water. Drain and mash. Sauté onions, green pepper, and chestnuts in butter. Add to squash. Fold in cheese, mayonnaise, sugar, and egg. Season to taste with salt and pepper. Pour mixture into greased 1½-quart casserole. Top with cracker crumbs and dust with paprika. Bake in preheated oven at 350° for 30 minutes. **Yield:** 6-8 servings.

Mrs. Doug Rivenbark (Penny)

♥ *The cardinal rule for cooking vegetables is to use as little water and as short a cooking time as possible.*

Squash Patties

1½ cups grated squash (any kind)   ⅓ cup chopped onion
1   egg, beaten   Salt and pepper to taste
2   Tablespoons flour

Mix all ingredients together. Drop by tablespoons onto a greased skillet (about 2 tablespoons oil) at medium high heat. Brown on both sides; remove and drain on paper towel. **Yield:** 7 patties.

Mrs. Jim Conine (Donna)

Squash Casserole

5 pounds squash, diced   1 can (6 ounces) pimientos
2 large onions, diced   2 Tablespoons firmly packed
1 teaspoon salt   brown sugar
1 teaspoon pepper   ¾ cup margarine
2 green peppers, diced   Cracker crumbs

Combine squash and onions. Place in boiler and add a little water. Cook until tender. Add salt and pepper. Drain off most of the water and place in 2 casseroles (9x13-inch each). Add green peppers, pimientos, brown sugar, and butter. Sprinkle cracker crumbs and melted butter over casseroles. **Yield:** 16-20 servings.

Mrs. Pete Bennett (Stephanie)

Squash Carrot Casserole

2 pounds summer squash, sliced   2 cup grated carrots
4 ounces herb stuffing mix   1 carton (8 ounces) sour cream
1 onion, diced   1 can (10½ ounces) cream of
2 ribs celery, sliced   chicken soup

Boil squash in salted water for 5 minutes. Place ½ of stuffing mix in buttered 9x13-inch casserole dish. Mix squash and remaining ingredients and layer on top of crumbs. Top with remaining stuffing mix. Bake at 375° for about 30 minutes. **Yield:** 10 servings.

Mrs. Dan Boyd (Terry)

Zucchini-Rice Chili Cheese Bake

3 medium zucchini, thinly sliced
1 cup uncooked rice
½ cup (7½ ounces) whole green
   chilies, chopped
¾ pound Monterey Jack cheese
1 large tomato, thinly sliced
Salt, dash

2 cups sour cream
½ cup chopped green onion
1 teaspoon garlic salt
½ cup chopped green pepper
1 teaspoon oregano, optional
Parsley

Steam zucchini until tender crisp, no longer than 5 minutes. Cook rice according to package directions. Place in a 3-quart greased casserole. Cover with green chilies, ½ of the cheese, zucchini, tomato slices, and salt.

Combine sour cream, onion, garlic salt, and pepper. Spoon over tomato layer. Top with remaining cheese. Bake at 350° for 45-50 minutes. Sprinkle with parsley. **Yield:** 12 servings.

Note: *Use more green chilies if you can take it!*

Mrs. Richard Keeling (Laurie)

Spicy Zucchini

4 cups chopped zucchini
1 cup chopped onion
½ cup water
5 Tablespoons butter, divided
½ teaspoon salt

⅛ teaspoon pepper
1 Tablespoon horseradish
1 egg, slightly beaten
1 cup cracker crumbs

Cook zucchini and onion in water about 15 minutes. Drain well. Mash zucchini with onion and add 2 tablespoons butter, salt, pepper, and horse-radish. Cool. Add egg and mix well. Pour into greased 1-quart baking dish. Brown cracker crumbs in 3 tablespoons butter. Spread crumbs over zucchini mixture. Bake at 350° for 30 minutes. **Yield:** 4 servings.

Mrs. Dan Boyd (Terry)

Easy Zucchini

2-3 medium zucchini
½ cup margarine
1 cup grated Cheddar cheese
1 carton (8 ounces) sour cream

1 cup herb stuffing mix
Paprika
Parmesan cheese

Cut ends off zucchini and slice each lengthwise three times. Boil 5 minutes in salted water and drain. Place in 8x8-inch ovenproof dish. Melt margarine. Add cheese until melted. Remove from heat and stir in sour cream. Pour over zucchini. Sprinkle with paprika. Spread a layer of stuffing mix, then sprinkle with Parmesan cheese. Bake at 325° for 25 minutes. **Yield:** 6 servings.

Mrs. Jim Thornton (Jackie)

♥ *If you oversalt vegetables, add a teaspoon vinegar and sugar, one at a time until the salty taste disappears.*

Zucchini Dish

1 large zucchini, sliced
1 large onion, diced
3 large tomatoes, diced
2 Tablespoons salad oil
1 can (17 ounces) whole kernel corn

Salt and pepper to taste
Garlic salt to taste
Large slice of Longhorn cheese, grated

Sauté zucchini, onions, and tomatoes in 2 tablespoons oil in large skillet. Add corn, salt, pepper, garlic salt, and simmer for 20 minutes. Sprinkle grated cheese over top and serve. **Yield:** 4-6 servings.

Mrs. Donald Hudson (Vickie)

Children's
Cancer Fund
of Dallas

Children's Cancer Fund of Dallas was formed in 1982 by a group of concerned parents of children being treated for cancer at Children's Medical Center of Dallas. The organization was formed for the purpose of raising funds for cancer research to be conducted at the University of Texas Southwestern Medical Center at Dallas, and at Children's Medical Center of Dallas' Hematology-Oncology Division, which has achieved national recognition for its treatment and research accomplishments during the past several years.

Dallas Junior Forum assists Children's Cancer Fund of Dallas through volunteer support and sponsorship of a variety of fund-raising events.

Desserts

Desserts are a bonus at the end of a meal,
And along with their taste, their looks appeal.
Some are rich with chocolate for their yummy taste,
But just watch how they go to your tummy and
  waist!

Apple Cake

1½ cups salad oil
2   cups sugar
3   eggs
2½ cups sifted flour
1   teaspoon salt
1   teaspoon soda
2   teaspoons baking powder
1   teaspoon vanilla extract

3   cups chopped apples, peeled
1   cup chopped pecans

Glaze:
2   Tablespoons butter, melted
2   Tablespoons milk
1   cup powdered sugar
1   teaspoon vanilla extract
¼   teaspoon lemon extract

Grease and flour tube pan. Pour oil into large bowl. Add sugar and eggs; beat well. In separate bowl, sift together flour, salt, soda, and baking powder. Gradually add flour mixture to creamed mixture, add vanilla. Fold in apples and nuts and pour into tube pan. Bake at 350° for 1 hour. After cake has cooled, invert onto serving plate and cover with glaze. **Yield:** 10 servings.

Mrs. James Samson (Malissa)

Poppy Seed Almond Cake

3   cups sifted flour
1½ teaspoons salt
1½ teaspoons baking powder
2¼ cups sugar
1½ Tablespoons poppy seeds
1½ cups milk
1⅛ cups salad oil
3   eggs
1½ Tablespoons vanilla extract

1½ Tablespoons almond extract
1½ Tablespoons butter extract

Glaze:
¼   cup orange juice
¾   cup powdered sugar
½   teaspoon vanilla extract
½   teaspoon almond extract
½   teaspoon butter extract

Preheat oven to 350°. Combine flour, salt, baking powder, sugar, and poppy seeds. Add remaining ingredients and mix well. Pour into 2 lightly greased 9x5-inch loaf pans. Bake for 1 hour. Combine ingredients for glaze. Punch 10-12 shallow holes into warm loaf with toothpick. Brush on glaze with pastry brush. After 1 minute, remove from pan. **Yield:** 2 loaves.

Mrs. Jim Conine (Donna)

Cinnamon Pull Apart Coffee Cake

1½-2 cups chopped pecans
¾ cup firmly packed brown sugar
Cinnamon to taste
1 package cloverleaf rolls (24 count), frozen

1 package (3½ ounces) butterscotch pudding (not instant)
½ cup butter

Spray entire area of bundt pan with vegetable spray. Sprinkle ½ cup pecans and half the brown sugar in bottom of pan. Cover with cinnamon. Pull apart frozen rolls and place in pan. Add another ½ cup pecans, remaining brown sugar, cinnamon, and dry pudding mix. Drizzle melted butter on top. Add more cinnamon and remaining pecans. Cover and allow to rise overnight. Bake at 350° for 30 minutes. **Yield:** 12-16 servings.

Mrs. Don Argenbright (Gail)

Delicious Coffee Cake

1 box (18 ounces) Duncan Hines butter recipe golden cake mix
2 teaspoons vanilla extract
1 teaspoon lemon extract
½ cup sugar
4 eggs

⅔ cup salad oil
1 cup sour cream
½ cup firmly packed light brown sugar
1½ teaspoons cinnamon

Combine cake mix, vanilla, lemon extract, sugar, eggs, oil, and sour cream. Beat for 4 minutes. Pour ½ of batter into greased and floured bundt pan. Mix brown sugar and cinnamon. Sprinkle ½ of this mixture over batter in pan and swirl. Add rest of batter, sprinkle with remaining sugar mixture, and swirl again. Bake at 350° for 50-60 minutes. **Yield:** 12-14 servings.

Mrs. Steven Sellers (Anne)

♥ *If you are short 1 egg while making a box cake, reach for the mayonnaise jar. Use a scant ¼ cup mayonnaise for the missing egg. Follow package directions and the cake will be delicious.*

Graham Cracker Coffee Cake

2 cups graham cracker crumbs	1 cup water
1 cup chopped pecans	3 eggs
¾ cup firmly packed brown sugar	½ cup salad oil
1½ teaspoons cinnamon	Glaze:
¾ cup butter, melted	2 cups powdered sugar
1 box (18 ounces) yellow pudding cake mix	3 Tablespoons milk

To make topping, mix crumbs, pecans, brown sugar, cinnamon, and butter. Set aside. Prepare cake mix with water, eggs, and oil. Beat 2 minutes. Grease 9x13-inch ovenproof dish. Put ½ of cake batter in dish and cover with ½ of topping. Repeat layers. Bake at 350° for 40 minutes. Mix powdered sugar and milk and glaze cake. **Yield:** 24 (2-inch) squares.

Mrs. William Hollon (Kasey)

Blackberry Cake

4 eggs	1 cup frozen blackberries, thawed
1 package (18 ounces) white cake mix	½ cup water
⅔ cup salad oil	
1 package (6 ounces) strawberry flavored gelatin	Icing:
	½-⅔ cup powdered sugar
	4-6 Tablespoons blackberry juice

Preheat oven to 350°. Mix all ingredients together. Bake in a greased bundt pan for 45-50 minutes. (It will bake to a golden brown if you grease the bundt pan with real butter.)
Icing: Mix a small amount of blackberry juice (obtained by squeezing the blackberries) to the powdered sugar making a very thick sauce. Dribble it on the cake. **Yield:** 16-24 slices.

Note: *Cake freezes beautifully.*

Mrs. Sam Norvell (Patsy)

Luscious Coconut Cake
Great Make-Ahead Dessert

1 box (18 ounces) yellow butter
  cake mix
1 cup milk
4 eggs
¼ cup butter, softened
2 packages (6 ounces each) frozen
  coconut, thawed

2 cups sugar
1 carton (8 ounces) sour cream
½ teaspoon almond extract
½ teaspoon vanilla extract

Combine cake mix, milk, eggs, and butter. Pour into a greased and floured 9x13-inch ovenproof dish. Bake at 325° for 35-45 minutes. Combine remaining ingredients. Mix well. Punch small holes into top of hot cake with a toothpick. Spread coconut mixture over cake. Cool and store in refrigerator for 2-3 days before serving. **Yield:** 12-16 servings.

Note: *This cake must be made 2-3 days ahead.*

Mrs. Nick Harper (Anne)

Cheesecake

3 eggs, well beaten
2 packages (8 ounces each) cream
  cheese, softened
1 cup sugar
¼ teaspoon salt
2 teaspoons vanilla extract
½ teaspoon almond extract
3 cups sour cream

Graham Nut Crust:
1¾ cups fine graham cracker
  crumbs
¼ cup finely chopped pecans
½ teaspoon cinnamon
½ cup butter, melted

Combine eggs, cheese, sugar, salt, and extracts. Whip well with mixer. Blend in sour cream. Set aside. Combine crust ingredients. Mix thoroughly and reserve 3 tablespoons. Press remainder on bottom and 2½ inches up on sides of 9-inch springform pan. Pour cheesecake into graham nut crust. Bake at 375° for 35 minutes or until set. Cool. Trim with reserved crumbs or cherries. Refrigerate overnight. **Yield:** 14-18 servings.

Mrs. Robert George (Linda)

Easy Cheese Cake

2 packages (8 ounces each) cream cheese	¾ cup plus 3 Tablespoons sugar
3 eggs	1½ teaspoons vanilla extract
	1 cup sour cream

Preheat oven to 350°. Combine cream cheese, eggs, ¾ cup sugar, and ½ teaspoon vanilla. Beat 5 minutes. Pour into a 9-inch pie pan sprayed with vegetable cooking spray. Bake at 350° for 25 minutes. Remove from oven and cool for 20 minutes. Combine sour cream, 3 tablespoons sugar and 1 teaspoon vanilla. Pour over cooled cake. Bake 10 minutes longer. Chill at least 4 hours. Serve plain or with your favorite topping. **Yield:** 6-8 servings.

Mrs. Steve Moi (Joanie)

♥ *Slicing cake is easier if you dip the knife into water before each slice.*

♥ *Ingredients for cakes should be at room temperature. Ingredients for pastry should be ice cold.*

Praline Cheesecake

1 cup graham cracker crumbs	1¼ cups firmly packed brown sugar
½ cup butter, melted	2 Tablespoons flour
¼ cup sugar	3 eggs
3 packages (8 ounces each) cream cheese, at room temperature	1½ teaspoons vanilla extract
	½ cup chopped pecans

Preheat oven to 350°. Combine cracker crumbs, butter, and sugar. Press into a springform pan. Bake for 10 minutes. Remove crust from oven and reduce heat to 300°. In a large bowl, beat cream cheese and brown sugar. Add flour. Add eggs, one at a time, beating after each one. Add vanilla. Pour into crust and top with pecans. Bake for 45 minutes. Turn off oven and leave cake in for 30 more minutes. Cool and refrigerate for at least 2 hours. **Yield:** 10-12 servings.

Mrs. Dan Boyd (Terry)

Miniature Cheese Cupcakes

Crust:
2¼ cups graham cracker
   crumbs
½ cup butter, melted
4½ Tablespoons sugar
1½ teaspoons vanilla extract

Filling:
2 packages (8 ounces each) cream
   cheese, softened
2 eggs
½ cup sugar
2 teaspoons vanilla extract

Combine crust ingredients. Put 1 tablespoon into each mini-cup and form crust. Cream filling ingredients. Pour 2 teaspoons or less into each cup. Bake at 350° for 8-10 minutes. They do not brown, just bake until set. **Yield:** 48 mini-cakes.

Mrs. Pete Bennett (Stephanie)

Mini-Cheesecakes
Quick, Quick

26-32 vanilla wafers
1 package (16 ounces) cream
   cheese, softened
3 eggs, separated
1 can (14 ounces) sweetened
   condensed milk

¼ cup lemon juice
¼ teaspoon salt
1 can (21 ounces) of your favorite
   flavor of pie filling

Put cupcake liners in muffin tins. Place a vanilla wafer in each. In a large bowl, beat cream cheese until light and fluffy. Add egg yolks and sweetened condensed milk. Beat until smooth. Stir in lemon juice. In another bowl, beat egg whites with salt to form soft peaks. Fold into first mixture. Fill muffin tins to ¼ inch from the top. Bake at 275° for 20 minutes. Cool in tins. Remove and chill. Before serving, remove paper and top with pie filling. **Yield:** 26-32 cakes.

Note: *Can be frozen successfully. Will keep in refrigerator for several days. Dark sweet cherries in heavy syrup may be substituted for pie filling.*

Mrs. William Hollon (Kasey)

Texas Cake

2 cups flour
2 cups sugar
½ teaspoon salt
2 eggs
½ cup sour cream or buttermilk
1 teaspoon baking soda
1 cup margarine
1 cup water
4 Tablespoons cocoa

Icing:
½ cup margarine
6 Tablespoons milk
4 Tablespoons cocoa
1 box (16 ounces) powdered sugar
1 teaspoon vanilla extract
1 cup chopped pecans

Combine flour, sugar, salt, eggs, sour cream, and baking soda. In a saucepan, boil margarine, water, and cocoa. Add to flour mixture. Mix well and
pour into a greased 18x12x1-inch cookie sheet. Bake at 350° for 20-25 minutes. **Icing:** In a saucepan, boil the margarine, milk, and cocoa. Mix powdered sugar, vanilla, and pecans. Combine the two mixtures and stir. Ice
cake in the cookie sheet as soon as it comes from the oven. **Yield:** 12-16
servings.

Mrs. James Sowards (Nancy)

Carol's Special Chocolate Cake
Excellent with Vanilla Ice Cream

2 cups flour
2 cups sugar
¾ cup cocoa
1 teaspoon salt
1 teaspoon baking powder
2 teaspoons baking soda

2 eggs
½ cup salad oil
1 cup milk
1 teaspoon vanilla extract
1 cup coffee, strong and cold

Combine and sift flour, sugar, cocoa, salt, baking powder, and baking soda
into large bowl. In small bowl, blend eggs, oil, milk, and vanilla. Add to
dry ingredients. Mix thoroughly. Add 1 cup cold coffee. Batter will be thin.
Bake in 9x13-inch greased and floured ovenproof dish at 350° for 40 minutes. **Yield:** 10-12 servings.

Note: *May use bundt pan.*

Mrs. Doug Arnold (Debbi)

♥ *Place a lace doily over the top of an unfrosted cake and sprinkle with powdered
sugar. Remove the doily gently so as not to disturb the design.*

Milky Way Cake

8 Milky Way bars	½ teaspoon salt
1 cup butter	1 cup buttermilk
2 cups sugar	2 teaspoons vanilla extract
2½ cups flour	4 eggs
½ teaspoon soda	1 cup chopped pecans

Melt Milky Way bars and ½ cup of butter in a double boiler. Set aside. Cream remaining ½ cup butter and sugar. Mix flour, soda and salt in one bowl. In another bowl, mix buttermilk and vanilla. Alternately add the flour and buttermilk mixtures to the creamed butter and sugar. Add eggs, one at a time. Then add candy mixture and pecans. Bake in greased tube pan at 325° for 1 hour 30 minutes. **Yield:** 16 servings.

Mrs. Thomas Hunter (Lynda)

Icing for Milky Way Cake

2½ cups sugar	6 ounces semi-sweet chocolate
1 cup evaporated milk	chips
½ cup margarine	1 cup marshmallow creme

In large, heavy saucepan, cook sugar and milk to softball stage. Stir constantly to prevent scorching. Add margarine, chocolate chips, and marshmallow creme. Stir until all are melted and mixture is smooth. Cool slightly before icing cake. **Yield:** Approximately 4 cups.

Note: *This makes more icing than you can pile on the cake! Leftover icing is good used as fudge. The cake is good without icing, but better and richer with it!*

Mrs. Ellwood Jones (Ann)

♥ *A cake will be less likely to stick if you put the pan on a wet towel to cool immediately after removing it from the oven.*

Mayonnaise Chocolate Cake

1½ cups mayonnaise	3 teaspoons baking soda
1½ cups cold water	1½ cups sugar
⅛ teaspoon salt	3 cups flour
7 Tablespoons cocoa	1½ teaspoons vanilla extract

Preheat oven to 350°. Grease 9x13-inch ovenproof dish. Cream together mayonnaise, water, salt, cocoa, baking soda, and sugar. Blend well. Add flour and vanilla. Mix well. Pour into ovenproof dish and bake for 25-30 minutes. **Yield:** 12-14 servings.

Note: *Sprinkle powdered sugar over top or add a scoop of vanilla ice cream.*

Mrs. Felix Mitchell (Valerie)

♥ *When using a glass pan for baking, set the oven temperature 25 degrees lower than specified. Glass heats faster than metal and holds heat longer.*

Chocolate Sheet Cake

2 cups flour	Icing:
2 cups sugar	½ cup margarine
½ cup margarine	4 Tablespoons cocoa
4 Tablespoons cocoa	6 Tablespoons milk
1 cup water	1 box (16 ounces) powdered sugar
½ cup buttermilk	1 cup chopped nuts
2 eggs, lightly beaten	1 teaspoon vanilla extract
1 teaspoon baking soda	
1 Tablespoon cinnamon	
1 teaspoon vanilla extract	

Mix together flour and sugar. In a saucepan, boil margarine, cocoa, and water. Add to flour and sugar and beat well. Add remaining ingredients. Mix well and pour into a greased and floured 9x13-inch ovenproof dish. Bake at 300° for 50 minutes. Cool. **Icing:** In a saucepan, bring margarine, cocoa, and milk to a boil. Stir in remaining ingredients and pour over cake. **Yield:** 12-16 servings.

Sharon Gardner

Joy's German Cake

1 package (18 ounces) German
  chocolate cake mix
½ cup margarine, softened
4 eggs

1 box (16 ounces) powdered sugar
1 package (8 ounces) cream cheese
1 teaspoon vanilla extract

Mix cake mix, margarine, and one egg. Spread into a greased and floured 9x13-inch ovenproof dish. Mix remaining ingredients and pour over cake mixture. Bake 20 minutes at 300° and then 20 minutes at 350° or until brown on top. **Yield:** 12-16 servings.

Mrs. Wallace Brown (Gayle)

Dump Cake

1 can (20 ounces) crushed
  pineapple, drained
1 can (21 ounces) cherry pie filling
1 box (18 ounces) yellow cake mix

1   cup butter or margarine,
    sliced
½-1 cup chopped pecans

Dump all ingredients into a 9x13-inch ovenproof dish in order listed. Bake 350° for 70 minutes. **Yield:** 15 servings.

Mrs. Thomas Hunter (Lynda)

Pumpkin Pecan Cake

1 box (18 ounces) yellow cake mix
8 ounces canned pumpkin
½ cup salad oil
¾ cup firmly packed light
  brown sugar
¼ cup water
1 teaspoon cinnamon
¼ teaspoon nutmeg

½ teaspoon allspice
4 eggs

Pecan Topping:
½ cup firmly packed dark
  brown sugar
¼ cup whipping cream
4 Tablespoons butter
½ cup chopped pecans

Combine all ingredients except eggs. Beat at medium speed with electric mixer for 1 minute. Add eggs one at a time, beating 1 minute between each egg. Pour into greased bundt pan. Bake at 350° for 1 hour. Combine topping ingredients and heat until all sugar is dissolved. Spoon over warm cake. **Yield:** 14-16 servings.

Note: *Freezes nicely. Great with whipped cream.*

Mrs. Sam Norvell (Patsy)

Yummy Pineapple Cake

Cake:
2   eggs
2   cups sugar
2   cups crushed pineapple,
     undrained
2   cups flour
2½ teaspoons baking
     powder

Topping:
1   cup sugar
1   can (5 ounces) evaporated milk
½   cup margarine
1   cup pecan pieces
1   cup coconut
½   teaspoon vanilla extract
½   teaspoon lemon extract

Beat eggs and sugar with mixer until light and fluffy. Stir pineapple in by hand. Sift together flour and baking powder. Gently stir into pineapple mixture and mix well. Spread into greased and floured 9x13-inch ovenproof dish. Bake at 350° for 25-30 minutes.

Topping: Just before cake is done, combine sugar, milk, and margarine in a pan over medium heat. Bring to a boil. Boil rapidly for 2 minutes. Remove from heat and add pecans, coconut, vanilla, and lemon extract. Set aside. When cake is done, pour topping immediately over hot cake. **Yield:** 9-12 servings.

Note: *May be made a day ahead. After adding topping, cake may be returned to oven for 10 minutes to brown coconut and nuts.*

Mrs. Bill Frank (Barbara)

Thanksgiving Cake

½ cup butter, softened
1   box (18 ounces) yellow cake mix
6   eggs
2   cups sugar
2   cans (16 ounces each) pumpkin

2   cups milk
½   teaspoon salt
2   Tablespoons pumpkin spice
1   carton (12 ounces) non-dairy
     whipped topping

Cut butter into dry cake mix. Set aside. Mix all other ingredients except non-dairy whipped topping. Pour pumpkin mixture into 9x13-inch ungreased pan, reserving 4 tablespoons for topping. Sprinkle dry cake mix over pumpkin mixture. Bake at 350° for 45-55 minutes. Combine reserved 4 tablespoons pumpkin mixture and non-dairy whipped topping. Use as garnish on cooled cake cut into squares. **Yield:** 14-16 servings.

Mrs. Sam Murray (Sandy)

Georgia B's Pound Cake
After a Fashion

1 cup shortening
2 cups sugar
6 eggs
2 cups flour (may use cake flour)

1 teaspoon vanilla extract
1 teaspoon lemon extract
1 teaspoon almond extract

Preheat oven to 350°. Cream shortening and sugar in mixer. Gradually add eggs, one at a time, alternately with flour. Blend in extracts. Pour into greased and floured tube pan. Bake 1 hour. (Check; may need to bake 10-15 minutes longer.) **Yield:** 12 servings.

Note: *Contains no salt. Nice served with strawberries and whipped cream.*

Mrs. Dennis Furlong (Dede)

Whipping Cream Pound Cake

3 cups sugar
1 cup butter
6 eggs

3 cups flour
1 teaspoon almond extract
1 cup whipping cream

Using electric mixer, cream sugar and butter. Mix in eggs, one at a time. Add flour, almond extract, and whipping cream. Mix well. Grease and flour a tube pan. Pour batter in and put into a cold oven. Bake at 325° for 1 hour 25 minutes. Remove from pan when cool. **Yield:** 12-16 servings.

Note: *Good with fresh fruit and whipped cream on top.*

Mrs. Bill Frank (Barbara)

Cream Cheese Pound Cake

1½ cups butter (do not use
    margarine)
1   package (8 ounces) cream
    cheese

3 cups sugar
6 eggs
3 cups cake flour
1 teaspoon lemon extract

Cream butter, cream cheese, and sugar. Add eggs, one at a time, beating after each. Add flour and extract. Pour into greased and floured bundt pan. Put into a cold oven, then set at 300°. Bake for 1 hour 30 minutes, or until done. **Yield:** 16-20 servings.

Mrs. Steve Moi (Joanie)

Cherry Nut Pound Cake

1 package (18 ounces) cherry
  cake mix
1 package (4 ounces) vanilla
  instant pudding
½ cup finely chopped nuts
⅓ cup salad oil
1 cup water

4 eggs
1 teaspoon almond extract

Glaze:
1 cup powdered sugar
2 Tablespoons milk, warm
¼ teaspoon almond extract

Preheat oven to 350°. Grease and flour 10-inch tube or fluted pan. In large bowl blend all ingredients except those for the glaze. Beat at medium speed for 2 minutes. Pour into pan and bake for 50-60 minutes. For glaze, sprinkle sugar slowly into milk and blend until smooth. Add almond extract and mix. Spread on cooled cake and let stand until glaze hardens. **Yield:** 18-20 servings.

Mrs. James Samson (Malissa)

♥ *Stale cake or cookies can be made into crumbs in a blender. Sprinkle over ice cream or puddings for a delicious topping.*

Piña Colada Cake

1 package (18 ounces) yellow
  cake mix
1 can (14 ounces) sweetened
  condensed milk
1 can (12 ounces) Piña Colada mix

1 container (8 ounces) non-dairy
  whipped topping
1 can (3½ ounces) shredded
  coconut

Bake cake according to package directions using a 9x13-inch ovenproof dish. As soon as it comes out of oven, punch holes in top of cake with a meat fork. Mix condensed milk and Piña Colada mix together and pour over cake. Chill overnight. Before serving, frost with non-dairy topping and sprinkle with coconut. **Yield:** 12 (3-inch) servings.

Mrs. Steve Moi (Joanie)

Marian's Rum Cake

1 cup butter or margarine	Icing:
1¾ cups sugar	1 cup sugar
5 eggs	½ cup water
1 teaspoon vanilla extract	½ cup light rum
2 cups flour	

Cream butter and sugar. Add eggs and vanilla. Gradually add flour. Pour into greased and floured 6½x10-inch oblong ovenproof dish. Bake at 325° for 1 hour.

Icing: Mix sugar, water, and rum and cook over medium heat until all sugar is dissolved. Punch holes in cake with a toothpick. Pour icing over warm cake. **Yield:** 9-12 servings.

Note: *Cake is delicious right away but gets better as it sits for a day or two.*

Mrs. Ellwood Jones (Ann)

Sad Cake

3 cups Bisquick mix	1 package (6 ounces) semi-sweet chocolate chips
4 eggs	1 can (3½ ounces) shredded coconut
1 box (16 ounces) brown sugar	1 cup chopped pecans
½ cup salad oil	

Combine all ingredients. Mix well. Pour into greased 9x13-inch ovenproof dish. Bake at 350° for 30 minutes. Cool and cut into bars or squares. **Yield:** 24 squares or 48 bars.

Note: *This cake rises, then falls.*

Mrs. James Layton (Vicki)

♥ *Dented measuring utensils give inaccurate measures. Use only standard measuring cups and spoons that are in good condition.*

Snow Cake

1 cup butter	2 boxes (12 ounces each) vanilla
2 cups sugar	wafers
4 egg yolks	1 large container (12 ounces)
1 can (20 ounces) crushed	non-dairy whipped topping
pineapple, drained	or 2 cups whipping cream,
2 cups chopped pecans or walnuts	whipped
4 egg whites	1-3 cups coconut, to taste

Cream butter and sugar. Add egg yolks, pineapple, and nuts. Beat well, until sugar is fully dissolved. Set aside. Beat egg whites in a separate bowl until stiff. Fold into butter mixture. Line the bottom of a 9x13-inch oven-proof dish with vanilla wafers. Spread evenly with ⅓ of cream mixture. Repeat until there are 3 layers of each. Top with whipped topping or whipped cream and sprinkle with coconut. Refrigerate, covered, at least 4 hours before serving. **Yield:** 12-16 servings.

Note: *Must be served cold. Should not stand at room temperature more than 1 hour; it will become runny.*

Mrs. Donald Robson (Karen)

Apple Crunch

8 medium apples, peeled	1 cup flour
1 teaspoon cinnamon	½ cup firmly packed brown sugar
1 teaspoon nutmeg	½ cup butter
½ cup sugar	½ cup chopped pecans, optional
½ cup water	

Lightly butter inside of 9-inch pie plate. Cut peeled apples into quarters, slice and place in dish. Sprinkle cinnamon, nutmeg, and sugar over apples. Pour ½ cup water over this evenly. Mix flour and brown sugar together. Sprinkle on top of apples. Drop by slices, ½ cup butter over apples. Add pecans. Bake at 350° for 25-30 minutes until golden brown. **Yield:** 6-8 servings.

Note: *Great served warm with vanilla ice cream.*

Mrs. Jim Thornton (Jackie)

Carmella DeSarno's Ricotta Pie
Authentic Italian

Crust:
¼ cup butter
2 cups flour
2 egg yolks
5 Tablespoons milk
½ cup powdered sugar
½ teaspoon vanilla extract
½ teaspoon lemon juice

Filling:
7 eggs, separated
2 cups sugar
3 pounds ricotta cheese
2 Tablespoons flour
½ cup lukewarm milk
2 teaspoons vanilla extract
½ teaspoon lemon juice

Preheat oven to 325°. Mix butter and flour with fork. Beat egg yolks well and add to flour mixture. Add remaining ingredients and mix well, using hands to knead slightly. Form into a ball and refrigerate dough about 1 hour. (Filling can be prepared during this time.) Remove dough from refrigerator and roll out into rectangle, approximately 12x15 inches. Press dough into bottom and sides of a 9x13-inch glass ovenproof dish. **Filling:** In a 3-quart mixing bowl, beat egg yolks well with sugar. Add remainder of ingredients, except egg whites, and mix well. Beat egg whites in clean, cold bowl until stiff, then fold into cheese mixture. Spread over pie crust. Bake for 1 hour. Turn off oven temperature and leave pie in oven another hour, without opening door. **Yield:** 20-24 servings.

Mrs. John Mearns (June)

Best Ever Buttermilk Pie

Crust:
1½ cups flour
½ teaspoon salt
¾ cup shortening
1 egg, well beaten
½ Tablespoon vinegar
2 Tablespoons water

Filling:
3 eggs
½ cup margarine, melted
1½ cups sugar
½ cup buttermilk
1 teaspoon vanilla extract

Cut flour, salt, and shortening together. Combine egg, vinegar, and water, and add to shortening mixture. Roll out on floured surface and place into 9-inch deep dish pie pan. Filling: Beat eggs until frothy and add to rest of filling ingredients. Mix well. Pour into unbaked pie shell. Bake at 350° for 10 minutes. Reduce heat to 325° and bake for 30 minutes or until center is set. **Yield:** 6-8 servings.

Mrs. Doug Rivenbark (Penny)

Aunt Matilda's Peach Cobbler

2 cups sliced peaches, drained
    but reserving liquid or use
    fresh peaches
1 Tablespoon cornstarch
½ cup sugar
¼ teaspoon salt
¾ teaspoon almond extract,
    optional
¼ teaspoon vanilla extract,
    optional

Cobbler dough:
1 cup sifted flour
1½ teaspoons baking powder
½ teaspoon salt
¼ cup sugar
¼ cup shortening
⅓ cup milk

Place peaches in greased 6x10-inch baking dish. Sprinkle cornstarch over fruit. Combine sugar, salt, ½ cup peach juice (not necessary if fresh peaches), almond extract, and vanilla extract. Pour over peaches. To make cobbler dough, sift flour, baking powder, salt, and sugar together. Cut in shortening. Add milk, stirring with a fork into a soft dough. Drop dough by small spoonfuls onto peaches and sprinkle with additional sugar, if desired. Bake at 375° for 40-45 minutes. **Yield:** 5-6 servings.

Mrs. Mallard Tysseland (Jill)

♥ *When cooking with fresh fruits, add a dash of salt and 2-3 teaspoons of fresh lemon juice to enhance the flavor and preserve the fruit.*

⽊ Southern Chocolate Pecan Pie

3 eggs
⅔ cup sugar
½ cup light corn syrup
½ cup dark corn syrup
⅓ cup margarine, melted

Salt, dash
1 cup pecan halves
¾-1 package (6 ounces) chocolate
    chips
1 unbaked 9-inch pie shell

Beat eggs and sugar. Add syrups, margarine, and salt. Stir in pecan halves. Sprinkle chocolate chips into bottom of unbaked pie shell and pour pie mixture over chips. Bake at 350° for 50 minutes. **Yield:** 6-8 servings.

Mrs. Jim Thornton (Jackie)

Pecan Pie

3 eggs, slightly beaten
1 cup light corn syrup
½ cup sugar
¼ teaspoon salt

1 cup pecan halves
1 Tablespoon flour
1 teaspoon vanilla extract
1 unbaked 9 or 10-inch pie crust

Beat eggs and add light corn syrup, sugar (with salt added to it), pecans, flour, and vanilla. Mix and pour into pie crust. Bake at 375° for 40 minutes. **Yield:** 6 servings.

Mrs. Thomas Hunter (Lynda)

Jaeson's Pie

1 package (8 ounces) cream
   cheese
1½ cups powdered sugar
1 cup chopped pecans
1 carton (8 ounces) non-dairy
   whipped topping

1 can (21 ounces) cherry
  pie filling
1 baked 9-inch graham cracker
  pie crust

Using an electric mixer, cream together the powdered sugar and cream cheese. Add pecans and mix well. Spread this into the prepared pie crust. Layer whipped topping over cheese mixture then top with a layer of cherry pie filling. **Yield:** 8 servings.

Mrs. Jim Thornton (Jackie)

Oreo Pie

½ cup margarine
19 Oreo cookies, crushed
2 cups coffee ice cream, softened
3 squares unsweetened chocolate
¾ cup sugar

1 can (5 ounces) evaporated milk
⅛ teaspoon salt
1½ teaspoons vanilla extract
Whipped cream, optional
Crème de cacao, optional

Melt ¼ cup margarine, add cookies and mix. Press into 10-inch pie pan. Add ice cream and freeze until firm. Melt remaining ¼ cup margarine and chocolate in double boiler. Stir in sugar. Slowly add milk. Mix salt and vanilla. Cook until sugar is dissolved. Cool. Pour over frozen pie and freeze hard. Set at room temperature for 15 minutes before serving. Top with whipped cream and ½ jigger of crème de cacao. **Yield:** 8 servings.

Mrs. Marvin Chronister (Donna)

French Silk Chocolate Pie

½ cup butter, softened
¾ cup sugar
1 square (1 ounce) unsweetened
   chocolate, melted and cooled
3 Tablespoons cocoa
1 teaspoon vanilla extract
2 eggs

1 baked 9-inch pie shell
1 cup whipping cream
¼ cup powdered sugar
1 teaspoon vanilla extract
1 package (3 ounces) slivered
   almonds, toasted

Cream butter and sugar until fluffy. Add chocolate, cocoa, and vanilla, and blend well. Add 1 egg and beat for 5 minutes. Add second egg and beat an additional 5 minutes. Pour mixture into baked pie shell and chill at least 2 hours. Combine whipping cream, powdered sugar, and vanilla. Beat until stiff peaks are formed. Garnish pie with whipped cream and toasted almonds. **Yield:** 6-8 servings.

Variation: *Chocolate sprinkles may be substituted for almonds.*

Mrs. Sam Murray (Sandy)

♥ *Chocolate that has turned gray still retains its fine flavor when melted.*

Chocolate Chip Pie

½ cup margarine, melted and
   cooled
2 eggs
1 cup sugar
½ cup self-rising flour
1 teaspoon vanilla extract

½ teaspoon salt
1 cup broken pecans
1 package (6 ounces) chocolate
   chips
1 unbaked 9-inch pie shell

Combine margarine, eggs, sugar, flour, vanilla, and salt. Gently add pecans and mix well. Add chocolate chips. Stir gently and pour into unbaked pie shell. Bake at 350° for 40-45 minutes. **Yield:** 6-8 servings.

Note: *Top with whipped cream if desired.*

Mrs. Jeff Farmer (Kaliko)

Fudge Pie
Chocolate Lover's Delight!

½ cup butter	1½ cups sugar
3 squares (1 ounce each) unsweetened baking chocolate	¼ teaspoon salt
	1 teaspoon vanilla
4 eggs	1 unbaked 9-inch pie shell
3 Tablespoons light corn syrup	Vanilla ice cream

Over low heat melt butter and chocolate. Beat eggs until light. To the eggs add corn syrup, sugar, salt, and vanilla. Stir in chocolate and mix well. Pour into pie shell and bake at 350° for 30-40 minutes. Top with vanilla ice cream. Best if served warm, but not necessary. **Yield:** 6-8 servings.

Mrs. Bill Frank (Barbara)

♥ *Chill dough 10 minutes in refrigerator to reduce the amount of flour needed when rolling out. Excess flour results in a tough dough.*

Heavenly Milk Chocolate Pie
A Dream Come True

¼ cup plus 2 Tablespoons flour	1¾ squares (1 ounce each) semi-sweet chocolate
1 cup water	2 eggs, beaten
1 scant cup sugar	2 Tablespoons margarine
1 cup evaporated milk	1 baked 9 inch pie crust, chilled
Salt, dash	Whipped cream to taste

Combine flour, water, sugar, milk, and salt in a saucepan and heat. Add 1½ chocolate squares. Cook, stirring constantly until it begins to boil. Remove from heat. Combine ¼ cup of the chocolate mixture and the eggs; blend. Pour back into saucepan and cook 10 minutes longer on low, stirring constantly. Remove from heat and stir in margarine until melted. Pour into cold, baked crust and cool. Top cooled pie with whipped cream. Shave remaining ¼ square chocolate over whipped cream. **Yield:** 6-8 servings.

Mrs. Terry Chambers (Dianne)

Easy Cherry Cake Pie

2 cans (21 ounces each) cherry
  pie filling
1 box (18 ounces) white cake mix

½ cup chopped pecans
½ cup plus 2 Tablespoons plus 2
  teaspoons margarine, melted

Preheat oven to 325°. Layer pie filling, cake mix sprinkled evenly, pecans and melted margarine in a 3-quart rectangular baking dish. Bake for 1 hour and 15 minutes. Cool and serve with ice cream or whipped topping. **Yield:** 12-16 servings.

Mrs. Thomas Hunter (Lynda)

Grasshopper Pie

1¼ cups crushed chocolate wafers
  (30-34)
⅓ cup butter, melted

20 large marshmallows
⅓ cup crème de menthe
2 cups whipping cream

Mix wafers and butter and press into a 9 or 10-inch pie pan, covering bottom and sides. Chill in freezer. Melt marshmallows and crème de menthe over low heat. Cool. Whip the whipping cream and add to marshmallow mixture. Place filling in pie crust and freeze until ready to serve. **Yield:** 8-10 servings.

Note: *You can add shavings of semi-sweet chocolate on top for decoration.*

Mrs. King Bourland (Carol)

Luscious Lemon Icebox Pie

4 egg yolks
1 egg white, stiffly beaten
1 can (15 ounces) sweetened
  condensed milk

½ cup lemon juice, freshly
  squeezed
1 baked 9-inch graham cracker
  crust

Beat egg yolks until lemon colored, fold in the egg white. Add condensed milk and slowly stir in lemon juice to taste. Pour into pie shell and refrigerate about 4 hours. **Yield:** 8-10 servings.

Note: *If desired, you may top with slightly sweetened whipped cream or meringue.*

Mrs. Doug Rivenbark (Penny)

Lemonade Pie

1 can (6 ounces) frozen lemonade
  concentrate
1 can (14 ounces) sweetened
  condensed milk

1 carton (12 ounces) non-dairy
  whipped topping
1 baked 9-inch graham cracker
  crust

Combine ingredients with mixer. Pour into graham cracker crust and chill for 1 hour. **Yield:** 8 servings.

Note: *Use green food coloring for color variety. Can also use pink lemonade and add a few drops of red food coloring.*

Mrs. Jim Thornton (Jackie)

Million Dollar Pie

1 can (16 ounces) sliced peaches,
  drained and cut up
1 can (8 ounces) crushed
  pineapple, drained
1 jar (6 ounces) maraschino
  cherries, drained and cut up
¼ cup lemon juice

1 can (14 ounces) sweetened
  condensed milk
1 cup whipping cream or 1 carton
  (8 ounces) non-dairy whipped
  topping
2 baked 9-inch graham cracker
  pie crusts

Combine all ingredients. Mix well and refrigerate for 3-4 hours. Pour into 2 pie crusts. Return to refrigerator until ready to serve. **Yield:** 12-16 servings.

Note: *Great early preparation dessert.*

Mrs. Steve Moi (Joanie)

♥ *Whipped cream will keep for a day or two if while whipping you add 1 teaspoon light corn syrup for each ½ pint of cream.*

Peanut Butter Pie

1 package (3 ounces) cream
  cheese
½ cup crunchy peanut butter
⅓ cup milk
¾ cup powdered sugar

½ of an 8 ounce carton non-dairy
  whipped topping
¼ cup chopped peanuts
1 baked 9-inch graham cracker
  crust

Soften cream cheese; add peanut butter, milk, and sugar. Mix until fluffy; then slowly fold in whipped topping. Pour into crust and sprinkle with peanuts. Freeze for 8 hours. Store in freezer. **Yield:** 8-10 servings.

Note: *Can be served with hot chocolate fudge sauce.*

Mrs. James Layton (Vicki)

Pineapple Pie

1¼ cups crushed pineapple,
  drained
¼ cup sugar
1 envelope unflavored gelatin

1 cup evaporated milk, chilled
½ teaspoon lemon juice
½ cup butter, melted
1½ cups graham cracker crumbs

In a small saucepan, heat pineapple and sugar until it comes to a boil. Set aside. Empty gelatin into a cup, stirring in just enough water to dissolve. Add to hot pineapple mixture, a little at a time. Cool in a pan of cold water. Beat 1 cup of the chilled evaporated milk until stiff. Add lemon juice and stir into pineapple. Combine butter and graham cracker crumbs. Press into a 9-inch pie plate. Pour pineapple mixture into pie shell and chill. **Yield:** 6-8 servings.

Mrs. Nick Harper (Anne)

Pineapple Macadamia Pie

⅓ cup shredded coconut
1 unbaked 9-inch pie shell
3 eggs
⅔ cup sugar
1 cup light corn syrup
¼ cup butter, melted
1 teaspoon vanilla extract

½ teaspoon salt
1 can (13½ ounces) pineapple tidbits, drained
1 cup macadamia nuts, rinse if salted
1 cup whipping cream
3 Tablespoons cream of coconut

Preheat oven to 350°. Press coconut into bottom and sides of pie shell. In large bowl, combine eggs, sugar, syrup, butter, vanilla, and salt. Beat thoroughly. Stir in pineapple and nuts. Pour into pie shell. Bake at 350° for 45 minutes or until set. Cool thoroughly on wire rack. Whip cream to soft peaks. Fold in cream of coconut. Slice pie into wedges and serve, passing coconut cream mixture separately. **Yield:** 6-8 servings.

Mrs. Sam Murray (Sandy)

♥ *Handle pie dough very little after water has been added. Excessive handling results in tough, unflaky crust.*

Pineapple-Cheese Pie
Good Dessert for a Heavy Meal

3 packages (3 ounces each) cream cheese, softened
2 eggs, beaten
10 ounces crushed pineapple, drained

1 Tablespoon plus 2 teaspoons vanilla extract
1 graham cracker crust
1 carton (8 ounces) sour cream
2 Tablespoons sugar

Beat cream cheese until smooth. Add eggs, pineapple, and 2 teaspoons vanilla; beat well. Pour into pie crust. Bake at 350° for 15-17 minutes. For topping, combine sour cream, sugar, and 1 tablespoon vanilla; beat well. Pour over pie and bake an additional 5 minutes at 350°. Cool, then refrigerate approximately 3 hours or until firm. **Yield:** 6-8 servings.

Mrs. Marvin Chronister (Donna)

Pumpkin Pie with a Punch

½ cup firmly packed brown sugar
½ teaspoon salt
2 teaspoons cinnamon
½ teaspoon ginger
½ teaspoon nutmeg
¼ teaspoon cloves
½ cup corn syrup

3 eggs, slightly beaten
1½ cups canned pumpkin
1½ cups whipping cream
¼ cup Southern Comfort
  or brandy
1 unbaked 9½-inch pie shell

Combine sugar, salt, spices, corn syrup, and eggs. Stir in pumpkin, cream, and liquor. Pour into pie shell. Bake at 425° for 15 minutes. Reduce heat to 350° and bake about 45 minutes longer or until an inserted knife comes out clean. Serve at room temperature or cold, with or without whipped cream. **Yield:** 8 servings.

Mrs. William Hollon (Kasey)

French Strawberry Pie

1 package (3 ounces) cream cheese
Milk
1 baked 9-inch pie crust
2 pints strawberries, washed and
  cored

1 cup sugar
3 Tablespoons cornstarch
⅓ cup water
1 cup whipping cream,
  whipped

Mix cream cheese with a little milk and spread over bottom of pie shell. Arrange 1 pint strawberries over cream cheese. In saucepan mash other pint of berries. Bring to a boil, gradually adding sugar. Blend cornstarch and water and add to strawberries. Cook slowly until thick. Cool and spread over berries. Chill and serve with whipped cream. **Yield:** 6-8 servings.

Mrs. Jerry Leatherman (Diana)

♥ *Hull strawberries after washing to keep them from absorbing too much water and becoming mushy.*

Pumpkin Ice Cream Pie

1 cup canned pumpkin
½ cup firmly packed brown sugar
½ teaspoon salt
½ teaspoon cinnamon
½ teaspoon ginger

¼ teaspoon nutmeg
1 quart vanilla ice cream, softened
1 graham cracker crust

Mix pumpkin, sugar, and spices. Fold in ice cream. Pour into graham cracker crust. Freeze. **Yield:** 8 servings.

Note: *Slivered almonds may be put on top of crust before adding ice cream mixture.*

Mrs. Mac Cravy (Sharon)

Sherbet Pie
Great Do-Ahead Dessert

18 almond macaroons, crumbled
1 carton (16 ounces) whipping cream, whipped
1 teaspoon vanilla extract
8 Tablespoons sugar

½ cup chopped walnuts
1½ pints orange sherbet, softened
1½ pints raspberry sherbet, softened
1½ pints lime sherbet, softened

Combine macaroons, whipping cream, vanilla, sugar, and nuts. Spread half of mixture in bottom of 9x13-inch dish. Stir each sherbet separately until smooth and of spreading consistency. Layer over macaroon mixture according to color preference. Top with remaining macaroon mixture. Place in freezer until firm. Let stand a few minutes before slicing. **Yield:** 16 servings.

Mrs. Winston Borum (Jimmie)

Cherry Pizza Pie

2 cans (16 ounces each) pitted bing cherries, undrained
1 cup sugar
2 Tablespoons tapioca
3 Tablespoons light corn syrup

1 box (18 ounces) yellow cake mix
1 cup chopped nuts
¾ cup margarine, melted
Cinnamon
Whipped cream

Pour cherries with juice into a greased 11x14-inch ovenproof pan. Sprinkle evenly with sugar, tapioca, corn syrup, and cake mix. Top with nuts; then margarine. Sprinkle with cinnamon. Bake at 325° for 50 minutes. Serve with whipped cream. **Yield:** 20-24 servings.

Mrs. Mike Diffenderffer (Judy)

Toffee Ice Cream Pie
A Real Favorite

½ gallon vanilla ice cream, softened
¾ cup crushed Heath bars
2 graham cracker pie crusts

Sauce:
1½ cups sugar
1 cup evaporated milk
¼ cup butter
¼ cup light corn syrup
½ cup crushed Heath bars

Combine ice cream and Heath bars. Pour ½ mixture into each pie shell. Freeze. Before serving, prepare sauce. In a saucepan, combine all sauce ingredients except the Heath bars. Heat until slightly thickened. Add Heath bars and stir. Slice pie and pour warm sauce over each piece. **Yield:** 6-8 servings.

Mrs. Bill Frank (Barbara)

Fruit Pizza
Beautiful to Look At

Pie crust dough for 2-crust pie

Sauce:
2 packages (8 ounces each) cream cheese, softened
1-1½ cups powdered sugar
1 Tablespoon grated lemon rind
½ cup half and half

Filling:
1 cup strawberries (or cranberries)
½ cup sugar
½ cup water

Fruit: (choose 4 or 5 fruits)
Bananas, sliced and dipped in lemon juice to retain color
Mandarin oranges
White seedless grapes
Pineapple chunks
Blueberries
Papaya
Strawberries
Kiwi fruit
(The amount of fruit depends on the placement on the pizza pan.)

Cover bottom of pizza pan with pie crust dough. Follow baking instructions until golden brown; cool. Beat sauce ingredients until smooth and refrigerate. After 10-15 minutes, put sauce on pie crust. Combine strawberries (or cranberries) with sugar and water to make filling. Boil until thick and sugary. If using cranberries don't let them pop. Refrigerate until cool. Spread this over sauce. In the center of the pan, form a circle of one of the fruits you have chosen. Continue forming circles with each of the other types of fruit. You will finish with about 5 rows of fruit. **Yield:** 15-18 servings.

Mrs. Jack Hamer (Pam)

Aunt Guy's Pie Crust

¾ cup shortening
¼ cup boiling water
1 Tablespoon milk

2 cups sifted flour
1 teaspoon salt

In a medium bowl, combine shortening, water, and milk. Break up shortening with a fork. Tilt bowl and with rapid cross-the-bowl strokes, whip until mixture is smooth and thick and holds soft peaks when fork is lifted. Sift flour and salt together into shortening mixture. Stir quickly with round-the-bowl strokes until dough cleans the bowl. Pick up and work into a smooth dough. Shape into a flat round. May chill slightly if desired. Use 2 pieces of wax paper to roll between. **Yield:** 1 crust.

Mrs. Ellwood Jones (Ann)

Swedish Pie Crust

1½ cups shortening
3 cups flour
½ teaspoon salt

1 egg
5 Tablespoons water
1 Tablespoon vinegar

Cut shortening into flour until size of small peas. Add remaining ingredients and mix. Form into 3 balls and roll each onto floured board the size of 9-inch pie pans. **Yield:** 3 crusts.

Note: *May be frozen until ready to use.*

Mrs. Joe Key (Christie)

Mounds

½ cup margarine, melted
2 boxes (16 ounces each) powdered sugar
1 can (14 ounces) sweetened condensed milk
1 can (3½ ounces) flaked coconut

2 cups chopped pecans
1 teaspoon vanilla extract
1 package (12 ounces) semi-sweet chocolate chips
1.6 ounces (½ bar) paraffin

Mix together margarine, powdered sugar, milk, coconut, pecans, and vanilla. Form dough into walnut size balls. Chill. In a double boiler, melt chocolate chips and paraffin. Dip balls into chocolate mixture and place on waxed paper. Refrigerate to store. **Yield:** Approximately 6 dozen.

Mrs. Bill Frank (Barbara)

Almond Joy Bars

2 packages (12 ounces each)
  chocolate chips
4 Tablespoons salad oil
2 cans (14 ounces each) sweetened
  condensed milk

2 envelopes unflavored gelatin
2 packages (14 ounces each)
  coconut
1 cup slivered almonds

Melt 1 package of chips and 2 tablespoons oil in double boiler. Pour on a 10x15-inch cookie sheet lined with wax paper. Refrigerate until cool. Cook sweetened condensed milk and gelatin until boiling, stirring constantly as it will burn. Remove from heat and stir in coconut and almonds. Mixture will be hard to stir. Spread over chocolate and cool. Melt remaining chips in 2 tablespoons oil and spread over top. Cool and cut into 1-inch squares. **Yield:** 150 bars.

Mrs. Winston Borum (Jimmie)

Buckeyes

2 cups chunky peanut butter
3 cups Rice Krispies cereal
1 box (16 ounces) powdered sugar
½ cup butter, softened

1 package (12 ounces)
   semi-sweet chocolate
1.6 ounces (½ bar) paraffin

Combine peanut butter, cereal, powdered sugar, and butter. Shape into bite-size balls. Chill. In a double boiler, melt the chocolate and paraffin. Coat peanut butter balls in chocolate mixture. Refrigerate. **Yield:** About 5 dozen.

Note: *Microwave can be used to melt the chocolate mixture. The chocolate sauce can also be used to dip strawberries!*

Mrs. William Hollon (Kasey)

♥ *The weather is a big factor in candy making. On a hot, humid day it is advisable to cook candy 2 degrees higher than on a cold, dry day.*

Walnut Caramels

1 cup butter
1 pound brown sugar
Salt, dash

1 cup light corn syrup
2 cups half and half
½ cup chopped walnuts

Butter sides of a heavy 5-quart Dutch oven. In same pan, melt the 1 cup butter. Mix in brown sugar and salt. Add corn syrup and mix well. Gradually add cream, stirring constantly over medium heat until firm ball stage (245°), about 30-35 minutes. Remove from heat. Place nuts into bottom of buttered 9-inch square baking pan. Pour caramel mixture over nuts. Cool and cut into squares. **Yield:** 36 squares.

Mrs. Sam Murray (Sandy)

Jo's Good and Easies

1 package (12 ounces) chocolate
 chips
1 package (6 ounces) butterscotch
 chips

1 jar (12 ounces) dry roasted
 peanuts, salted or unsalted

Melt chips together in double boiler or microwave. Stir in peanuts. Drop onto wax paper by teaspoonfuls. Refrigerate and let harden. **Yield:** 3-4 dozen.

Note: *If you like butterscotch flavor, reverse chip measures.*

Mrs. John Mearns (June)

Aunt Maggie's Fudge

1 cup butter or margarine
1 can (12 ounces) evaporated milk
5 cups sugar
1 package (12 ounces) chocolate
 chips

1 jar (7 ounces) marshmallow
 cream
2 teaspoons vanilla extract
1½ cups chopped nuts

In a heavy 4-quart saucepan, melt butter. Add milk and sugar. Bring to a boil over medium-high heat. When it boils to where you can't stir down the bubbles, start timing for 10 minutes. Stir constantly. Turn off heat, add the chocolate chips, and stir until melted. Add marshmallow cream, vanilla and nuts. Beat until cool and pour into a buttered 9x13-inch pan. Score while warm. **Yield:** 54 squares.

Mrs. Jerry Leatherman (Diana)

Fudge Meltaways

First Layer:
½ cup butter
1 square (1 ounce) unsweetened chocolate
¼ cup sugar
1 teaspoon vanilla extract
1 egg, beaten
2 cups graham cracker crumbs
1 cup coconut
½ cup chopped walnuts

Second Layer:
¼ cup butter
1 Tablespoon milk or cream
2 cups powdered sugar, sifted
1 teaspoon vanilla extract

Third Layer:
1½ squares (1½ ounces) unsweetened chocolate, melted

Melt butter and chocolate for first layer in saucepan or microwave. Blend sugar, vanilla, egg, graham cracker crumbs, coconut, and nuts into butter-chocolate mixture. Mix thoroughly and press into 7½x11½-inch baking dish or 9-inch square pan. Refrigerate. For a second layer, cream butter, milk, powdered sugar, and vanilla extract. Spread over crumb mixture. Chill. Melt chocolate for third layer and pour over chilled mixture and spread evenly. Store in refrigerator. Cut into squares before meltaways are completely firm. **Yield:** 3-4 dozen bite-size squares.

Mrs. Jerry Washam (Geraldine)

Peanut Butter Fudge

1 cup margarine
1 package (12 ounces) chocolate chips

1 pound crunchy peanut butter
1 box (16 ounces) powdered sugar

Melt margarine and chocolate chips in microwave. Stir in peanut butter and powdered sugar. Pour into a greased 9x13-inch dish. Chill and cut into squares. **Yield:** 70 squares.

Mrs. Jim Thornton (Jackie)

Microwave Peanut Brittle
A Big Hit

1 cup white sugar	1 teaspoon margarine
½ cup white corn syrup	1 teaspoon vanilla extract
1 cup raw peanuts	1 teaspoon baking soda

Combine sugar and syrup and pour into a 1½-quart casserole. Microwave on high for 4 minutes. Stir in peanuts. Microwave 4 more minutes on high. Add margarine and vanilla and stir. Microwave 2 more minutes on high. Add baking soda and gently stir until light and foamy. Pour onto lightly buttered cookie sheet. Let cool ½-1 hour. Break into small pieces and store in airtight container. **Yield:** 20-30 pieces.

Mrs. James Layton (Vicki)

♥ *Raw eggs separate more easily while still cold from the refrigerator, but let whites reach room temperature to get maximum volume when beating.*

Frosted Date Turtles
Date Hater's Love

1 box (8 ounces) dates, chopped	¼ cup margarine
1 can (14 ounces) sweetened condensed milk	1 package (3 ounces) cream cheese
1 cup chopped pecans	2 cups powdered sugar
Town House crackers	1½ teaspoons vanilla extract

Heat dates and condensed milk over low heat for 5 minutes, or until thickened. Add pecans, and remove from heat. Spread each cracker with mixture (using 1½-2 packages crackers). Bake at 350° for 8 minutes, remove from pan and cool. Frost with icing.

Icing: Cream butter or margarine with cream cheese. Add powdered sugar and vanilla, beat well, and ice each cracker. **Yield:** 40-50 crackers.

Note: *May freeze or keep refrigerated.*

Mrs. Mac Cravy (Sharon)

Pecan Log

3 Tablespoons butter or
  margarine, melted
4 Tablespoons milk
1 package (14.5 ounces) creamy
  white frosting mix

28 vanilla caramels (8 ounces)
1½ cups chopped pecans

Combine butter and 2 tablespoons milk. Stir in frosting mix until well blended. Form into two 8x1½-inch logs. Wrap each in foil and chill for 2 hours. Melt caramels with remaining 2 tablespoons milk on low heat. Spread melted caramel on top and sides of chilled rolls, reserving part of mixture. Sprinkle 1 cup pecans on 2 sheets of foil. Invert 1 log onto each sheet. Spread remaining caramel mixture on each log. Coat logs evenly with ½ cup pecans and reshape as needed. Wrap each log well and chill before serving. When ready to serve remove from refrigerator and let stand for about 30 minutes. Slice into ¼-inch pieces. **Yield:** 64 slices.

Mrs. Jim Conine (Donna)

Microwave Pralines

1½ cups firmly packed brown
  sugar
⅔ cup half and half
⅛ teaspoon salt

2 Tablespoons butter or
  margarine
1½ cups pecan halves

Combine sugar, half and half, and salt in a deep 3-quart microwave casserole; mix well. Stir in butter. Microwave at High for 7-9½ minutes or until mixture reaches soft ball stage (235°); stirring once. Mix in pecans and cool about 1 minute. Beat by hand until mixture is creamy and begins to thicken (about 3 minutes). Drop by tablespoonfuls onto waxed paper. Let stand until firm. Wrap when cool. **Yield:** 2 dozen.

Mrs. James Layton (Vicki)

♥ *To test your microwave for accuracy, place 8 ounces of tap water in the oven and microwave for 3 minutes. Water should boil in this time at sea level.*

Toffee with Black Walnuts

1 cup butter
2 cups firmly packed brown sugar
Lemon juice, dash
1 cup black walnut pieces

1 bar (4 ounces) Baker's sweet
  chocolate
1 cup ground black walnuts

In a heavy pan, melt butter. Add sugar and lemon juice, bringing to a slow boil. Cook 10 minutes watching carefully because mixture burns easily. Remove from heat. Add 1 cup of black walnut pieces. Mix. Pour onto buttered cookie sheet. Cool. Break into pieces. Dip in melted chocolate and roll in 1 cup ground walnuts. **Yield:** Approximately 4 dozen.

Note: *Do not substitute margarine for butter, as it will separate.*

Mrs. William Hollon (Kasey)

Jodie's Truffles
For Those of You with Champagne Taste

8 squares (1 ounce each)
  semi-sweet chocolate
⅓ cup milk
⅓ cup butter

2 egg yolks, slightly beaten
¼ teaspoon vanilla extract
Unsweetened cocoa

In a saucepan, melt chocolate with milk and butter over low heat. Stir until smooth and remove from heat. Blend ¼ cup hot mixture into egg yolks, then whisk yolks into chocolate in saucepan. Add vanilla; beat well. Pour into small bowl, cover and refrigerate until firm. Form teaspoonfuls into round balls. Roll in cocoa; shake off excess. **Yield:** 2½ dozen.

Note: *Store in refrigerator up to 3 weeks. Freeze up to 2 months. Great after dinner with coffee!*

Mrs. John Mearns (June)

♥ *Whole raw egg yolks may be stored, covered with water and refrigerated, for up to three days. Raw egg whites remain fresh for up to 10 days, refrigerated and covered with a tight-fitting lid.*

Buttermilk Pralines

3 cups sugar
1 teaspoon baking soda
⅛ teaspoon salt
1 cup buttermilk

¾ cup light corn syrup
2 Tablespoons butter
2 cups pecans

Combine all ingredients, except pecans, in a 4-quart pan. Cook to soft ball stage. Add pecans and beat until mixture loses its gloss. Drop onto wax paper. **Yield:** 3 dozen.

Mrs. Winston Borum (Jimmie)

Grandma's Pecan Balls

1 cup butter
½ cup powdered sugar
½ teaspoon salt

2 teaspoons vanilla extract
2 cups sifted flour
2 cups finely chopped pecans

Cream together butter and powdered sugar. Add remaining ingredients and mix well. Chill for 2 hours or overnight. Shape dough into 1-inch balls and place on ungreased cookie sheet. Bake at 350° for 12-15 minutes. While cookies are still warm, roll in additional powdered sugar. **Yield:** 4 dozen.

Note: *Pretty cookie – similar to sand tart.*

Mrs. Pete Bennett (Stephanie)

Italian Nut Balls

¾ cup sugar
1 teaspoon salt
¾ cup butter
2 egg yolks, reserve whites
½ teaspoon vanilla extract

½ teaspoon almond extract
2 cups flour
¾ cup chopped nuts
Red or green jelly

Mix first 6 ingredients about 1 minute. Lightly spoon in 2 cups flour, blend. Roll into 1-inch balls. Roll balls into reserved egg whites then in chopped nuts. Place on greased cookie sheet. Poke finger into each ball making an indention. Bake at 350° for 10-12 minutes. Remove from cookie sheet and place jelly into each indentation while warm. Cool. **Yield:** 3 dozen.

Mrs. John Mearns (June)

Oatmeal Chocolate Chip Cookies

1 cup shortening	1 teaspoon salt
¾ cup firmly packed brown sugar	1 teaspoon baking soda
	1 cup finely chopped nuts
¾ cup granulated sugar	1 package (12 ounces)
2 eggs, beaten	chocolate bits
1 teaspoon hot water	2 cups oatmeal, uncooked
1½ cups flour	1 teaspoon vanilla extract

Cream shortening and sugars. Add eggs one at a time. Add hot water and sifted dry ingredients. Add nuts, chocolate bits, oatmeal, and vanilla extract. Drop by teaspoon on greased cookie sheet. Bake at 375° for 8-10 minutes. **Yield:** 100 small cookies.

Mrs. James Sowards (Nancy)

Super-Duper Chocolate Cookies

½ cup margarine or shortening	4 eggs, unbeaten
4 squares unsweetened chocolate or ¾ cup cocoa plus 2 Tablespoons shortening	2 cups flour
	⅛ teaspoon salt
	2 teaspoons baking powder
2 cups sugar	½ cup chopped nuts
2 teaspoons vanilla extract	Powdered sugar

Melt margarine and chocolate. Add sugar and vanilla and mix well. Add eggs; beating after each one. Sift together flour, salt, and baking powder and add to chocolate mixture. Stir in nuts. Chill dough for several hours. Form into small balls (about 1 teaspoon) and roll in powdered sugar. Place on greased cookie sheet. Bake at 350° for 12-15 minutes. **Yield:** About 6 dozen.

Note: *These freeze well after baking.*

Mrs. Ellwood Jones (Ann)

♥ *To make baking powder, mix 2 tablespoons cream of tartar, 1 tablespoon baking soda, and 1 tablespoon cornstarch. Measure the same as the commercial mix.*

Small Chocolate Tarts
Kids Love These

1 roll (20 ounces) refrigerated
   peanut butter cookie dough
1 jar (12 ounces) fudge sauce

Pecan halves or maraschino
   cherries

Slice cookie dough thin and press into miniature muffin tins. Bake as directed on package. When cool fill each cup with fudge sauce and top with a pecan or cherry. **Yield:** 3 dozen.

Note: *May use a chocolate kiss or peanut butter cup placed on warm cookie instead of fudge sauce.*

Mrs. Wallace Brown (Gayle)

♥ *If crisp cookies soften in storage, place them in a 300° oven for about 5 minutes.*

Chocolate Peanutty Surprises
Great Christmas Cookie

1 cup creamy peanut butter
½ cup butter or margarine,
   softened
1 cup firmly packed brown sugar
2 eggs
1 cup flour

1 teaspoon baking powder
1 teaspoon cinnamon
1 package (14 ounces) milk
   chocolate kisses
Powdered sugar

Cream peanut butter, margarine and brown sugar. Beat in eggs. Combine flour, baking powder, and cinnamon. Add gradually to creamed mixture until well blended. Chill dough at least 30 minutes for easy handling. Mold 1 teaspoon dough around each chocolate kiss. Place on ungreased cookie sheet and bake at 350° for 10-12 minutes. Remove from oven and cool slightly. Roll in powdered sugar. **Yield:** 5 dozen.

Mrs. Mark Layton (Beth)

Aunt Minnie's Boiled Cookies

2 cups sugar
3 Tablespoons cocoa
½ cup margarine
½ cup milk

½ cup peanut butter
3 cups oatmeal
1 teaspoon vanilla extract
½ cup chopped nuts

Boil together sugar, cocoa, margarine, and milk for 1 minute. Add peanut butter, oats, vanilla, and nuts. Drop by tablespoon on waxed paper or spread on greased pan and cut into squares. **Yield:** Approximately 4 dozen.

Mrs. Ellwood Jones (Ann)

Chocolate-Corn Flake Cookies
Super Easy!

2 large (8 ounces each) Hershey
  bars
2 squares unsweetened baking
  chocolate

5 cups corn flakes, crushed
1 cup raisins
1 cup chopped walnuts

Melt chocolates and cool slightly. Crush corn flakes. Add corn flakes, raisins, and nuts to chocolate. Drop by teaspoonfuls onto waxed paper. Let cool (overnight is best). **Yield:** 4½-5 dozen.

Note: *Chocolate can be melted in the microwave at a medium power setting. Cooling process may be hastened by placing in the refrigerator until firm.*

Mrs. John Mearns (June)

"Leave Me Alone" Cookies
Pretty Cookie for a Party

2 egg whites, beaten
¾ cup sugar
½ teaspoon vanilla extract

1 package (6 ounces) semi-sweet
  chocolate chips
1 cup finely chopped pecans

Preheat oven to 350°. Beat the egg whites until stiff. Add sugar gradually. Beat at high speed for 5 minutes. Fold in vanilla, chocolate chips, and pecans. Drop from a teaspoon on a foil-lined cookie sheet. Put in the oven and turn the heat off. Leave in the oven overnight or approximately 7 hours. **Yield:** 3 dozen meringue-like cookies.

Mrs. Doug Rivenbark (Penny)

Marilyn's Lemon Drops

1 container (4½ ounces) non-dairy
   whipped topping
1 box (18 ounces) lemon cake mix

1 egg
Powdered sugar

Mix all ingredients and shape into balls. Roll in powdered sugar. Bake at 350° for 8-10 minutes. **Yield:** 3 dozen.

Mrs. Wallace Brown (Gayle)

Pecan Butter Rounds

2   cups butter
1½ cups sifted powdered sugar
1   Tablespoon vanilla extract

3½ cups sifted cake flour
1½ cups chopped pecans
Powdered sugar, sifted

Cream butter until soft. Add powdered sugar and vanilla. Blend in flour slowly. Fold in pecans. Chill (1 hour or more). Form teaspoon size balls and place on cookie sheet. Bake at 350° for 15-20 minutes. Cool. Sift powdered sugar over cookies. **Yield:** 7 dozen.

Mrs. William Hollon (Kasey)

Pineapple Cookies

½ cup margarine
1 cup firmly packed brown sugar
¼ teaspoon salt
2 cups sifted flour
¼ teaspoon baking soda
1 teaspoon baking powder

1 egg
¾ cup crushed pineapple, drained
1 cup chopped pecans
1 teaspoon vanilla extract
About 50 maraschino cherry
   halves or candied cherries

Combine all ingredients except nuts, vanilla, and cherries. Mix thoroughly. Add nuts and vanilla and stir well. Drop by teaspoons onto cookie sheet. Press down on center and top with cherry half. Bake at 375° for 10-12 minutes. **Yield:** 4 dozen.

Mrs. Bill Frank (Barbara)

Stained Glass Cookies

1 package (12 ounces) chocolate chips
½ cup margarine
1 package (10½ ounces) small colored marshmallows

1 cup chopped nuts
1 teaspoon vanilla extract
1 package (10 ounces) coconut

Melt chocolate and margarine over medium heat and cool. Add marshmallows, nuts, and vanilla. Place on wax paper and form into two logs. Roll logs over coconut, wrap in wax paper and refrigerate. Slice when firm. **Yield:** 2 dozen.

Mrs. Ted Denbow (Connie)

Cut-Out Cookies

½ cup butter or margarine
½ cup sugar
2 eggs
1 teaspoon vanilla extract

Food coloring, optional
2¾ cups flour
2 teaspoons baking powder

Combine butter, sugar, eggs, vanilla, and food coloring. Mix thoroughly. Add flour and baking powder. (The batter will be very stiff so it's best to add the last bits of flour by hand.) Do not chill dough. Roll out to ¼-inch thick. Cut into shapes. Bake at 400° for 6-7 minutes on an ungreased cookie sheet. **Yield:** 2 dozen (2-inch) cookies.

Note: *These are not too sweet, so an icing is good on them. This is an easy dough for children to use because it is stiff and does not get too sticky.*

Mrs. Ellwood Jones (Ann)

Blueberry Delight

1 angel food cake
1 can (21 ounces) blueberry pie
  filling
1 package (6 ounces) instant
  vanilla flavored pudding

2 cups milk
1 cup sour cream
1 carton (20 ounces) non-dairy
  whipped topping

Cut cake in half. Break both halves into bite-size pieces and place ½ into bottom of 9x13-inch pan. Pour pie filling over cake pieces. Place other half of cake pieces over pie filling. Prepare vanilla pudding using the milk. Add sour cream and mix. Pour mixture over cake. Top with non-dairy whipped topping and refrigerate. **Yield:** 9-12 servings.

Note: *May be topped with chopped pecans.*

Mrs. Jim Conine (Donna)

♥ *Store soft cookies in a tightly covered container. It helps to place a slice of bread in the container. Store crisp cookies loosely covered.*

Brownies
Easy

½ cup butter, melted
4 squares (1 ounce each) baking
  chocolate
4 eggs
2 cups sugar

1 cup chopped pecans
1 cup flour
1 teaspoon vanilla extract
Salt, pinch

Melt butter and chocolate. Stir in remaining ingredients. Spread into a greased 9x13-inch ovenproof dish. Bake at 325° for 30 minutes. **Yield:** 12-16 brownies.

Mrs. William Hollon (Kasey)

Caramel-Filled Brownies

1 package (14 ounces) caramels	¾ cup margarine, softened
⅔ cup evaporated milk, divided in half	1 cup chopped nuts
	1 teaspoon vanilla extract
1 package (18 ounces) German chocolate cake mix	1 package (12 ounces) semi-sweet chocolate chips

Combine caramels and ⅓ cup evaporated milk. Cook over low heat, stirring until caramels are melted. The microwave may be utilized for this step. Combine cake mix, margarine, ⅓ cup evaporated milk, nuts, and vanilla. Press ½ of cake mixture into greased and floured 9x13-inch ovenproof dish. Bake at 350° for 6 minutes. Sprinkle with chocolate chips and pour caramel mixture over chips. Crumble remaining cake dough over caramel mixture. Bake 15-18 minutes. Cool and cut into squares. **Yield:** 24 squares.

Note: *Freezes well.*

Mrs. King Bourland (Carol)

Chocolate Mint Brownies

Bottom Layer:	Middle Layer:
1 cup sugar	2 cups powdered sugar
½ cup butter	½ cup butter
4 eggs, beaten	2 Tablespoons crème de menthe
1 cup flour	
½ teaspoon salt	Glaze:
1 can (16 ounces) chocolate syrup	1 package (6 ounces) chocolate chips
1 teaspoon vanilla extract	6 Tablespoons butter

Bottom Layer: Combine all ingredients and put into a greased 9x13-inch ovenproof dish. Bake at 350° for 30 minutes.
Middle Layer: Mix all ingredients and spread over cake that has cooled.
Glaze: Melt chocolate chips and butter and pour over middle layer. (This may be melted in a microwave oven for approximately 2 minutes). Refrigerate. **Yield:** Approximately 2 dozen.

Note: *This freezes well.*

Mrs. Jeff Farmer (Kaliko)

Vi's Blonde Brownies

½ cup butter or margarine,
    melted
1½ cups lightly packed brown
    sugar
2 eggs
1 teaspoon vanilla extract

1 cup flour
1 teaspoon baking powder
½ teaspoon salt
¾ cup semi-sweet chocolate chips
1 cup chopped pecans, optional
Powdered sugar

Combine butter, brown sugar, eggs, and vanilla and set aside. Mix flour, baking powder, salt, and fold into first mixture. Add chocolate chips and pecans. Pour into an 8x8-inch square ovenproof dish. Bake at 350° for 25 minutes. Let cool, dust with powdered sugar, if desired, and cut into squares. **Yield:** 16-20 servings.

Mrs. Wallace Brown (Gayle)

Cream Cheese Brownies

Chocolate Layer:
4 ounces German sweet chocolate
3 Tablespoons butter
2 eggs
¾ cup sugar
½ teaspoon baking powder
¼ teaspoon salt
½ cup unsifted flour
1 teaspoon vanilla extract
¼ teaspoon almond extract
½ cup chopped nuts

Cream Cheese Layer:
1 package (3 ounces) cream
    cheese, softened
2 Tablespoons butter
¼ cup sugar
1 egg
1 Tablespoon flour
½ teaspoon vanilla extract

Melt chocolate and butter over low heat. Stir, then cool. Beat eggs until light in color. Slowly add sugar and beat until thickened. Stir in baking powder, salt, and flour. Blend in cooled chocolate mixture, vanilla and almond extracts, and nuts. Set aside. Cream the cheese with the butter. Gradually, add sugar, creaming until fluffy. Blend in egg, flour, and vanilla. Spread ½ of chocolate mixture in a greased 8 or 9-inch square ovenproof dish. Top with cheese mixture. Spread remaining chocolate over top. Zigzag knife through batter for a marble effect. Bake at 350° for 35-40 minutes. **Yield:** About 16 brownies.

Note: *Store in refrigerator.*

Mrs. Ellwood Jones (Ann)

Marshmallow Brownies

4 eggs, beaten	Icing:
2 cups sugar	6 Tablespoons butter
1 cup butter	1 can (5 ounces) evaporated milk
4 Tablespoons cocoa	6 cups powdered sugar
1½ cups flour	¾ cup cocoa
2 cups chopped pecans	Salt, pinch
Salt, pinch	
2 teaspoons vanilla extract	
1 package (10½ ounces) miniature marshmallows	

Combine eggs and sugar. Melt butter, add cocoa and mix. Stir into eggs. Combine flour, pecans, salt, and vanilla. Add to egg mixture and mix well. Pour into a 9x13-inch ovenproof dish. Bake at 350° for 25 minutes. While this is baking, combine the icing ingredients and heat in double boiler or slowly in saucepan. When brownies are baked, remove from oven and cover the top with the marshmallows. Pour the hot icing over all. Cool. **Yield:** 20 brownies.

Mrs. Sam Murray (Sandy)

Texas Gold Bars

1 box (18 ounces) yellow cake mix	2 packages (8 ounces each) cream cheese, softened
1 egg, beaten	1 box (16 ounces) powdered sugar (reserve some to sprinkle on top)
½ cup margarine, melted	
2 eggs, beaten	
1 teaspoon vanilla extract	

Mix first 3 ingredients, and press into a 9x13-inch ovenproof dish. Mix remaining ingredients until smooth. Spread over cake mix. Bake at 325° for 1 hour. Sprinkle powdered sugar over top and cut into bars. **Yield:** 12-16 servings.

Mrs. Joe Key (Christie)

Coffee Nut Bars

Bottom Layer:
½ cup butter
½ cup firmly packed brown sugar
1 cup flour

Top Layer:
2 eggs, beaten
1 cup firmly packed brown sugar

1 teaspoon vanilla extract
2 Tablespoons flour
1 teaspoon baking powder
½ teaspoon salt
1 cup coconut
1 cup chopped nuts

Mix butter, brown sugar, and flour. Pat into bottom of a greased and floured 9x13-inch ovenproof dish. Bake at 350° for 10 minutes. Mix together ingredients for top layer. Spread over cooked bottom layer. Return to oven and bake 25 minutes, until brown. Cut into small bars or squares. **Yield:** 24 bars.

Mrs. Pete Cantrell (Wyvonne)

Eleanor's Bars
Great After School Snack

Bottom Layer:
½ cup firmly packed brown sugar
1 cup flour
½ cup butter, melted

Top Layer:
1 cup firmly packed brown sugar

1 cup flaked coconut
1 cup chopped pecans
½ teaspoon baking powder
¼ teaspoon salt
2 Tablespoons flour
2 eggs, slightly beaten

Preheat oven to 350°. Mix bottom layer ingredients and pat into 7x11-inch ovenproof dish. Bake 15 minutes or until it starts to turn light brown. Mix all top layer ingredients in bowl. Spread over cooked bottom layer. Return to oven and cook for 15 minutes. Cool before cutting. **Yield:** Approximately 15 squares.

Mrs. Dennis Furlong (Dede)

Lemon Bars

Crust:
2 cups flour
½ cup powdered sugar
1 cup margarine,
    melted

Filling:
4 eggs, beaten
2 cups sugar
½ cup lemon juice
¼ cup flour
½ teaspoon baking powder

Combine flour and powdered sugar. Add melted margarine and mix well. Press evenly into a 9x13-inch ovenproof dish. Bake at 350° for 20-25 minutes or until lightly browned. Beat eggs, sugar, and lemon juice together. Combine flour and baking powder and stir into egg mixture. Pour over crust and bake at 350° for 25 minutes. Sprinkle with powdered sugar and cut into bars. **Yield:** 35 bars.

Mrs. Doug Rivenbark (Penny)

Pecan Bars

10 Tablespoons butter, softened
1½ cups flour
⅓ cup sugar
½ cup firmly packed brown
    sugar
½ cup light corn syrup

2 Tablespoons flour
3 eggs
1 teaspoon vanilla extract
¼ teaspoon salt
½-1 cup pecans

Fold butter into flour and white sugar. Press firmly into 9-inch ungreased pie tin. Bake at 350° for 15-20 minutes. Combine remaining ingredients and beat until well blended. Pour over crust. Bake at 350° for 30-35 minutes until golden brown. **Yield:** 8 servings.

Mrs. Jack Hamer (Pam)

Quick Crescent Pecan Pie Bars

1 can (8 ounces) refrigerated
  quick crescent dinner rolls
1 egg, beaten
½ cup chopped pecans
½ cup sugar

½ cup corn syrup
1 Tablespoon butter or
  margarine, melted
½ teaspoon vanilla extract

Preheat oven to 375°. Lightly grease 9x13-inch ovenproof dish. Separate the crescent dough into two large rectangles. Press rectangles over bottom and ½ inch up sides of prepared pan to form crust, then seal any perforations. Bake crust at 375° for 5 minutes. In medium bowl, combine remaining ingredients. Pour over partially baked crust. Bake at 375° for 18-22 minutes until golden brown. Cool, then cut into bars. **Yield:** 2 dozen bars.

Mrs. Jim Conine (Donna)

Easy Graham Cracker Squares
A Family Favorite

32 graham cracker squares,
  crushed
1 package (12 ounces) semi-sweet
  chocolate chips

1 can (14 ounces) sweetened
  condensed milk
1 teaspoon vanilla extract
Salt, dash

Combine all ingredients in a large bowl. Mix well. Spread on a greased 10½x15-inch cookie sheet. Bake at 350° for 15 minutes. Cool and cut into squares. **Yield:** 15-18 servings.

Note: *Keeps well in tin.*

Mrs. Mallard Tysseland (Jill)

Seven Layer Cookie

½ cup margarine
1 cup graham cracker crumbs
1 package (6 ounces) semi-sweet chocolate chips
1 package (6 ounces) butterscotch chips

1 cup shredded coconut
1 cup chopped pecans
1 can (14 ounces) sweetened condensed milk

Melt margarine in 9x13-inch ovenproof dish. Sprinkle graham cracker crumbs over margarine. Layer the chips, coconut, and pecans. Pour the can of condensed milk on top. Bake at 350° for approximately 30 minutes. Cool completely before cutting. **Yield:** Approximately 2 dozen squares.

Note: *These keep well and may be made ahead.*

Mrs. Bill Frank (Barbara)

Chocolate Decadence

16 squares (1 ounce each) semi-sweet chocolate
¾ cup butter
¾ cup powdered sugar

1 Tablespoon flour
4 eggs, separated
1 teaspoon vanilla extract
1 cup sour cream

Preheat oven to 375°. Melt chocolate and butter in medium saucepan. Gradually blend in sugar and flour, stirring constantly. Remove from heat. With wire whisk or beater, blend in egg yolks one at a time, beating well after each. Stir in vanilla. Beat egg whites in separate bowl until stiff, then fold into the chocolate mixture. Remove one cup of the mixture and blend with the sour cream, set aside. Pour remaining mixture into a lightly greased 8-inch ovenproof dish. Top with chocolate and sour cream mixture. Bake 25 minutes. (Center will not appear set). Cool completely and cover. Chill at least 4 hours. Cut into squares to serve. **Yield:** 16 squares.

Note: *Squares may be frozen. Wrap individually in foil to freeze. Before serving, unwrap and thaw for 30 minutes at room temperature.*

Mrs. Robert George (Linda)

♥ *If beaten egg whites do not slide when the bowl is turned upside down, they are stiff enough.*

Chocolate Hungarian Torte

Torte:
7 large eggs, separated
¼ teaspoon salt
1½ cups powdered sugar
¼ cup plus 2 Tablespoons
   unsweetened cocoa
1½ teaspoons vanilla extract
1 container (12 ounces) non-
   dairy whipped topping

Chocolate Glaze:
4 Tablespoons butter
4 squares unsweetened chocolate
2 cups powdered sugar
5 Tablespoons boiling water
Salt, dash
2 teaspoons vanilla extract
Toasted sliced almonds, optional

Torte: Beat egg whites with salt until stiff but not dry. Beat in sugar, 1 tablespoon at a time. Fold in cocoa. Beat yolks until thick and lemon colored. Fold into the cocoa mixture. Add vanilla and fold until mixed. Spread batter in a 17x11x1-inch jelly roll pan lined with waxed paper that is well greased. Bake at 350° about 25 minutes. Turn out on towel sprinkled with powdered sugar. Very gently peel off waxed paper. Cool. Cut crosswise into four equal portions. Stack into layers, spreading whipped topping between each layer. Spread chocolate glaze over cake.

Glaze: Melt butter and chocolate together. Remove from heat and add remaining ingredients. Beat until smooth, glossy, and cooled. Drizzle over cake. Sprinkle with toasted almonds if desired. Chill until ready to serve.
Yield: 12-16 servings.

Mrs. Doug Rivenbark (Penny)

Chocolate Mousse

8 squares (1 ounce each)
   semi-sweet chocolate
½ cup butter
3 Tablespoons water

5 eggs, separated
1 teaspoon instant coffee
5 Tablespoons sugar
Whipped cream

Melt chocolate, butter, and water in double boiler, stirring constantly. Cool completely. Add egg yolks, coffee, and sugar. Beat egg whites until stiff. Fold into chocolate mixture and refrigerate. Serve with whipped cream.
Yield: 6-8 servings.

Note: *May be made 1-2 days in advance.*

Mrs. William Hollon (Kasey)

Four Layer Delight
Almost Sinful!

1 cup flour
½ cup margarine
1 cup chopped pecans
1 cup powdered sugar
1 package (8 ounces) cream cheese
1 container (16 ounces) non-dairy whipped topping

3 small packages (3½ ounces each) instant chocolate pudding mix
4½ cups milk
Chocolate bar, grated

First Layer: Mix flour, margarine, and ½ cup pecans together. Spread with fingers into 9x13-inch ovenproof dish. Bake at 350° for 20 minutes or until brown. Let cool completely.

Second Layer: Mix powdered sugar, cream cheese, and 1 cup whipped topping. Spread over crust very carefully.

Third Layer: Combine pudding and milk. Beat until thick. Spread over second layer.

Fourth Layer: Spread remaining whipped topping over pudding. Top with grated chocolate. Refrigerate 24 hours before serving. Sprinkle remainder of nuts over top. **Yield:** 14-16 servings.

Mrs. Pete Bennett (Stephanie)

Pumpkin Roll

3 eggs
1 cup sugar
⅔ cup canned pumpkin
¾ cup flour
1 teaspoon cinnamon
1 teaspoon baking powder

Filling:
1 cup powdered sugar
4 Tablespoons butter
2 packages (3 ounces each) cream cheese, softened
½ teaspoon vanilla extract

Beat eggs with sugar for 5 minutes. Add pumpkin, flour, cinnamon, and baking powder. Mix well. Grease and flour a 10x15x1-inch cookie sheet and place waxed paper inside pan. Pour in mixture and bake at 375° for 15-20 minutes. Then *immediately turn over on dish towel*, peel off waxed paper, and roll up lengthwise in towel. Cool 1 hour. To make filling, cream together the 4 filling ingredients. Unroll pumpkin roll and spread with filling. Re-roll in waxed paper and refrigerate or slice into 1-inch rolls and serve. **Yield:** 15 servings.

Mrs. Mac Cravy (Sharon)

Strawberries with Devonshire Cream
Quick, Easy and Excellent!

1 package (8 ounces) cream
  cheese
1 cup whipping cream

½ teaspoon vanilla extract
Powdered sugar to taste
Strawberries, 1 cup per person

Beat cream cheese until softened in a small bowl. Gradually add cream until mixture is smooth. Stir in vanilla. Add sugar to desired sweetness. Wash and hull strawberries. Keep berries and cream mixture in refrigerator until ready to serve. Dish strawberries into individual bowls or goblets and spoon cream over them. **Yield:** 1½-2 cups cream.

Mrs. Joe Key (Christie)

Strawberry Surprise

¾ cup margarine, softened
3 Tablespoons firmly packed
   brown sugar
2½ cups coarsely crushed pretzels
1 package (6 ounces) strawberry
   flavored gelatin
2 cups boiling water

3 packages (10 ounces each) frozen
  strawberries, undrained
1 package (8 ounces) cream
  cheese, softened
1 cup sugar
1 cup whipping cream, whipped

Cream margarine and brown sugar until smooth. Stir in pretzels. Pat into a 9x13-inch ovenproof baking dish. Bake at 350° for 10 minutes. Set aside to cool. Dissolve gelatin in boiling water. Stir in strawberries. Chill until slightly thickened. Beat cream cheese and sugar until smooth. Fold in whipped cream. Spread over crust. Top with gelatin mixture. Chill until firm. **Yield:** 10-12 servings.

Mrs. Thomas Hunter (Lynda)

Kahlúa Mousse

1 container (12 ounces) non-
   dairy whipped topping
2-3 teaspoons instant coffee

5 teaspoons cocoa
6 teaspoons sugar
4 ounces Kahlúa liqueur

Add all dry ingredients to whipped topping and blend. Stir in Kahlúa with spatula. Spoon into footed dessert glasses. Chill and serve. **Yield:** 6 servings.

Mrs. Jeff Farmer (Kaliko)

Fresh Fruit Pudding Compote
Pretty in a Glass Bowl

1¾ cups cold milk
1 Tablespoon crème de cacao
1 cup non-dairy whipped topping

Fresh fruits
1 package (3 ounces) French vanilla instant pudding mix

Pour milk and liqueur into bowl. Add pudding mix and beat slowly for 1 minute. Add whipped topping and beat until just blended. Arrange fruits in bowl and top with pudding. **Yield:** 6-8 servings.

Note: *More liqueur could be added.*

Mrs. James Sowards (Nancy)

Blender Pots-de-Crème

1 package (6 ounces) semi-sweet chocolate chips
2 Tablespoons sugar
2 eggs

1 teaspoon vanilla extract
Salt, pinch
¾ cup milk

Place first 5 ingredients in blender. Heat milk to boiling and pour into blender; blend 1 minute. Pour into fancy cups or champagne glasses. Chill and serve. **Yield:** 8 servings.

Mrs. Dennis Furlong (Dede)

Rum Tortoni

½ cup chopped almonds
½ cup chopped maraschino cherries
½ cup coconut

1 quart vanilla ice cream, softened
3 teaspoons rum extract

Toast almonds and cherries lightly in oven; cool. Combine with coconut. Stir into ice cream. Stir in rum extract. Pour into container and freeze overnight. Scoop into individual serving bowls. **Yield:** 4 servings.

Mrs. Mac Cravy (Sharon)

Pumpkin Cream

Ginger snaps	½ teaspoon ginger
1 can (20 ounces) pumpkin	½ teaspoon nutmeg
1 cup sugar	½ gallon vanilla ice cream,
1 egg	softened
1 teaspoon cinnamon	Non-dairy whipped topping

Cover bottom and sides of 9x13-inch dish with ginger snaps. Mix all ingredients well except ice cream and whipped topping. Blend in softened ice cream and pour this mixture over ginger snaps. Spread with whipped topping and freeze. **Yield:** 12-15 servings.

Mrs. Greg Smith (Katie)

Chocolate Cookie Frozen Dessert

1 package (16 ounces) Oreo cookies, crushed	1 jar (11 ounces) Kraft chocolate fudge topping
½-¾ cup real butter, melted	1½ cups chopped pecans
½ gallon vanilla ice cream, sliced	1 carton (8 ounces) non-dairy whipped topping

Layer ingredients in order given in a 9x13-inch pan. Freeze. **Yield:** 15-20 servings.

Note: *Fudge topping spreads easier if pan is put in freezer after ice cream is layered.*

Mrs. Thomas Hunter (Lynda)

Frozen Caramel Dessert

1 bag (9 ounces) small Heath bars, crumbled	½ cup sour cream
28 caramels	1 cup whipping cream
⅓ cup Amaretto liqueur or dark rum	

In a buttered 1½-quart dish, spread candy crumbs, reserving a small amount for topping. Melt caramels with the liqueur or rum in a saucepan. Cool to room temperature. Stir in creams. Whip until thick. Pour into dish and top with reserved candy crumbs. Freeze. Serve with chocolate sauce, if desired. **Yield:** 6 servings.

Mrs. Dan Boyd (Terry)

Frosty Strawberry Squares

1 cup flour	1 cup sugar
¼ cup firmly packed light brown sugar	2 cups fresh sliced strawberries
	2 Tablespoons lemon juice
½ cup chopped nuts	1 cup whipping cream, whipped
½ cup butter, melted	Whipped cream for garnish
2 egg whites	Strawberry halves

Combine flour, brown sugar, nuts, and butter. Spread in a shallow pan. Bake at 350° for 20 minutes. Sprinkle ⅔ of these baked crumbs into a 9x13-inch ovenproof dish. Combine egg whites, sugar, strawberries, and lemon juice in a large bowl and beat at high speed to form stiff peaks. Fold in whipped cream. Spoon over crumbs and top with remaining ⅓ crumbs. Freeze 6 hours or overnight. Garnish with whipped cream and strawberry halves. **Yield:** 8 servings.

Note: *If frozen strawberries are substituted for the fresh, reduce to ⅔ cup.*

Mrs. Jack Hamer (Pam)

♥ *Before beating egg whites bring them to room temperature.*

Pat McGinnis's Ice Cream Delight

1 cup butter or margarine	4 eggs, beaten
3 cups powdered sugar	¾ cup crushed chocolate wafers
3 squares (1 ounce each) unsweetened baking chocolate, melted	½ gallon vanilla ice cream, softened
	Chocolate shavings

Cream butter and sugar. Add chocolate and eggs. Cover bottom of 9x13-inch glass dish with crushed chocolate wafers. Pour chocolate mixture over wafers. Spread ice cream on top. Sprinkle with chocolate shavings or a few wafer crumbs. Freeze. **Yield:** 24 servings.

Note: *May also top with chopped pecans.*

Mrs. Bill Frank (Barbara)

Mrs. Smith's Ice Cream
For 6-quart freezer.

8 eggs
2 cups sugar
2 can (12 ounces each) evaporated
  milk

2 cups whole milk
2 cups half and half
Vanilla extract to taste

Beat eggs and sugar well, about 2 minutes. Stir in milk, half and half, and evaporated milk. Add vanilla. Pour into freezer, plug in or crank away. **Yield:** 10-12 (1 cup) servings.

Note: *May add in 2-3 cups fresh strawberries or peaches; eliminate whole milk.*

Mrs. Greg Smith (Katie)

Strawberry-Banana Ice Cream

2 cans (14 ounces each)
  sweetened condensed
  milk
36 ounces strawberry soda

2 packages (10 ounces each) frozen
  strawberries or 2 cups mashed
  fresh berries
6 bananas, mashed

Mix all ingredients. Pour into ice cream freezer. Freeze according to manufacturer's directions. **Yield:** 1 gallon.

Note: *May substitute orange pop and cut up mandarin oranges as a variation.*

Mrs. James Layton (Vicki)

Sinful Hot Fudge Sauce

½ cup margarine or butter
4 squares (1 ounce each)
  unsweetened chocolate

Salt, pinch
3 cups sugar
1⅔ cups evaporated milk

Melt margarine and chocolate in top of a double boiler. Add salt, sugar, and milk alternately until smooth. Heat until starts to bubble. **Yield:** 1 quart.

Note: *Sauce will keep indefinitely in refrigerator.*

Mrs. James Layton (Vicki)

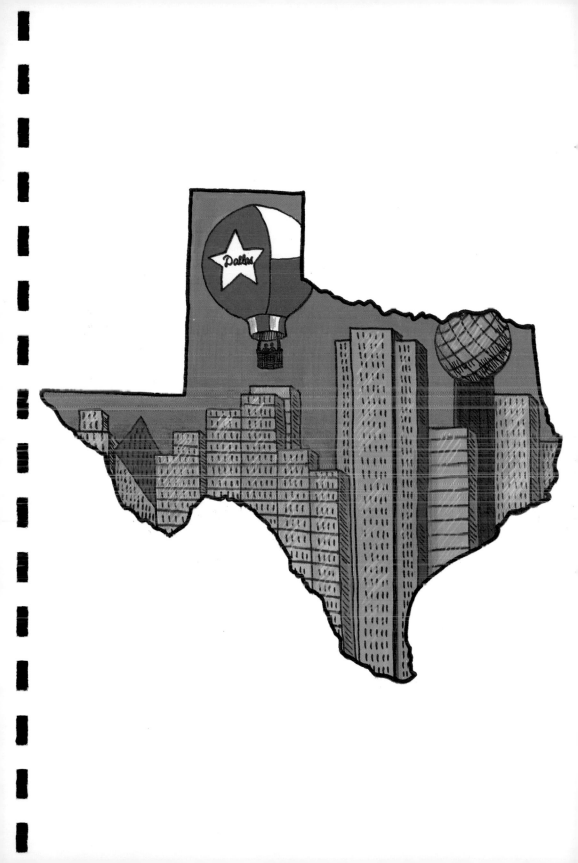

DALLAS **Children's** ADVOCACY CENTER

Their hope is in your vision

The Dallas Children's Advocacy Center is an innovative approach to improving the treatment of child victims of sexual and physical abuse in Dallas County. The program offers a coordinated, multi-disciplinary intervention system involving agencies — police, prosecutors, child protective workers, therapists and medical personnel — working together as a team in a single location. The team's goals are to minimize each child's trauma, provide immediate and long-term treatment and services, and to ensure proper investigation of cases.

With funding made possible from the sales of Deep In The Heart, Dallas Junior Forum has provided substantial initial funding for this innovative approach to treatment.

Hodgepodge

For a special taste, we often embellish
The foods we serve with a sauce or relish.
We make jellies, goodies and fruit that is curried,
And the recipes work for those who are hurried.

Texas Sauce for Corn on Cob

½ cup butter
½ cup whipping cream
1 cup grated American cheese

¼ teaspoon paprika
½ teaspoon salt
¼ teaspoon pepper

Melt butter in a double boiler. Add remaining ingredients. Cook over low heat, stirring until cheese is melted and mixture is well blended and hot. Keep mixture warm so it will not get too thick. Add a small amount of milk if it thickens too much. Roll hot cooked corn in sauce, turning until cob is coated. **Yield:** 1 cup.

Note: *This sauce is also great served over broccoli, cauliflower, and other vegetables.*

Mrs. Jack Hamer (Pam)

♥ *It is best to use a wire whisk, not an electric mixer, when making a sauce.*

♥ *Freeze leftover creamed soups in ice cube trays. Substitute them for sauces when you are in a hurry.*

Barbeque Sauce

½ cup vinegar
⅓ cup salad oil
4 Tablespoons Worcestershire sauce
1 large onion, chopped
3 large cloves garlic, chopped
1½ teaspoons salt

1 teaspoon paprika
½ cup ketchup
¼ teaspoon dry mustard
1½ teaspoons pepper
¾ cup firmly packed brown sugar
Juice of 1 lemon

Combine all ingredients in a saucepan. Simmer for 1 hour or longer. Use on chicken, ribs, chops or anything that is going on the grill. **Yield:** 2½ cups.

Note: *It is not necessary to simmer the full hour if time does not permit.*

Mrs. Brian Byrne (Veronica)

Delicious Barbeque Sauce
Great on Hamburgers and Chicken

¼ cup vinegar
½ cup water
1 Tablespoon mustard
2 Tablespoons sugar
1 teaspoon salt
1 teaspoon pepper
½ lemon, juiced

1 onion, sliced
¼ cup margarine
½ cup ketchup
1 teaspoon liquid smoke
1 Tablespoon Worcestershire sauce

Combine first 9 ingredients in medium saucepan. Stew for 20 minutes. Add ketchup, liquid smoke, and Worcestershire sauce. **Yield:** 2 cups.

Note: *1 tablespoon lemon juice concentrate equals juice of ½ lemon.*

Mrs. Pete Bennett (Stephanie)

Flank Steak Marinade

2 cups sherry
1 cup soy sauce

1 cup olive oil
2 green onions, chopped

Blend all ingredients together. Marinate steak 4-6 hours. **Yield:** 4 cups or enough to marinate 3-4 pounds steak.

Mrs. Greg Smith (Katie)

Seafood Cocktail Sauce

½ cup ketchup
½ lemon, cut into pieces
½ Tablespoon prepared horseradish

¼ cup chili sauce
½ teaspoon Worcestershire sauce

Put all ingredients in blender. Blend on low speed. Refrigerate. **Yield:** ¾ cup sauce.

Mrs. William Hollon (Kasey)

New Orleans Rémoulade Sauce for Shrimp

½ cup vinegar
4 Tablespoons horseradish
  mustard
2 Tablespoons ketchup
1 Tablespoon paprika
1 teaspoon salt

½ teaspoon pepper
1 cup salad oil
½ cup chopped celery
½ cup chopped green onion
Garlic purée, dash

Mix all ingredients in blender. Pour over peeled, boiled shrimp and refrigerate at least 1 hour before serving on a lettuce leaf or in a cocktail server. **Yield:** Enough sauce to cover 2 pounds of shrimp.

Mrs. Jerry Brown (Linda)

Blender Hollandaise

3 egg yolks
1 Tablespoon lemon juice
½ teaspoon salt

2 drops Tabasco sauce
½ cup butter, melted

In a blender, combine all ingredients, except butter. Mix well. Slowly pour in butter while blender is on low speed. **Yield:** ⅔ cup.

Mrs. Roy Watson (Charlene)

Jalapeño Pepper Jelly

¾ cup jalapeño peppers (seeded)
¾ cup green pepper
1¼ cups vinegar

6½ cups sugar
1 bottle (4 ounces) Certo
Wax for jelly

Chop first 4 ingredients in blender. Place in pan and bring to boil, boiling for 5 minutes. Cool. Return to heat and cook 2 more minutes, stirring occasionally. Add bottle of Certo and cook, stirring for 5 minutes. Pour into 4-ounce jelly jars. Top with melted wax. **Yield:** 6 (4-ounce) jars.

Mrs. Marvin Chronister (Donna)

Cranberry Relish

4 cups fresh cranberries	¼ teaspoon ginger
2 oranges, peeled and sectioned	¼ teaspoon cinnamon
½ cup raisins	2 Tablespoons orange juice
½ cup chopped walnuts	2 Tablespoons vinegar
1¼ cups sugar	

In a 3-quart casserole, combine all ingredients. Mix well. Cover with waxed paper and microwave on high for 9-11 minutes, or until berries burst and liquid is slightly thickened. Stir every 4 minutes. **Yield:** 4 cups.

Note: *If storing, place berries in sterilized jars, cover immediately. Process in boiling water.*

Mrs. Jim Conine (Donna)

♥ *Cooking times will always vary in microwave cooking, proportionate to the amount of food cooked.*

Barbeque Powder
Spice up Your Life

1 box (26 ounces) salt	2 ounces garlic powder
9 ounces paprika	1 box (16 ounces) brown sugar
6 ounces pepper	

Combine all ingredients. Mix well. Sprinkle over chicken, ribs, baked beans, hamburgers, or any item of choice. **Yield:** 7½ cups.

Note: *This powder makes a great Christmas gift for teachers, neighbors, or friends. Put in jar and tie with pretty ribbon.*

Mrs. Winston Borum (Jimmie)

Seasoning Mix
Makes a great gift

2 cups grated Parmesan cheese
2 teaspoons salt
½ cup sesame seeds
½ teaspoon garlic salt
1 Tablespoon instant minced
   onion

2 Tablespoons parsley flakes
½ teaspoon dried dill seed
2 Tablespoons poppy seeds
3 Tablespoons celery seeds
2 teaspoons paprika
½ teaspoon cracked pepper

Combine all ingredients in a small bowl. Mix well. Store in a cool, dry place. Sprinkle on baked potato, Italian bread, vegetables or salads. **Yield:** 3 cups.

Note: *Will keep for 3-4 months.*

Mrs. Robert Lusk (Sharon)

Texas Trash
Great Christmas Gift

1 box (12 ounces) shredded rice
  cereal
1 box (15 ounces) shredded wheat
  squares cereal
1 box (10 ounces) round toasted
  oat cereal
1 bag (9 ounces) pretzel sticks
1 pound pecan pieces

1 can (12 ounces) peanuts
4 Tablespoons butter
½ cup bacon drippings
2 Tablespoons Worcestershire
   sauce
1 teaspoon Tabasco sauce
2 teaspoons garlic powder

Combine the first 6 ingredients in a large ovenproof baking pan. Set aside. Combine remaining ingredients in a saucepan and heat until melted. Pour over cereal. Toss well. Bake at 200° for 1-2 hours, stirring occasionally. **Yield:** 20-25 servings.

Note: *May increase Worcestershire sauce to 4 tablespoons.*

Mrs. Thomas Hunter (Lynda)

Granola

1 cup honey	1 cup instant milk
1 cup salad oil	1 cup sesame seeds
5 cups old-fashioned oatmeal	1 cup sunflower seeds
1 cup soya flour	1 cup slivered almonds
1 cup wheat germ	1 cup shredded coconut

Mix together honey and oil. Combine remaining ingredients in a bowl. Pour honey and oil mixture over and toss well. Spread on 2 cookie sheets and bake at 300° for 30 minutes, stirring occasionally. Store in jars or plastic bags. **Yield:** 10 cups.

Mrs. Jack Hamer (Pam)

Sugared Popcorn
An Old Scottish Recipe

⅓ cup popcorn	3 Tablespoons bacon drippings
¼ cup water	⅓ cup sugar

Put unpopped corn into water; set aside. Heat bacon drippings and sugar in a large saucepan. After sugar dissolves add popcorn and water. Be careful of splattering. Cover and shake to pop corn. **Yield:** Approximately 7 cups.

Note: *I discovered "sweet" popcorn at the movies in Edinburg, Scotland. It is good for family nights around the television, gift-giving, and football outings.*

Mrs. Winston Borum (Jimmie)

Caramel Corn

2 cups firmly packed brown sugar	½ cup white corn syrup
1 cup margarine	1 teaspoon baking soda
1½ teaspoons salt	1 teaspoon vanilla extract
	7-8 quarts popped corn

Combine sugar, margarine, salt, and corn syrup in a medium or large saucepan. Cook over low heat until mixture boils. Boil 5 minutes. Add soda and vanilla and stir quickly. Pour over popped corn. Mix well. Spread on cookie sheet. Bake at 200° for 1 hour, stirring every 15 minutes. Remove from cookie sheet immediately and cool on wax paper. **Yield:** 7-8 quarts.

Mrs. Greg Smith (Katie)

Microwave Caramel Corn
Great Holiday Gift

1 cup firmly packed brown sugar
¼ cup light corn syrup
½ teaspoon salt

1½ Tablespoons margarine
½ teaspoon baking soda
3-4 quarts popped corn

Place brown sugar, corn syrup, salt, and margarine in microwave-proof dish. Cook on high power in microwave for 1 minute, or until margarine melts. Stir. Cook 2 more minutes. Add baking soda, blending well (mixture will foam up).

Place popped corn into brown grocery bag. Pour syrup over corn. Close the bag and shake the contents well until corn is well coated. Place bag in microwave and cook 1½ minutes more. Spread out on cookie sheet to cool. **Yield:** 4 quarts.

Note: *Quickly made in the microwave. Easy cleanup with the grocery bag!*

Mrs. Sam Murray (Sandy)

♥ *To clean your microwave, place a wet towel in the oven and microwave for 3-4 minutes. It will easily wipe clean with the towel after the steam has set for a few minutes.*

Sweet Spiced Pecans

2 egg whites
1 Tablespoon water
½ cup sugar
½ teaspoon allspice

½ teaspoon cinnamon
½ teaspoon salt
½ pound pecan halves

Beat egg whites with water until fluffy. Mix sugar, spices, and salt in large bowl. Drop pecans first in egg mixture, then in spice mixture, and spread out on a large cookie sheet lined with heavy duty foil. Bake at 300° for 1 hour, stirring every 15 minutes. Allow to cool, then break up and place into glass jars for storage. Serve with fresh fruit salad, over ice cream or as a snack. **Yield:** ½ pound pecans.

Mrs. Thomas Hunter (Lynda)

Minted Pecans

2 cups sugar
Salt, dash
¾ cup evaporated milk

1 Tablespoon butter
1 Tablespoon peppermint extract
4 cups pecan halves

Mix first 4 ingredients in saucepan. Stir over low heat until dissolved, about 5 minutes. Boil over medium heat for 7 minutes. Add extract, then pecans. Coat pecans well. Lay out on waxed paper quickly. **Yield:** 4 cups.

Mrs. Greg Smith (Katie)

Curried Fruit
A Nice Holiday Dish

½ cup butter
¾ cup firmly packed brown sugar
2 teaspoons curry powder
1 can (29 ounces) pear halves
1 can (16 ounces) peach halves
1 can (17 ounces) apricot halves

1 can (16½ ounces) pitted bing cherries
2 cans (11 ounces each) mandarin oranges
2 bananas, sliced

Melt butter in a small saucepan. Add sugar and curry, mix well. Drain fruit well and arrange in a 9x13-inch ovenproof baking dish. Pour curry mix over fruit. Bake at 350° for 30 minutes. **Yield:** 8-10 servings

Note: *This can be assembled and refrigerated a day early.*

Mrs. Sam Norvell (Patsy)

Pineapple Curried Fruit

2 Tablespoons plus 2 teaspoons
  butter
¾ cup firmly packed light brown
  sugar
1 Tablespoon curry powder
¼ teaspoon cinnamon
¼ teaspoon nutmeg

¼ cup pineapple juice
1 can (15¼ ounces) sliced
  pineapple
1 can (16 ounces) apricots
1 can (16 ounces) peaches
1 can (16 ounces) pears
6-8 medium cherries

Melt together in pan the first 6 ingredients. Cook over medium heat for about 15 minutes. Arrange all fruit in one layer on greased 9x13-inch oven-proof baking dish. Pour sauce over and cook at 325° for 1 hour, uncovered. **Yield:** 8 servings.

Note: *If sauce does not cover fruit, juice from the other fruit cans may be added.*

Mrs. King Bourland (Carol)

♥ *Nuts with cheese and fruit make a perfect conclusion to a meal.*

Fudgesicles
Kids Love These!

1 package (3½ ounces) instant
  chocolate pudding mix
½ cup sugar

½ cup cream
2 cups milk

Mix all ingredients as directed on pudding package. Pour into molds and freeze. **Yield:** 12-16 popsicle molds.

Note: *Can use ice cube trays or paper cups with popsicle sticks put in them.*

Mrs. Ellwood Jones (Ann)

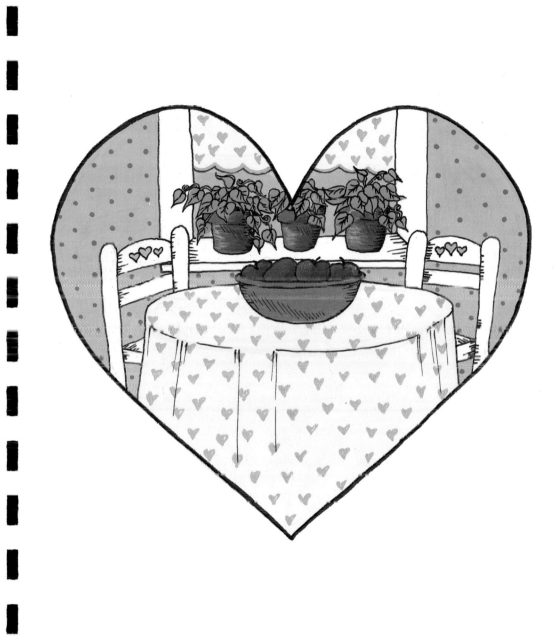

Notes

Menus

When you're planning a meal for family or friend,
Preparing a menu is how it begins.
So, if you want foreign, or seafood, or something
   that's grilled,
Here are menu suggestions that are flavor-filled.

Meal planning is sometimes a tedious and time con-suming task. Let's face it, it's hard to think of new ideas! We have put together some menus to guide you in your planning, and to serve as suggestions for you.

The menus use recipes that can be found within the pages of Deep In the Heart. We hope that these menu ideas will help you in planning some special meals for your family and friends.

Company's Coming

Asparagus Roll-ups
Cream of Carrot Soup
Caesar Salad
Fillets with Crabmeat Stuffing – serves 6-8
Champagne Broccoli
Strawberries with Devonshire Cream

Shrimp Dip
Mandarin Salad
Chicken Kiev – serves 8
Fantastic Rice
Asparagus Au Gratin
Blender Pots-de-Crème
Pecan Butter Rounds

Mushrooms Eleganté
Super Spinach Salad II
Veal Scallopini with Mushrooms – serves 6-8
Juna's Fettucini
Baked Puff Tomatoes
Rum Tortoni

Lunch Bunch

Strawberry Soup
Mary's Salmon Turnovers – serves 12
Super Spinach Salad 1
Pennsylvania Applesauce Bread
Kahlúa Mousse

Iced Avocado Soup
Swiss Quiche – serves 6-8
Fresh Fruit with Fruit Salad Dressing
French Puffs
Fudge Pie

Zucchini Cream Soup
Hawaiian Chicken Salad – serves 6
Asparagus with Sour Cream
Orange Muffins
Frosty Strawberry Squares

Shrimply Delicious with Avocado Half – serves 4-6
Tomato Aspic
Country Club Muffins
French Strawberry Pie

Family Fare

Meatloaf Supreme – serves 4-6
Tossed Salad with Dijon Dressing
Oven Fries
Green Peas with Celery and Olives
Apple Crunch

Ham and Cheese Log
Mary's Salad
"Six Weeks" Muffins
Seven Layer Casserole – serves 6-8
Chocolate Cookie Frozen Dessert

Broccoli Mushroom Dip
Copper Pennies
Melt-In-Your-Mouth Muffins
Luttrell's Crispy Chicken – serves 4
Sour Cream Cheese Potatoes
Aunt Matilda's Peach Cobbler

Marinated Vegetable Salad
Do-Ahead Brisket – serves 6-8
Mama's Best Beans
Green Chile Rice
Milky Way Cake and Icing

Especially for the Kids

Strawberry Gelatin Juice Punch
Frozen Banana Salad
Foiled Frankfurters – serves 8
Chuckwagon Carrots
Fudgesicles

Sausage Swirls
Frozen Fruit Salad
Macaroni and Cheese – serves 4-6
Vegetable of Choice
Buckeyes

Pizza Dip
Emerald Glow Salad
Chicken Pot Pie and I Don't Care – serves 6
Easy New Potatoes
Chocolate-Cornflake Cookies

Cheese Crispies
Raspberry-Applesauce Salad
Chipper Trout – serves 4-6
Oven Fries
Myra's Crumb Broccoli
Small Chocolate Tarts

Straight off the Grill

Tuna and Watercress Tapenade
Mary's Salad
Marinated Pork Tenderloin – serves 4-6
Stuffed Tomatoes
Scrumptious Baked Squash
Fresh Fruit Pudding Compote

Curry Clam Dip
Golden Salad Dressing over Salad Greens
Marinated Chicken Breasts – serves 4-6
Easy Zucchini
Tuta Robert's Curried Rice
Mrs. Smith's Ice Cream

Quick Bacon Squares
Wagoner's Grilled Flank Steak – serves 4-6
Mushrooms Bourguignon
Baked Tomatoes
Almond Asparagus
Pineapple Macadamia Pie

Catch of the Day

Quick Cheese Puffs
Saucy Shrimp – serves 6-8
Hot Rice
Spinach Stuffed Tomatoes
Green Beans and Tomatoes
Green Beans and Almonds
Heavenly Milk Chocolate Pie

Carol's Cheese Roll
Artichoke Soup
Heavenly Broiled Fish – serves 6
Fresh Vegetable of Season
Snow Pea Surprise
Southern Chocolate Pecan Pie

Tomato Toasties
Green Bean and Avocado Salad
Crab Au Gratin – serves 6-8
Quick – Easy Carrots with Wine
Brandy Alexanders

Our Feathered Friends

Salmon Ball
Holiday Cranberry Salad
Windsor Canadian Goose – serves 4-6
Fantastic Rice
Green Beans Au Gratin
Sherbet Pie

Caviar Pie
Super Spinach Salad I
Saucy Quail – serves 4
Rice with Mushrooms
Nutty Carrots
Snow Cake

Cream Cheese Crab Bars
Spinach Salad with Honey Mustard Dressing
Chicken and Wild Rice – serves 4-6
Broccoli Cauliflower Casserole
Chocolate Mousse

South of the Border

Mexican Layer Dip
Avocado Salad Bowl
Spoon Cornbread
Crabmeat Rellenos con Queso – serves 4-6
Spanish Rice
Pat McGinnis's Ice Cream Delight

Mexican Dip
Gazpacho
Festive Cornbread Salad
Chicken Enchiladas – serves 4-6
Jalapeño Rice Texas Style
Piña Colada Cake

Tortilla Roll-ups
Jalapeño Hushpuppies
Mexican Fiesta – serves 20
Mexican Corn Casserole
Microwave Pralines

Gazpacho Dip
Chicken Flautas – serves 6
Guacamole Dip
Diced Tomatoes and Lettuce Garnish
Frozen Caramel Dessert

Viva Italiano

Parmesan Artichokes
Italian Olive Salad
Our Family Spaghetti – serves 6
Layered Cheese Vegetable Bake
Praline Cheesecake

Little Pizza Appetizers
Italian Olive Salad
Manicotti – serves 6
Skillet Squash
Carmella DeSarno's Ricotta Pie

Spinach Balls
Mock Caesar Salad
Lasagne Bolognese – serves 12
Garlic Bread
Fruit Pizza

Let's Go Oriental

Pineapple Cheese Ball
Oriental Spinach Salad
Sweet and Sour Pork – serves 4-6
Gail's Sukiyaki – serves 4
Golden Rice
Walnut Caramels

Sue's Easy Stuffed Mushrooms
Sweet and Sour Cabbage
Chicken Chop Suey – serves 4
Polynesian Pork – serves 4-6
Hot Rice
Pineapple Cookies

Teriyaki Steak Roll-ups
Oriental Salad
Pineapple Chicken with Orange Rice – serves 4
Snow Peas and Water Chestnuts
Luscious Lemon Icebox Pie

Common Food Equivalents

Food	Weight or Amount	Approximate Yield or Measure
Apples	1 pound (3 medium)	3 cups sliced
Bacon	8 slices cooked	½ cup crumbled
Bananas	1 pound (3 medium)	2½ cups sliced, 2 cups mashed
Beans, dried	1 pound (2½ cups)	6 cups cooked
Butter or Margarine	1 pound	2 cups
Cabbage	1 pound	4½ cups shredded
Carrots	1 pound	3 cups, shredded
Celery	2 ribs	1 cup, sliced
Cheese, American or Cheddar	1 pound	4-5 cups, shredded
Cheese, other	4 ounces	1 cup shredded
Chicken	3½ pound fryer	3 cups cooked, diced
Coffee	1 pound	80 Tablespoons (40-45 cups)
Crab	1 pound, in shell	¾-1 cup flaked meat
Cream, whipping	½ pint	2 cups, whipped
Crumbs, fine		
Saltine	24 crackers	1 cup fine crumbs
Bread	4 slices	1 cup fine crumbs
Graham cracker	14 crackers	1 cup fine crumbs
Vanilla wafers	22 wafers	1 cup fine crumbs
Flour, All purpose	1 pound	4 cups sifted
Green Pepper	1 large	1 cup, diced
Lemon	1 medium	2-3 Tablespoons juice, 2 teaspoons grated rind
Lettuce	1 pound head	6¼ cups torn
Meat	1 pound	2 cups, diced
Mushrooms	8 ounces, raw	1 cup, sliced, cooked
Nuts, shelled	1 pound	4 cups, chopped
Onion	1 medium	½ cup chopped
Orange	1 medium	⅓ cup juice and 2 Tablespoons grated rind
Pasta		
Macaroni	1 pound	4 cups dry
	1 cup (4 ounces)	2¼ cups, cooked
Noodles	4 ounces uncooked	2 cups, cooked
Spaghetti	7 ounces, uncooked	4 cups, cooked

Peaches	1 pound (4-6 peaches)	2½ cups sliced
Potatoes, white	1 pound (3 medium)	2 cups cooked, cubed
Potatoes, sweet	3 medium	3 cups sliced, cooked
Rice	1 pound	2⅓ cups uncooked
	1 cup	3½ cups, cooked
Shrimp	1½ pounds, fresh, unpeeled	2 cups, cooked, peeled and deveined
Strawberries	1 pint	2 cups, sliced
Sugar		
Brown	1 pound	2½ cups firmly packed
Powdered	1 pound	3½ cups unsifted
Granulated	1 pound	2 cups
Squash, summer	1 pound (4 small)	1½ cups, cooked
Tomatoes	1 pound (4 small)	1½ cups cooked

Measurements

Dash	⅛ teaspoon
1 Tablespoon	3 teaspoons (½ ounce)
2 Tablespoons	⅛ cup (1 ounce)
4 Tablespoons	¼ cup (2 ounces)
5 Tablespoons + 1 teaspoon	⅓ cup
8 Tablespoons	½ cup (4 ounces)
16 Tablespoons	1 cup (8 ounces)
1 cup	½ pint (8 ounces)
2 cups	1 pint (16 ounces)
4 cups	1 quart (32 ounces)
1 quart	2 pints
2 quarts	½ gallon (4 pints)
4 quarts	1 gallon
16 ounces	1 pound
1 pound butter	2 cups or 4 sticks

If at all possible, it is best to use the ingredient called for in a recipe. Occasionally it may be necessary to use a substitute ingredient. Use the following table when you need a handy substitution.

Substitutions

For These	Use These
1 square unsweetened chocolate	3 Tablespoons cocoa plus 1 Tablespoon butter or margarine
1 whole egg	2 egg yolks plus 1 Tablespoon water
2 large eggs	3 small eggs
1 cup buttermilk or sour milk	1 Tablespoon white vinegar or lemon juice plus milk to fill cup (let stand 5 minutes)
1 cup commercial sour cream	1 Tablespoon lemon juice plus evaporated milk to equal 1 cup
1 cup yogurt	1 cup buttermilk or sour cream
½ cup butter or margarine	7 Tablespoons vegetable shortening
1 Tablespoon cornstarch	2 Tablespoons all purpose flour
1 teaspoon baking powder	½ teaspoon cream of tartar plus ¼ teaspoon baking soda
1 cup cake flour	1 cup all purpose flour minus 2 Tablespoons
1 cup self rising flour	1 cup all purpose flour plus 1 teaspoon baking powder and ½ teaspoon salt
1 clove fresh garlic	1 teaspoon garlic salt or ⅛ teaspoon garlic powder
⅓ cup chopped raw onion	2 Tablespoons instant minced onion
1 Tablespoon fresh herbs	1 teaspoon ground or crushed dry herbs
2 teaspoons fresh minced herbs	½ teaspoon dried herbs
1 pound fresh mushrooms	6 ounces canned mushrooms
1 cup diced cooked chicken	1 can (5 ounces) boned chicken
Juice of 1 lemon	3 Tablespoons bottled juice
Juice of 1 orange	⅓-½ cup canned juice
1 cup barbeque sauce	1 cup ketchup plus 2 teaspoons Worcestershire sauce
1 Tablespoon dry sherry	1 Tablespoon dry vermouth
15 ounce can tomato sauce	6 ounce can tomato paste plus 1 cup water

Index